Writing Clear Sentences

ROBERT B. DONALD   **BETTY RICHMOND MORROW**

LILLIAN GRIFFITH WARGETZ   **KATHLEEN WERNER**

Community College of Beaver County, Pennsylvania

PRENTICE-HALL, INC., Englewood Cliffs, New Jersey 07632

Library of Congress Cataloging-in-Publication Data

Writing clear sentences.

Includes index.
1. English language—Sentences.   2. English
language—Grammar   3. English language—
Rhetoric.   I. Donald, Robert B.
PE1441.W77   1987   808'.042   86–3192
ISBN 0-13-970401-9

Editorial/production supervision and
  interior design: Serena Hoffman
Cover design: Ben Santora
Manufacturing buyer: Harry P. Baisley

PRINTED IN THE UNITED STATES OF AMERICA

10   9   8   7   6   5   4   3   2   1

ISBN   0-13-970401-9   01

PRENTICE-HALL INTERNATIONAL (UK) LIMITED, *London*
PRENTICE-HALL OF AUSTRALIA PTY. LIMITED, *Sydney*
PRENTICE-HALL CANADA INC., *Toronto*
PRENTICE-HALL HISPANOAMERICANA, S.A., *Mexico*
PRENTICE-HALL OF INDIA PRIVATE LIMITED, *New Delhi*
PRENTICE-HALL OF JAPAN, INC., *Tokyo*
PRENTICE-HALL OF SOUTHEAST ASIA PTE. LTD., *Singapore*
EDITORA PRENTICE-HALL DO BRASIL, LTDA., *Rio de Janeiro*
WHITEHALL BOOKS LIMITED, *Wellington, New Zealand*

Contents

Exercises

Preface

Writing Clear Sentences is a student-centered textbook designed to help the basic writer. It focuses on the positive: students are encouraged to discover the value of writing as a way of thinking rather than as a meaningless task imposed upon them by an English teacher.

The first chapter builds self-confidence by showing students how much they already know about writing. By drawing on their knowledge of spoken English, students discover that they already have a great deal of "sentence sense." Subsequent chapters deal with problems common to basic writers. Throughout these chapters, the focus is on effective writing as opposed to grammatical correctness.

Although each chapter builds on what students learned in previous chapters, the book as a whole is composed of self-contained units, and thus provides a flexible sequence of topics for the individual instructor. Concise explanations, relevant examples, and practical assignments replace abstract grammatical terminology. The exercises in each chapter are written at both the sentence level and the paragraph level; many of them tell a little story or provide information on a single topic.

Writing Clear Sentences is based upon the belief that improvement in writing involves more than reading a text and completing the exercises; inexperienced writers become better writers through *practice*. Therefore, through a writing-across-the-curriculum approach, *Writing Clear Sentences* provides students with the opportunity to practice different types of writing for different types of audiences. The Writing from Reading sections included after each chapter provide students with ample opportunity to write. Reading skills are integrated with writing skills so that students see writing as an active rather than a passive process. By experiencing writing as a dialogue between reader and writer, students learn the importance of communicating with an audience.

Assignments in the Writing from Reading sections deal with a broad range of topics. Students see how writing is related to such areas as math, physics, marketing, medicine, music, history, and sociology. Critical thinking skills are developed through activities such as brainstorming, role playing, and problem solving. Students condense, summarize, analyze, interpret, and evaluate information. They explore, they create, they think.

In short, the Writing from Reading sections are designed to show students that writing is not a static medium, that writing applies in a variety of contexts—from pie charts to poetry. Assignments call for both formal and informal writing. Sometimes students work alone; sometimes they work in small groups. Sometimes they write about their private world; sometimes they write about their working world. All of the assignments are so designed that, while the students are developing their writing skills, they are also improving their reading comprehension, oral communication, and critical thinking skills.

To conclude, *Writing Clear Sentences* encourages students to take ownership of their writing. It incorporates recent research on language and composition without discarding traditional techniques that work in the classroom. Above all, it does not talk down at inexperienced writers; it talks *to* them.

Every book is more than a product of its authors, for it also represents the help and cooperation of colleagues. We are grateful to Dr. William K. Bauer, President of Beaver County Community College, and to Dr. Margaret J. Williams, Vice President for Academic Affairs, for their ongoing support of our endeavors. We are also indebted to our indispensable librarian, Linda Ciani, and to our illustrator, Rodney Dennis, for being there when we needed them. A special thanks also goes to Sylvia Hines and Mary Williams, two of the world's greatest secretaries.

We are especially grateful to our perceptive reviewers: John B. Baird, Catawba Valley Technical College; Carol Cinclair, Brookhaven College; Gertrude B. Hopkins, Harford Community College; and Alice Maclin, Dekalb Community College. In addition, we extend our sincere thanks to Phil Miller, Serena Hoffman, Jane Baumann, and Gary Gutchell of Prentice-Hall. We still think they're magic.

Finally, we thank our students—those who have permitted us to use their writing, and those who share the learning process with us in the classroom. For permission to use the selections reprinted here, the authors are grateful to the publishers and copyright holders.

Writing
Clear
Sentences

1

Discovering What You Already Know

If you are like most students, you probably know much more about English than you think you do. It is not unusual to hear students expressing anxiety about writing: "English is my worst subject. I don't know anything about grammar." But you use your knowledge of sentences every day. Every time you talk to someone, you demonstrate a certain sentence sense—an understanding of what a sentence is, what it does, and what it sounds like. Consider the following conversations:

Your Mechanic:	You say you only hear that noise when you put the car in reverse?
You:	Right.
Your Mechanic:	Oh.
Your Mother:	Don't you think you ought to call the dentist and check on your X-rays?
You:	Whatever you say, Mom.
Your Mother:	Ask him about the new dental insurance forms, too.
You:	O.K.

In both brief conversations, the basic unit of communication is the sentence. Even though some of the statements don't look like sentences, they function as sentences—that is, they convey complete thoughts. The fragments, even the one-word responses, for example, are really abbreviated sentences.

$$\begin{array}{cc} & \text{S} \quad \text{V} \\ \text{Right.} & = \text{That is right.} \end{array}$$

$$\begin{array}{cc} & \text{S} \quad \text{V} \\ \text{Oh.} & = \text{Oh, I see.} \end{array}$$

$$\begin{array}{cc} & \text{S} \qquad \text{V} \\ \text{Whatever you say, Mom.} & = \text{I will do whatever you say, Mom.} \end{array}$$

$$\begin{array}{cc} & \text{S} \quad \text{V} \\ \text{O.K.} & = \text{O.K., I will.} \end{array}$$

Whether you are talking or writing, you are using the same basic unit of communication—the sentence—to convey your thoughts to someone else. Writing, then, is really not a solitary activity. In writing, as in speaking, a dialogue is taking place—a silent dialogue between the writer and the reader. In fact, this silent dialogue often produces the best writing. When writers forget about their audience—when they fail to see writing from their readers' point of view—their writing becomes incoherent. Good writers anticipate their readers' questions; they provide transitional markers to show the readers how one thought is connected to another; they choose words and punctuation carefully, so that their readers will know exactly how they feel about something.

Talking and writing are simply different forms of the same activity: communicating through language. In the spoken word, a dialogue takes place between a speaker and a listener. In the written word, a dialogue takes place between a writer and a reader. The differences between a speaker-listener exchange and a writer-reader exchange are really not as complex as they sometimes seem. When you talk, you employ a number of techniques to let your listeners know how you feel about something: the tone of voice you use, the expression on your face, the way you move your hands. All of these things have an effect on your listeners. They help get your point across. When you are writing, however, you have to pay more attention to things that will have an effect on your readers. For instance, the kind of words you use and the punctuation marks you select can convey a certain tone of voice to your readers. Consider the following example.

Suppose that after breaking the dining room lamp and spilling chocolate milk all over the living room carpet, your younger brother, Matthew, catches a snake, brings it into the house, and promptly deposits it on the kitchen floor. Suppose that your exasperated mother then walks into the kitchen. Upon seeing the snake, her face turns red; she pounds her fist on the table and shouts angrily, "Get that thing out of here!" Your little brother would probably have no difficulty getting the message. Even if your mother had just glared at the snake, pointed her finger toward the kitchen door, and shouted "Out!" Matthew would have understood. Translated in Matthew's

mind, the message would be clear: "Mom is really mad. I'd better get this snake out of the kitchen right now."

Thus, in spoken English even one-word statements can really be implied sentences. They can communicate complete thoughts. In written English, however, one-word statements are rarely sufficient. If your mother had to leave a note for Matthew, just writing "Out" on a piece of paper would not provide enough information. Without seeing his name, Matthew wouldn't even know the message was directed at him. Even the longer spoken sentence that your mother used—"Get that thing out of here!"— would not be sufficient. The words "thing" and "here" could be interpreted in various ways. Maybe Matthew had dragged more than one "thing" into the kitchen, and "out of here" could be interpreted as simply out of the kitchen, but not necessarily out of the house. Reading the spoken words might have led Matthew dutifully to transport the snake to his bedroom. In order for your mother to get the same message across in writing, she would have to be more explicit:

Matthew! Get this filthy snake out of the house IMMEDIATELY!

By underlining Matthew's name, characterizing the snake as "filthy," capitalizing and underlining the word "immediately," and concluding with an exclamation mark, your mother would have conveyed her tone of voice effectively. She produced an effect similar to the one she would have produced by talking directly to Matthew (looking at the snake, pointing toward the door, and shouting "Out").

3

The important thing to remember about writing, as opposed to talking, is that a reader needs more information than a listener. In other words, things that can be implied through speech have to be directly stated in writing. You can't leave out a subject or a verb and expect the readers to supply them. You can't use vague words like "thing" and expect the readers to know what you're talking about. You can't assume that your readers understand how strongly you feel about something if you don't show them with words or punctuation. It is simply a matter of putting yourself inside your readers' minds and seeing things from their perspective. Anyone who can communicate in spoken English has some sense of what a sentence is, and anyone who understands what a sentence is can learn to write.

EXERCISE 1A: IMPLIED SENTENCES

Each of the following conversations has brief responses that suggest complete thoughts. For each of the italicized statements, write out the sentence that is being implied.

Husband: Let's do something special for your mother's birthday this year.

Wife: *Like what?*

_____

Husband: I was thinking of flying her to Florida to see her sister. You know, she hasn't seen Mary Ellen since Uncle Bill died.

Wife: That's a terrific idea! *Only problem is getting her on the plane.* She hates to fly.

_____

Husband: Yeah, but she'd love to see Mary Ellen.

Wife: *True.*

_____

Husband: Well, it's something worth thinking about anyway.

Wife: *Right.*

_____

Doctor: How often do you get these headaches?

Patient: Oh . . . *at least once a month.*

_____

Doctor:	*Severe?*

Patient:	Yeah, really bad.

Teacher:	What kind of animal is that you're drawing there, Garret?
Garret:	*A froad.*

Teacher:	Oh, I've never seen a froad before.
Garret:	It's a cross between a frog and a toad.
Teacher:	*Very clever.*

Teacher:	Where do froads live?
Garret:	*In my closet.*

Garret:	Sometimes they like to come to school with me. *Wanna' see one?*

Teacher:	I'd love to.
Garret:	*O.K. . . . tomorrow.*

SENTENCES

Whether or not you can define a sentence or whether you even call something a sentence, you know what a sentence is: *the basic unit of grammar.* Which of the following is a sentence?

1. Wagging dog the tail his went by.
2. Eleanor shopped for clothes at the Mall.
3. Dieting tired of was she.

You know that you show the beginning of a sentence by capitalizing the first letter, and you know that you show the ending of a sentence by adding a period. You probably also know that a sentence contains a subject and a verb. All the examples above have all the criteria of a sentence (capital letter, period, subject, and verb), but you had no trouble picking out the sentence (2), did you?

Even if a careless writer forgets to capitalize the first letter and/or omits the period, the reader can still usually figure out where one sentence ends and another begins. Try picking out the sentences in this example:

Going to school in the summer is a drag I'd rather be doing the things I do best I think summers should be used for exercising the other muscles instead of the brain swimming is great fun and it exercises every muscle in the body basketball builds leg muscles and increases both stamina and quickness baseball improves eye-hand coordination and improves wrist strength even a quiet game of golf improves muscle tone in one's arms, legs, and back so here I sit in a classroom when I want to be running in the sunshine this class had better be exciting.

You also know how to name the key words in sentences. If you had to, you could reduce most sentences to the two or three words that express the gist of your message: the *subject, verb*, and *completer* (a word or phrase that is sometimes needed to finish a thought). You would probably never write in this way, and you wouldn't ordinarily speak this way, unless you were in danger or in an emergency.

S   V   C
Pat went home from school early today.

    S   V   C
My *brother*, a former mill worker, *graduated* from *college* last Thursday.

                                            S   V   C
After visiting my uncle in the hospital last week, my *mother quit smoking*.

                           S   V
The long shallow twisting *stream* that winds through eastern Ohio *is called*
    C
Meander Creek.

You also can recognize the purposes of sentences. If someone says, "Could you tell me what time it is?" you know that person is seeking information. If someone says, "That movie stinks!" you know he or she is expressing an opinion. If someone says, "I like you better every time I see you," you know he or she is expressing feelings of affection. If you show up for a date in formal clothes instead of a sweat suit, you recognize that your friend is expressing surprise when he or she says, "What happened?" or "Is it really you?" If someone tells you to "Go to the third traffic light and turn right to find McDonald's," you know he or she is conveying information. If your father says, "Get home on time," you know he is issuing a command. You can recognize the purpose of a sentence by the way its words are put together and by the way it is punctuated.

**EXERCISE 1B: RECOGNIZING THE PURPOSES
OF SENTENCES**

For each of the following sentences, decide what purpose was intended: informing or seeking information, expressing opinions or feelings, or commanding.

1.   Do not walk on the grass. _____

2.   Where are the car keys? _____

3.   There is no excuse for your behavior._____

4.   Go three miles along Route 65 and turn left at Exit 4 to reach Mapleton.

_____

5.   Help! _____

6.   The library book is lying on the hall table. _____

7.   This meal is delicious. _____

8.   I regret missing your phone call. _____

9.   My heart's in the highlands. _____

10.   I hate hard rock._____

You see, you do know a lot about sentences. Does that mean you don't need any more instruction? No, of course not. No one knows it all. But, you *do* know a lot about language already, and you *can* learn much more.

WRITING FROM READING

Reading without Words

Reading without words may sound impossible at first, but if you think about it for a minute, you will realize that you do it constantly. Probably the first thing you do when you wake up in the morning is to glance at a clock. You may look out the window and "read" the thermometer on your garage. If you have a toothache and you have to see your dentist, the dentist will probably "read" your X-rays before he or she works on your teeth. If your car has

7

a stick shift, there is probably a diagram on the knob to show you where to push the stick for each of the gears. And if you need to go someplace in your car, you can't drive a mile without "reading" a number of signs like these:

All of these "readings" convey information very swiftly, even though that information may be rather complicated. Indeed, ideas that range from being very simple to being very complex can be successfully communicated through different types of pictures, diagrams, maps, graphs, tables, and so on.

One very common, simple graph with which you are probably familiar is the *pie chart*.

SOURCES OF ENGLISH VOCABULARY IN AN AVERAGE PIECE OF WRITING

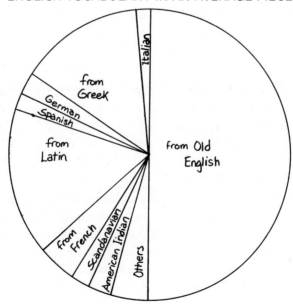

By reading this chart, you learn that in an average piece of writing, half of the words are native—that is, they come from Old English. The next largest number of words comes from Latin. Smaller percentages come from Greek, French, Scandinavian, and American Indian; still other percentages come from languages whose contributions are too small to be recognized on the chart.

The following pie chart provides Bob, a baker, with a quick overall picture of his average daily sales.

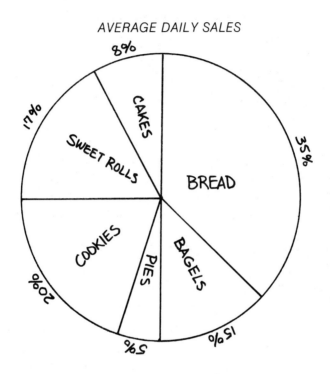

AVERAGE DAILY SALES

Bob is building a new addition onto his bakery, but before he expands his business, he needs a clear picture of his customers' buying habits. After reading the pie chart, what could you tell Bob? Do you have any suggestions that might help Bob improve his business? Jot down your thoughts and then compare them with those of your classmates. See if they read the pie chart the same way you did. Did they arrive at different conclusions or make different suggestions?

9

2

Simple Sentences

A sentence is usually defined as *a group of words containing a subject and a verb and whatever else is necessary to express a complete thought.* Each of the following groups of words meets that basic definition:

Frogs croak.	Subject–Verb
Elephants are mammals.	Subject–Verb Completer
Janice hit John on the nose.	Subject–Verb–Completer

However, you already know that complete thoughts are often expressed *without* subjects and verbs. In fact, even a one-word command—a verb alone—may be considered a sentence:

Look! Stop! Wait! Hurry!

So, is the definition of a sentence a good one? The answer lies in recognizing that it is difficult to provide a completely satisfactory definition of a sentence, but it is easy to know when you have written one. In certain contexts, for example, a simple "Yes" or "No" may act as a sentence. In speaking, brief word groupings such as "Next time" or "Not tonight" serve as sentences (complete communications). Of course, in spoken communication you have all kinds of signals, clues, and aids, such as tone of voice, facial expression, gestures, and other kinds of body language that frequently accompany the words themselves. Even a shake of the head, a slight shrug, or a thumbs-down signal may have the effect of a complete sentence.

In writing, however, you don't have signals and clues to add to your message to make it clear. What you say in writing must be said *by the words themselves* as you have arranged them. With very few exceptions, then, written sentences should be complete: a subject-verb statement or a subject-verb-completer statement.

RECOGNIZING SUBJECTS

The subject of the sentence is a *noun* or a *noun substitute* (a pronoun or a noun phrase). Nouns are names given to

Things:	a dog, a chair, a rose, a computer
Events:	the 1984 Olympics, the assassination of John F. Kennedy, your high school graduation
People:	Joe, Susan, gang, class
Places:	Pittsburgh, Alaska, beach, park
Emotions:	love, hate, anger, fear
Ideas:	freedom, tradition, bravery, communism

Nouns can refer to things and people that are, to things and people that no longer are (like the Pony Express and Abraham Lincoln), and even to things that never were (like mermaids and fairy godmothers).

Noun substitutes are usually pronouns (I, you, he, she, it, they, who, which, what, everyone, each, somebody, this, that, these, those, etc.) or noun phrases (growing up, finding a job, hunting quail, being an astronaut). (Pronouns are explained in more detail in Chapter 9, and noun phrases are discussed later in this chapter.) The main point to remember is that the subject of a sentence is what the rest of the sentence is about. The sentence tells you what the subject *is* or *does*. For example:

Janet is an effective speaker.

In this sentence, the phrase "is an effective speaker" tells you about Janet. It tells you what Janet *is*.

Sparky broke his chain and streaked after the cat.

This sentence tells you about Sparky. It tells you what he *did*.

EXERCISE 2A: RECOGNIZING NOUNS

Underline all the nouns in the following sentences. Then identify each noun as a person, place, thing, event, emotion, or idea. The number of nouns in each sentence is given at the end of the sentence.

1. Life was hard for the miners of western Pennsylvania during the first half of the century. (5)

    _____

2. The miners got up at 4:00 in the morning. The bus left for the mine by 5:15. (6)

    _____

3. The work was hard on their muscles and their health. Heavy coal strained the muscles in their arms. (6)

    _____

4. The miners often worked in a stooped position because of low ceilings, which strained their backs. (4)

    _____

5. Black lung, a respiratory disease, was common. Most miners had suffered some lung damage. For many, black lung was fatal. (5)

    _____

6. And the pay was poor. As late as 1947, a miner received $13.06 per day. (5)

    _____

7. Worst of all, the work was dangerous. Between 1908 and 1938, 37,064 men died from slate falls and 8,045 men from explosions. (7)

    _____

8. The treatment of the dead men by mine officials was horrible. These officials took the body to the wife's home and deposited it on the porch. (7)

    _____

9. Then, their job ended. Each wife had to wash the body of her dead husband to prepare it for burial. (5)

    _____

10. Since the homes were owned by the mining company, the widows were forced to move unless another miner could be persuaded to live in the house. Only working miners were allowed to live in the company houses. (7)

EXERCISE 2B: RECOGNIZING SUBJECTS

Underline the subject in each of the following sentences.

1. Freedom makes life worth living.

2. Cheating is dishonest and self-defeating.

3. Liza is the number one tennis player on the team.

4. Epcot Center is a fascinating place to visit.

5. Learning to write well requires concentration and practice.

6. Bruno ran out of the theatre during the gruesome murder scenes.

7. Afterwards, they decided not to protest the game.

8. Each of the members was questioned individually.

9. Linda's spitefulness ruined our friendship.

10. Billy's two-year-old brother is a riot.

11. Exercising strengthens the heart muscles.

12. He talked for hours.

13. That typewriter hasn't been touched in over fifty years.

14. Despite my objections, Anna Mae drove up to the haunted house alone.

15. The ugly man contest was held at the local pub.

16. According to Fogel's book, *Duck Soup* ranks high among fans of the Marx Brothers.

17. Compassion often leads to understanding.

18. Vietnam changed his life.

19. Dubliners raised over $50,000 for Colin's liver transplant.

20. On his way to the podium, Senator Dempsey tripped over a chair and landed in the punch bowl.

RECOGNIZING NOUN SUBSTITUTES

Some sentences have subjects that don't look like nouns. In these sentences, the subject (what the rest of the sentence tells you about) is not expressed by a single word (a noun), but rather by a combination of words (a noun phrase). These noun phrases usually begin with a word that, at first glance, looks more like a verb than a noun. For example:

> looking for a job . . .   to look for a job . . .
>
> saving $100 a month . . .   to save $100 a month . . .
>
> buying a car . . .   to buy a used car . . .

Notice that the words *looking, saving,* and *buying* all consist of a verb plus *ing*:

> look + ing   sav(e) + ing   buy + ing

Notice, however, that when an *ing* is attached to a verb, that verb can function as a noun referring to an act or a process or an idea—for example, the *process* of looking for a job as opposed to a specific action taking place (I looked for a job yesterday.).

>   N
> *To look for a job* is time-consuming.
>   N
> *Looking for a job* is time-consuming.
>   V
> I *looked* for a job for four weeks.

Now notice that the words *to look, to save,* and *to buy* can also serve as subjects. Most verbs can be used as noun substitutes if you add *ing* or place *to* before them. Each of these noun phrases, then, can serve as perfectly good subjects:

>   S   V   C
> *Looking for a job* taxed all my energies.
>   S   V   C
> *To look for a job* is exhausting.

$$\overset{\text{S}}{\textit{Saving \$100 a month}} \overset{\text{V}}{\text{forced}} \overset{\text{C}}{\text{me to change my priorities.}}$$

$$\overset{\text{S}}{\textit{To save \$100 a month}} \text{on my salary} \overset{\text{V}}{\text{is}} \overset{\text{C}}{\text{impossible.}}$$

Saving $100 a month forced me to change my priorities.

To save $100 a month on my salary is impossible.

Buying a used car was a real learning experience.

To buy a used car is to buy trouble.

EXERCISE 2C: NOUN PHRASES AS SUBJECTS

Following the example, create your own sentences using noun phrases as subjects.

EXAMPLE: Eating

Eating pepperoni pizza

Eating pepperoni pizza is Snoopy's favorite pastime.

1. Marrying

    _____

    _____

2. Studying

    _____

    _____

3. Losing

    _____

    _____

4. Winning

    _____

    _____

5. Celebrating

    _____

    _____

15

EXAMPLE: To eat

To eat at Tomaine Tommy's

To eat at Tomaine Tommy's requires an adventurous spirit.

6. To marry

_____

_____

7. To study

_____

_____

8. To lose

_____

_____

9. To win

_____

_____

10. To celebrate

_____

_____

EXERCISE 2D: IDENTIFYING NOUNS AND SUBJECTS

Underline all the nouns in the following sentences. Then circle the subject of each sentence (nouns and noun substitutes).

1. Choosing a career is often a difficult task, but a little research can help. Consider the area of salaries, for example.

2. Salaries differ widely. Half of the people in the United States make more than $18,700 a year. The other half make less. Only 1 percent of the people in the U.S. make over $60,000 per year.

3. A contractor's aide makes about $5,000 per year. A cab driver makes about $7,800. A savings and loan teller earns about $9,000 per year.

4. A food service worker can earn $15,000 whereas a high school counselor may earn almost $30,000.

5. Some professional athletes receive big salaries. Million dollar contracts are not uncommon.

6. Dave Winfield, a baseball player, will earn $25 million in ten years. Basketball's Magic Johnson will receive $1 million a year for twenty-five years.

7. John McEnroe earned $5 million in 1983. The biggest contract for an athlete, for $40 million, was signed by Brigham Young quarterback Steve Young.

8. Steve's contract is for forty-four years. Will he still be playing football in his sixties?

9. Athletes do not make the really big money, though. Top business executives make far more.

10. William Anderson of NCR made $13 million in one year. Frederick W. Smith, founder of Federal Express, made $54 million in 1982.

11. Charles Lazarus of Toys "R" Us received $44 million in 1982. Three others in the same corporation made more than $7 million in one year.

12. Salaries do differ widely, but salary is only one part of a job.

RECOGNIZING VERBS

You already know that the subject is one of the most important parts of a sentence. The verb is the other necessary part of the sentence.

Action: They *threw* the ball.

Invisible Action: The dog *remembered* me.

State of Being: She *is* a lawyer

Sometimes verbs show action:

They *threw* the ball fifty yards.

Maria *slapped* her thigh.

Fog *crept* in through the valley.

Sometimes verbs show action that is invisible:

The dog *remembered* me.

The teacher *thought* the class was ready.

Debbie *loves* grapes.

Sometimes verbs express a condition or state of being:

She *is* a lawyer.

Randy *appears* ill.

Steak *will be* perfect for the barbecue.

In these last three sentences, each of the verbs tells what the subject *is* (condition or state or being). All of the major verbs of being (called *linking verbs*) are forms of the verb *to be*:

I *am*	We *are*
You *are*	You (plural) *are*
He, she, it *is*	They *are*

As you know, these linking verbs have other tenses:

past: *was, were, has been, have been*

future: *will be, shall be*

EXERCISE 2E: VERBS

See if you can supply the missing verbs in each of the following popular sayings.

1. Beauty _____ only skin deep.

2. Misery _____ company.

3. Nobody _____ a crybaby.

4. The early bird _____ the worm.

5. Haste _____ waste.

6. Love _____ blind.

7. Time _____ all wounds.

8. Kids _____ the darnedest things.

9. A rolling stone _____ no moss.

10. Money _____.

EXERCISE 2F: IDENTIFYING NOUNS, SUBJECTS, AND VERBS

Underline all the nouns in the following sentences. Then, in each sentence, mark an *S* over the subject and a *V* over the verb.

1. The Olympics have an interesting history.

2. They were started over 2,500 years ago by the Greeks.

3. The year was 776 B.C.

4. The Olympics were held every four years at Olympia, a beautiful plain on the mainland of Greece.

5. Each of the first thirteen Olympic Games lasted only one day and consisted of *one* race of 630 feet.

6. Later, wrestling, boxing, jumping, and throwing were added.

7. Only men attended, sometimes 40,000 of them.

8. The contestants performed naked.

19

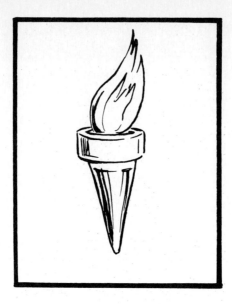

9. Winners at the Olympics became famous and were honored throughout Greece.

10. For almost 1,200 years, the Games did a lot of good.

11. Wars, for instance, were stopped for the games.

12. Therefore, spectators could travel in safety to and from the games.

13. However, like many other things, the Olympics became corrupt.

14. Athletes began to accept money.

15. The games became dishonest.

16. In 393 A.D., after almost 1,200 years and 300 Olympics, the Games were discontinued.

17. For 1,500 years after that, there were no Olympic Games.

18. In 1898, largely because of the efforts of Pierre de Coubertain, a French noble, the modern Olympics were started.

19. In 1898, the modern Olympics were revived in Olympia.

20. Since then, Olympics have been held in many major cities of the world.

21. However, wars no longer stop because of the Games.

22. In 1916, 1940, and 1944, the Games were cancelled because of the World Wars.

23. Four major changes have taken place in the modern Olympics.

24. First, the number of women athletes has increased enormously.

25. Second, winter sports became a part of the Olympics in 1924.

26. Third, 149 events, excluding winter sports, now replace the original race.

27. Fourth, records are broken continuously.

28. A record holder in a 1956 Olympics might not qualify for the national team today.

COMPOUND SUBJECTS AND VERBS

One definition of a simple sentence states that it has only one subject-verb combination. This does *not* mean that the simple sentence can have *only* one subject and one verb. On the contrary, the simple sentence can have several subjects and several verbs, as long as the subjects are together and the verbs are together.

A simple sentence can have two subjects.

   S   S
Joe and *Sue* went to McDonald's.

It can also have two verbs.

            V   V
Joe and Sue *went* to McDonald's and *bought* cheeseburgers.

Even if many subjects and verbs are added, a sentence remains simple—as long as the subjects remain together and the verbs remain together.

   S   S   S   S   S
Bill and *Tom* and *Fran* and *Esther* and the *rest* of the gang went skating.
     V   V   V   V   V
Clara *caught* a fish, *skinned* it, *cleaned* it, *fried* it, and *ate* it—all in thirty-five minutes.

However, if the subjects are separated by verbs, the sentence is no longer simple.

   S   V   S   V
Jerry grilled the steaks, and *Janet made* the salad.

EXERCISE 2G: COMPOUND SUBJECTS AND VERBS

In the following simple sentences, underline all the subjects and verbs. Place an *S* above each subject and a *V* above each verb.

1.   The thunder, lightning, and wind terrified the vacationers.

2.   The storm howled and raged all night.

3.   The waves rolled across the beach and reached the driveway.

4.   Bill and Barbara quarreled over leaving their cabin and argued about safety.

5.   Bill said nothing, quietly packed his car, and drove away in silence.

6.   The back roads and even the highway were flooded and cluttered with fallen branches.

7.   Barbara sat alone in the cabin and trembled with fear.

8.   Both Bill and Barbara regretted their quarrel.

9.   They both worried about each other.

10.   They felt foolish and decided not to quarrel again.

EXERCISE 2H: SENTENCE COMBINING

Following the example, combine each group of simple sentences to make one or two clear, concise simple sentences.

EXAMPLE: The book lay on the desk.

   The book was a textbook.

   The desk was the student's.

   He was a freshman.

   The textbook lay on the freshman's desk.

1.   This is my favorite poem.

   It is a sonnet.

   This sonnet was written by Shakespeare.

   It is numbered 73.

2. The *Just-So Stories* were written by Rudyard Kipling.

   They are children's stories.

   Adults enjoy them, too.

   They pretend to tell how animals got their present forms.

   _____

3. Joe's new car stands in the driveway.

   It is a dark red station wagon.

   It is a Horizon.

   Joe is proud of it.

   _____

4. The teacher's office is untidy.

   Books bulge out of bookcases.

   Papers clutter his desk.

   Pipe ashes dust everything.

   _____

5. Last week's snow is still heaped in piles.

   The piles are crusted.

   They are also dirty.

   _____

6. Today's snow covers everything.

   It looks like a soft blanket.

   It covers the dirt.

   The world looks pretty again.

   _____

7. We are a third through the new semester.

   It is the spring semester.

   It is my last semester.

   _____

8. The story was difficult to understand.

The hero's purpose was not clear.

It raised questions in my mind.

They are still there.

_____

9. Our cabin stood in a little clearing.

The lake bordered the clearing.

The lake was deep blue.

It reflected the sky.

_____

10. We used the cabin in hunting season.

We used it for get-away weekends.

We often use it for Thanksgiving.

We once used it for a winter vacation.

_____

VIRTUES AND LIMITATIONS
OF THE SIMPLE SENTENCE

What sets the simple sentence apart from all other forms of sentences is chiefly its unity, its oneness. It expresses a single idea:

It rained on Sunday.
Jim had a quarrel with his girlfriend.
Hummingbirds and bees hovered and zigzagged around the honeysuckles.

This singleness makes the simple sentence especially valuable for two purposes. First, if you have something to say that really is a single thought, the simple sentence is best because the simplicity of the sentence form fits the simplicity of the sentence meaning. Thus, the readers *know* without question what thought you mean. There are no added thoughts to distract them. Especially if you are expressing an emotion, you would probably not want to add more information to your main thought. You would not be very effective, for example, if you wrote:

Because you have a lot of money and drive a nifty sports car and are a neat dresser and a marvelous dancer, I love you.

All of those things might be true, but you probably would be more persuasive if you said simply:

I love you.

Second, the simple sentence is short, and brevity is a virtue. Using more words than you need tends to make you a boring writer.

The simple sentence, then, can be a very effective way to express your ideas. It has the virtue of being simple and direct, easy to understand, and strong. If you choose clear and specific subjects, verbs, and completers, and if you add modifiers that sharpen, verify, and clarify them, you can do a lot with the simple sentence.

The simple sentence does, however, have limitations. For one thing, a long series of simple sentences sounds choppy. A long paragraph made up entirely of simple sentences quickly gets monotonous. More important, you often want to present more than a simple thought. You may wish to show an idea that has two or more closely related thoughts.

Using only simple sentences, you cannot show that one idea is more important than another. Also, you cannot easily show relationships between ideas using only simple sentences. Every thought stands alone, and all are equally important. In Chapters 14 and 15, we will discuss other types of sentences and sentence combining. As you learn these other types of sentences, you will be able to avoid using simple sentences exclusively in your writing.

WRITING FROM READING

Reading without Words—Again

Although, of course, the most important sense of *reading* is to follow printed words across a page, there are many other senses of *reading*. Reading, in these other senses, just indicates that you receive information from something. Farmers, for example, *read* the weather to foresee whether it will rain or storm or be hot and dry. (Farmers also listen to weather forecasters on the radio and television, where professional forecasters *read* charts and illustrations and satellite pictures to reach conclusions about what the weather will be.)

During the early days of our country, many people believed in a religion called deism. Deists believed that God was everywhere and that to see God all you had to do was "to read the book of the creatures." They believed, in other words, that the world of created things—stars and snowflakes, mountains and flowers—all "proclaim the glory of God." They believed that "reading" creation and meditating on the wonder and mystery of created things led you to a conviction of God's presence everywhere.

On a less philosophical and more practical level, another kind of "reading" that is essentially not based on words is reading a map. You can gather much information from maps if you know how to read them. The first thing you need to remember when you look at a map is that the top is north and the bottom is south; the right-hand side is east and the left-hand side is west.

If you have read a wonderful novel called *The Adventures of Huckleberry Finn,* you will recall that Huck and Jim are running away in order for Jim to free himself from slavery. But they are escaping on a raft that floats downstream on the Mississippi River, which flows from north to south. This obviously means that they are heading south, deeper and deeper into the slave states, and farther and farther away from Jim's freedom! If they had had a map and knew how to read it, they would not have made this serious mistake.

Maps differ in some details, but most maps are basically the same; the differences are explained in a tiny chart or code at the bottom of the page. Find a map of the United States and see what kinds of information you can gather.

For example, you can see that the United States presents a symmetrical picture. Reading from right to left, from the Atlantic to the Pacific Ocean, there first is a broad strip of coastal plain. Then a string of mountains runs from north to south. In the center of the country, west of the mountains, there is a vast, flat area cut almost in the center by the great river system of the Missouri-Mississippi River. Westward, beyond the Great Plains, there rises up another mountain chain, also running from north to south. And beyond the mountains is another coastal plain that parallels the Pacific Ocean.

Maps are not only informative, but they are also fascinating to many people because they communicate such a sense of place. Looking at a map of the southwest United States, you spot the city of Taos and remember what a wonderful time you had there looking at the Indian ruins. Or looking at a map of New England, you see the little island of Nantucket off the Massachusetts coast, and you hope you can go there next year.

Three recent popular books have been based on the idea of "get a good map and set out." The earliest was John Steinbeck's *Travels with Charley*. Steinbeck pored over his map to determine where to go to understand America. Once he decided, he and his poodle Charley took off in a small van and, following the directions he received from his map, they covered the country. A second book with a similar purpose was written by William Least Heat Moon, an Indian, who wanted to see the back country of the United States. Moon didn't want to go whizzing along superhighways dotted with fast-food stands and suburban malls. So, he looked at his trusty map and noticed that secondary roads were marked in blue ink. He called his book of fascinating observations *Blue Highways*.

A third traveler to write a book based on a map was Peter Jenkins who, with his dog, *walked* across the United States following the directions on his map. Jenkins's book is called *A Walk Across America*.

Go to the nearest library and find a good atlas. First, make a list of the types of maps you can find, such as political map, relief map.

_____   _____

_____   _____

_____   _____

_____   _____

Next make a list of the types of information you can gather from maps, such as: What is the distance between two cities? What are the state capitals?

Then, based on what you can see on your map(s), write a paragraph about a vacation trip that would be fun to take.

Finally, pretend that you are a salesperson and make up a sales itinerary that you could reasonably cover starting on a Monday morning and getting home in time for the weekend. Your itinerary will differ depending on what you are selling—for example, seed potatoes or computer software.

3 *Verbs*

The second element of the simple sentence is the *verb*. Most simple sentences follow one of two possible patterns:

1. *Subject*   *Verb*
    The baby   cried.
    The mother   worried.
                 or

2. *Subject*   *Verb*   *Completer*
    The car   struck   the jaywalker.
    The boys   jogged   quickly.

In the first pattern, the subject does (or is) something; there is an actor and an action. In the second pattern, the subject does (or is) something about which the writer says something more. (Completers will be discussed in a later chapter.) What is done, the action, is determined by the verb.

TENSE

Verbs express both *action*—for example: swim, think, eat, remember—and *condition*—for example: be, seem, appear. Almost equally important, they show the *time* of the action or condition. Time as expressed in verbs is called *tense*. The four most frequently used tenses are the *present* (what's happen-

Past: I *was* an acorn.   Present: I *am* a sapling.   Future: I *will be* an oak tree.

ing now); the *future* (what will happen); the *past* (what has happened); and the *past perfect* (what has happened before the past action).

Present:	He walks.
Future:	He will walk.
Past:	He walked.
Past perfect:	He had walked.

Your sentence sense will usually tell you what tense to use.

If it *happens* now, it *is* present tense.

If it *will happen* tomorrow, it *will be* future tense.

If it *happened* yesterday, it *was* past tense.

If it *had happened* the day before yesterday, it *would have been* past perfect tense.

The important thing to remember about using tense is that you must be consistent. You confuse your reader if you jump from one tense to another. People often make this error by switching from the past to the present or from the present to the past.

Incorrect:	He *walked* to the window and *calls* down to his brother.
Correct:	He *walks* to the window and *calls* down to his brother.

or

He *walked* to the window and *called* down to his brother.

Occasionally, there is a logical reason to switch tenses within one sentence. Consider this example:

The chemistry professor said, "Water *is composed* of hydrogen and oxygen."

In this case, the professor said the statement in the past, but it still is true in the present. If there is such a logical reason, then you can shift tenses. Otherwise, you must remain in the same tense.

Present

	Singular	Plural
First person (speaker)	I call	we call
Second person (person spoken to)	you call	you call
Third person (person spoken about)	he, she, it *calls**	they call

Future

	Singular	Plural
First person	I will call	we will call
Second person	you will call	you will call
Third person	he, she, it will call	they will call

Past

	Singular	Plural
First person	I called	we called
Second person	you called	you called
Third person	he, she, it called	they called

Past Perfect

	Singular	Plural
First person	I had called	we had called
Second person	you had called	you had called
Third person	he, she, it had called	they had called

PRINCIPAL PARTS OF VERBS

To use any verb correctly, you must be aware of what are called its principal parts. You can find these principal parts in the dictionary entry following the verb itself.

Infinitive: to know	I need *to know* the answer.
Present tense, third person singular: knows	She *knows* my mother.
Past tense: knew	He *knew* math well.

---

* Notice that the form has changed, but *only* in the third person singular of the present tense of the main verb and the present tense of the helping verb for the present perfect tense.

31

Present participle: knowing	The next best thing to *knowing* something is *knowing* where to find it.
Past participle: known	I have *known* him for years.
Infinitive: to learn	I need *to learn* this chart.
Present tense, third person singular: learns	The child *learns* through play.
Past tense: learned	He *learned* his lesson.
Present participle: learning	He is *learning* his multiplication tables.
Past participle: learned	He has *learned* his multiplication tables.

Knowing these principal parts and the helping verbs, you can make up any possible verb form.

EXERCISE 3A: IDENTIFYING VERBS

Underline the verbs in the following sentences.

1. She was afraid of him.
2. Mr. Ciello has been teaching for thirty years.
3. Every day after class, the gang went to the drugstore.
4. Fear dominated the classroom on the day of the first test.
5. Everyone loved the comedians in the review.
6. Someone across the street called to me.
7. The apartment was expertly decorated.
8. Travel is my favorite recreation.
9. Ernie traveled with his father and his son to Greece this year.
10. Who gave you the black eye?

EXERCISE 3B: IDENTIFYING VERBS

Underline the verbs in the following sentences.

1. Recognizing verbs is easy.
2. Crowds at the USFL football games are often small.

3. She churned through the water on her way to an Olympic gold medal.

4. Following surgery, he developed a whole new way of life.

5. Hairstyles of the sixties look funny to us today.

6. A shaman is an Indian witch doctor.

7. Three pedestrians were killed in the accident.

8. Flashdancing may be the fad of the eighties.

9. Hot dogs, lathered in mustard and spiced with onions, taste great!

10. Of all the emotions, vengeance is the worst.

HELPING VERBS (AUXILIARIES)

One sentence part that a writer must be aware of is the helping verb, also called the auxiliary. Its name explains what it does: it helps the main verb make its meaning clear. It can do this by altering mood, tense, or emphasis. It also helps in forming questions and making negative statements.

Mood shows possibility or potential. Auxiliaries that indicate mood include *may, can, must, might, could, would,* and *should.*

Your sentence sense will tell you that the following sentences differ in meaning because of the helping verb used:

He *may* go.   (He has a choice.)

He *can* go.   (He is physically able to go.)

33

He *must* go.   (Something or someone is forcing him.)

He *might* go.   (Past tense of *may*.)

He *could* go.   (Past tense of *can*.)

He *would* go.   (Past tense of *will*.)

He *should* go.   (Past tense of *shall*; it suggests an obligation to go.)

The helping verbs also indicate *tense*, which means time.

> the future: shall, will.
>> I *shall* go tomorrow.
>> I *will* go tomorrow.
> the past: have, has, had.
>> I *have* gone many times.
>> He *has* gone many times.
>> He *had* gone many times before he met you.

The helping verbs can supply emphasis, using the words *do, does, did*.

> He *did* go.
> *Do* go away.

These same helping verbs combined with *not* can make negative statements.

> He *did not* go.
> *Do not* go away.

They also help form questions.

> *Did* he go?
> *Does* he go away tomorrow, *do* you think?

EXERCISE 3C: HELPING VERBS

In the following sentences, decide what the helping verb indicates: possibility, tense, emphasis, necessity, choice.

EXAMPLE: Do turn down that radio.   *emphasis*

You must surrender.   *necessity*

1.   He did not send the telegram. _____

2.   We should send a message for him. _____

3.   No one will know what to do. _____

4.   His parents have had no word from him at all. _____

5.   He does irritate me by his carelessness. _____

6.   His parents never have corrected him about this. _____

7.   They should not have ignored such careless unkindness. _____

8.   They can't influence him now. _____

9.   Friends and family will suffer from his carelessness in the future. _____

10. I guess that we simply must forgive him or give him up. _____

EXERCISE 3D: IDENTIFYING HELPING VERBS

Underline the helping verb in each of the following sentences.

1.   We have laughed all through the movie.

2.   Do come to my party.

3.   I must go home now.

4.   They never have put their house in good shape.

5.   We will announce the winner tomorrow.

6.   Do you know who the choices are?

7.   He did not sing well.

8.   She had received the notice two months before she answered it.

9.   We do respect your wishes; we always have respected your wishes.

10. They have had bad luck ever since they married.

EXERCISE 3E: IDENTIFYING HELPING VERBS

Circle the correct helping verb in each of the following sentences.

1.   (May, Can) I leave the class?

2.   I (may, might) be able to leave tomorrow.

3.   I (should, should have) left yesterday.

4.   He (will, would) never play baseball next week.

5. You (can, may) lift your own weight.

6. They (do not, did not) want to go to the movies tonight.

7. We (had, have had) tests every day last week.

8. He (does, did) chatter for hours this afternoon.

9. (Do, Does) he understand the problem?

10. We (may, can) persuade the voters if we are good speakers.

ACTIVE AND PASSIVE VERBS (VOICE)

Verbs are primarily used to show action, as in such sentences as "Jack *jumped* over the candlestick" or "The bomb *exploded*." Most of the time you want your verbs to be active because the action lends vigor and clarity to your writing.

Action verbs show rather than tell. In the active voice, the doer of an action, the actor, is the subject of the verb.

```
    actor
subject    action
 Fred     kicked the door.
```

```
      actor
      subject     action
The supervisor    rang  the alarm.
```

Active Voice: Fred *kicked* the door.

Passive Voice: The door *was kicked* by Fred.

In the passive voice, the real actor is not the subject.

>   subject   action   actor
> The   door   *was kicked* by Fred.

>   subject   action   actor
> The   alarm   *was rung* by the firefighter.

Using the passive voice slows down the sentence without adding meaning or clarity. Therefore, you will usually choose the active voice.

Sometimes, however, the passive voice is effective, as in the following cases.

1.   When the doer of the action is unknown or unimportant:

    Dr. Livingston was hunted by many searchers.

    In this sentence, the focus is on Dr. Livingston. The identity of the searchers is of little importance.

2.   When the writer wants to emphasize the receiver of the action:

    Dr. Livingston was finally found by Stanley.

  In this sentence Livingston is more important than Stanley.

EXERCISE 3F: USING ACTIVE VERBS

Rewrite the following sentences to make them *active* rather than *passive.* If the passive voice is used effectively, mark the sentence with a *C* (correct).

1.   The players were applauded by the fans.

    _____

2.   The class was dismissed by the instructor.

    _____

3.   The bridge was built in 1954.

    _____

4.   The toddler was hurt by his fall.

    _____

5.   The book was read by the class.

    _____

6.   The dynasty was founded by Suleiman the First.

    _____

7. Job was punished by God without reason.

    _____

8. The stronger man was beaten by the weaker.

    _____

9. "Ode on a Grecian Urn" was written by Keats.

    _____

10. The senator was elected by a two-thirds majority.

    _____

LINKING VERBS

Not all verbs are active or passive; some are *linking verbs* that don't act on anything. They simply indicate a condition by linking or connecting the subject with the words that come after the verb. They are almost the same as the "equals" mark in mathematics. Logically, then, the two sides of the sentence are interchangeable.

> I *am* a student.   A student *am* I.

The most common linking verbs are the many forms of the verb *to be*, but *to become, to seem,* and *to appear* are also common linking verbs. Verbs that express the five senses are also usually linking verbs: *to feel, to look, to smell, to taste,* and *to sound.*

Other Uses of the Verb *To Be*

Various forms of the verb *to be* can help shape the passive voice.

> *Active:*   The general praised the soldier.
>
> *Passive:* The soldier *was* praised by the general.
>
> *Active:*   The audience applauds the violinist.
>
> *Passive:* The violinist *is* applauded by the audience.

EXERCISE 3G: RECOGNIZING ACTION VERBS

Underline the verb (the word that shows action) in each of the following sentences.

1. Carlos's wild pitch hit the umpire.

2. She supports a family of five.

3. We followed the Appalachian Trail and the Blue Ridge Parkway.

4. Phillip carried two briefcases on every trip.

5. Herbie's ice cream melted in the blazing sun.

6. Marie drove a rental car from the airport to her grandmother's house.

7. They drove their parents mad.

8. Juan stole third base.

9. Caroline drives a hard bargain.

10. People often speak before they think.

EXERCISE 3H: RECOGNIZING LINKING VERBS

Underline the linking verb in each of the following sentences.

1. Things looked gloomy for Harold.

2. Mrs. Juarez's daughter is now a doctor.

3. The Smiths are her next-door neighbors.

4. That course of action is completely wrong.

5. Mary suddenly became ill.

6. He looks quite distinguished.

7. She has become very pretty.

8. The weather seemed unusually warm for March.

9. The sun scarcely appears.

10. To have fish more often would be good for them.

WRITING FROM READING

Discovering the Fringe Benefits of Learning

Writing is a skill that is often associated solely with English composition class. In reality, however, what you learn in composition class can help you in other classes as well—not just because writing may be a part of your grade in other classes, but because the concepts governing writing apply to areas other than English. The following thoughts, for example, written by a professor of physics, illustrate one way in which the principles of written communication apply to the science of physics:

The solution to a physics problem is an essay, even though it may largely be written in mathematical symbolism. It should begin with a topic sentence or sentences (i.e., a description of the physical situation under consideration), then proceed through a body that identifies the relevant principles governing the situation. Next comes a chain of logic (generally, but not always, mathematical) leading to a conclusion. Often, more than one conclusion is legitimately possible . . . If there is a service the English faculty can provide, it would be to emphasize that the principles of written communication and rhetoric apply equally well to the analysis of a passage from Shakespeare or the solution of a heat-transfer problem in thermodynamics.

Dr. Ernest Zebrowski, Jr.

Can you think of some instances in which what you learned in one class helped you understand what you were studying in another? Get together with some of your classmates and have a brainstorming session. See how many different examples you can think of as a group. Students with academic interests different from yours might suggest links between subject areas that you have never thought of. After you have finished brainstorming, write down your thoughts on paper.

4

Recognizing Other Sentence Parts

COMPLETERS

In Chapters 2 and 3, you learned the importance of subjects and verbs. You learned, in fact, that some sentences effectively communicate a complete thought with nothing but a subject and a verb.

> We lost!
> You lied.
> Money talks.

Your sentence sense tells you that, without any other words, these thoughts are complete. However, most sentences need more than a subject and a verb to communicate a thought clearly. For example:

> George punched.
> The doctor wrote.

Your sentence sense tells you that these thoughts are incomplete. George punched *whom?* The doctor wrote *what?* These sentences could be completed in numerous ways:

> George punched his *boss.*
> George punched *Mr. Thackery* so hard that his hand ached all week.
> George punched *him.*

The doctor wrote an illegible *prescription.*

The doctor wrote a *letter* to my employer.

The doctor wrote a fascinating *book* about medical malpractice.

Notice that, in each sentence, the key word that completes the action of the verb is a noun or a pronoun (*boss, him, prescription*). These noun completers (sometimes called *direct objects*) work best with action verbs because they complete the action suggested by the verb. You can't form a clear picture in your mind with "George punched," but you *can* picture George punching another person. Similarly, "The doctor wrote" means little until you can picture the doctor writing a prescription, a letter, or a book.

Completers, then, are often necessary parts of a sentence, and they are just as easy to recognize as subjects and verbs are. Just asking *Who?* or *What?* after the verb usually leads you directly to the completer. For example, consider the sentence, "The nurse dispensed the medication." Now ask, "The nurse dispensed *what?*" "The medication" is the completer.

Remember, however, that not all verbs are action verbs. As you learned in Chapter 3, some verbs don't act on anything. These linking verbs simply connect the subject with the words that come after them:

The water was *cold.*

Fred is a *mechanic.*

With linking verbs, the completers are often adjectives (*cold*) or sometimes adverbs (*here*). The most common linking verbs followed by adjective completers are the forms of the verb *to be* (*is, was, are, were,* etc.). *To seem, to appear,* and *to become* are also common linking verbs followed by adjective completers: Tony seemed *angry.* . . . Mahoney appeared *ill.* . . . Levi became *nervous.* The linking verbs that express the five senses—*to feel, to look, to smell, to taste,* and *to sound*—are also usually followed by adjective completers.

EXERCISE 4A: DISTINGUISHING NOUN COMPLETERS FROM ADJECTIVE COMPLETERS

Complete the following sets of sentence beginnings. Notice that the first sentence in each set contains a linking verb and that the second contains an action verb. When you finish the exercise, examine your completers. Notice how your choice of completers was affected by different types of verbs.

EXAMPLE: The horse <u>was</u> _____<u>excited</u>_____ . (adjective completer)

It <u>kicked</u> _____<u>the fence</u>_____ . (noun completer)

1.   Elvira *appeared* _____ .

She *spilled* _____ .

2.   The child's story *was* _____ .

It *shocked* _____ .

3.   Richard *became* _____ .

He *resented* _____ .

4.   I *am* _____ .

I just *ate* _____ .

5.   The Tigers *were* _____ .

They *beat* _____ .

6.   Mike's voice *sounded* _____ .

It certainly *impressed* _____ .

7.   Warm milk *tastes* _____ .

It *nauseates* _____ .

8.   Melinda *looks* _____ .

She *bleached* _____ .

9.   The patient *felt* _____ .

He *closed* _____ .

10.   The workers *are* _____ .

They are *picketing* _____ .

EXERCISE 4B: RECOGNIZING SUBJECTS, VERBS, AND COMPLETERS

Try finding the subject-verb-completer in the following sentences. Underline the subject, verb, and completer. Mark the subject *S,* the verb (including helping verbs) *V,* and the completer *C.* (Remember, not all sentences have completers.)

43

EXAMPLE: Old movies, with stars like Charlie Chaplin and Buster Keaton,
         V   C
         are my favorites.

              S   V   C
         Muhammed Ali knocked out most of his opponents in fewer than five rounds.

1. Antarctica is our least known continent.

2. Some interesting things have been learned about it, though.

3. Ice, 7,000,000 cubic miles of it, covers this distant continent.

4. In some places, the ice is 14,000 feet (over 2½ miles) thick.

5. During the winter, Antarctica remains dark around the clock.

6. Spring arrives in September.

7. Houses are built inside tunnels carved out of the ice.

8. The tunnels protect the houses from the fierce winter storms.

9. Cold air must be circulated through the tunnels to prevent the ice from melting.

10. Things change fast in Antarctica.

11. An airport can float out to sea in minutes.

12. The temperature seldom rises above freezing.

13. Explorers have found mummified seals, possibly thousands of years old, preserved in the almost bacteria-free air.

14. Cooks serve visitors twenty-year-old steaks.

15. In fact, food left there by previous expeditions many years before can be eaten safely.

Using Clear and Specific Completers

Next to the subject and verb, the completer is the most important word in a sentence; therefore, you should choose a completer carefully. A clear and specific completer helps you get your message across to your readers. For example, suppose you wrote:

I bought a *car.*

What would your reader see? An old jalopy? A big luxury car? A sleek sports model? How much have you conveyed to your readers? By adding a few adjectives, you can give your reader a clearer image:

I bought a *metallic blue 1978 Corvette.*

EXERCISE 4C: MAKING COMPLETERS SPECIFIC

Improve the following sentences by making the underlined completer more specific. Then add details to make the completers even more specific.

EXAMPLE: Gene bought a vehicle.

Gene bought an antique car.

Gene bought a black Ford roadster in mint condition.

A vehicle.

A black Ford roadster in mint condition.

1.   John bought some clothes.

John bought _____.

John bought _____.

2.   The leaves clogged the plumbing.

The leaves clogged _____.

The leaves clogged _____.

3.   The fox chased the animal.

The fox chased _____.

The fox chased _____.

45

4. Admiral Robinson wrote a book.

   Admiral Robinson wrote _____.

   Admiral Robinson wrote _____.

5. Jill painted her room.

   Jill painted _____.

   Jill painted _____.

6. The bear climbed the tree.

   The bear climbed _____.

   The bear climbed _____.

7. Hurricane Josephine hit the coast.

   Hurricane Josephine hit _____.

   Hurricane Josephine hit _____.

8. The test scores revealed information.

   The test scores revealed _____.

   The test scores revealed _____.

9. Elliot's wife owns a store.

   Elliot's wife owns _____.

   Elliot's wife owns _____.

10. The restaurant served homemade desserts.

    The restaurant served homemade _____.

    The restaurant served homemade _____.

EXERCISE 4D: SUPPLYING CLEAR AND SPECIFIC COMPLETERS

Make the following sentences come alive by adding clear and specific completers.

1. The substitute quarterback threw _____

2. The volunteer at the hospital forgot _____

3. The police followed _____

4. The apple was _____

5. My father made _____

6. Tomorrow I'll take _____ .

7. The student got _____ from the teacher.

8. My little brother built _____ .

9. Jean hit _____ .

10. The nurse saved _____ .

11. Pat and Joe adopted _____ .

12. Americans like _____ .

13. I hate _____ .

14. My uncle knows _____ .

15. At the party, I met _____ .

16. The handicapped child needs _____ .

17. Bob baked _____ for the wedding.

18. The old man carried _____ .

19. The President's words startled _____ .

20. Good completers are _____ .

PREPOSITIONAL PHRASES

In all of your speaking and writing, you depend heavily on phrases like the following to modify the subject or verb and to complete the meaning of your sentences. All of these phrases are *prepositional phrases.*

throughout the country	*at* the bridge	*across* the river
on the road	*from* the beginning	*into* the trees
by the door	*for* my birthday	*among* ourselves
out the gate	*during* the winter	*behind* the curtain
over the hill	*beside* the stream	*along* the way
below the surface	*beneath* the stars	*down* memory lane
in the Bible	*above* the clouds	*between* you and me
against the world	*during* the war	*without* you

A prepositional phrase always consists of two parts: (1) the preposition, and (2) the object of the preposition—a noun or pronoun.

Sometimes groups of words function as a single preposition: *in accordance with, together with, in spite of, by means of, in front of,* and so on.

In spite of the storm, the patrol boat began its search.

Also, prepositional phrases are frequently strung together in a series:

Joel sat *by* the river bank *with* his feet *in* the cool water.

Prepositions can best be described as *relationship* words. Their function is to connect sentence parts and to show such relationships as who, what, where, when, why, and under what conditions.

The word *to* is not only a preposition but also a part of the infinitive. An infinitive is always the word *to* plus a verb, such as *to know, to assemble, to fly*.

EXERCISE 4E: RECOGNIZING PREPOSITIONAL PHRASES

Underline the prepositional phrases in the following articles from the U.S. Constitution.

THE FOUR FREEDOMS

Congress shall make no law respecting an establishment of religion, or prohibiting the free exercise thereof; or abridging the freedom of speech or of the press; or the right of the people peaceably to assemble and to petition the Government for a redress of grievances.

INCOME TAX

The Congress shall have power to lay and collect taxes on incomes, from whatever sources derived, without apportionment among the several states and without regard to any census or enumeration.

SEARCH AND SEIZURE

The right of the people to be secure in their persons, houses, papers, and effects, against unreasonable searches and seizures, shall not be violated, and no warrants shall issue but upon probable cause, supported by oath or affirmation, and particularly describing the place to be searched, and the persons or things to be seized.

The right of citizens of the United States to vote shall not be denied or abridged by the United States or by any state on account of sex.

Congress shall have power, by appropriate legislation, to enforce the provisions of this article.

Notice how much of the Constitution consists of prepositional phrases. Our rights as American citizens are defined in terms of brief but powerful prepositional phrases: freedom *of religion,* freedom *of speech,* freedom *of the press.* Thus, although you should use subjects, verbs, and completers as the key words in your sentences, be sure to also include prepositional phrases to clarify details and get your message across clearly.

EXERCISE 4F: USING PREPOSITIONAL PHRASES

Write a sentence using each of the following prepositional phrases.

1.   until the end of time _____

_____

2.   for the good of humanity _____

_____

3.   in the moonlight _____

_____

4.   after the war _____

_____

5.   between you and me _____

_____

6.   about Joe and her _____

_____

7.   to Stella and him _____

_____

8.   with an uneasy feeling _____

_____

9. about six miles above the Earth _____

    _____

10. in accordance with the treaty _____

    _____

EXERCISE 4G: PREPOSITIONAL PHRASES AS MODIFIERS

In each of the following sentences, circle the subject and the verb. Then draw a double line under each prepositional phrase and an arrow to the noun or verb that the phrase modifies.

EXAMPLE: A long (line) of devout followers (waits) in the blistering sun for the holy man.

1. One of the richest people in America is Gordon Getty.

2. There are many examples of furious battles over different interpretations of scriptural passages.

3. A strong odor of boiled cabbage sticks in your nostrils for days afterward.

4. She worked in the tavern across the street.

5. George C. Scott won an Academy Award for his role in *Patton.*

6. In quiet moments after his father's death, he dreamed about his future as a major league pitcher.

7. None of the rich kids was as happy with life as Al was at that moment.

8. The boss asked about Phyllis and me.

9. What is told to you and me in strict confidence should not be repeated by either one of us.

10. My older brother ran away from home before me, and my younger brother ran away from home after me.

WRITING FROM READING

Making Good Choices

Sometimes we become so familiar with a piece of writing that we take it for granted. We don't appreciate the author's writing skills because we never think about how he or she chose the words or how he or she arranged the words. Consider, for example, how often you have heard or read the following words:

> We hold these truths to be self-evident, that all men are created equal, that they are endowed by their Creator with certain unalienable rights, that among these are life, liberty, and the pursuit of happiness.

But do you know what unalienable means? What is an "unalienable right"? Why did Thomas Jefferson choose that word over all the other adjectives he could have used? If something is unalienable, it cannot be sold or transferred to anyone else. It is something that can never be taken away from the person to whom it belongs. That's why Jefferson chose the word "unalienable."

Do you think he made the best choice? Consider the possibilities. Focus specifically on the three words in the phrase: "certain unalienable rights."

Work in small groups with four or five of your classmates and revise Jefferson's phrase. With the aid of a dictionary and a thesaurus, substitute synonyms for "certain," "unalienable," and "rights," and see how each of your revisions affects the meaning of the preamble to the Declaration of Independence. How, for example, does the impact of

> . . . that men are endowed by their Creator with *certain unalienable rights* . . .

compare with

> . . . that men are endowed by their Creator with *some natural claims* . . . ?

51

Talk to the other groups in your class and see if they have arrived at similar conclusions about the choice of a particular word. After you have exhausted all of the possibilities you can think of, try the same exercise with the phrase: "life, liberty, and the pursuit of happiness."

The arrangement of a writer's thoughts also has a powerful effect on the reader. Jefferson not only chose his words carefully; he arranged them effectively. If you read the following revisions aloud, you will see that they are less effective than Jefferson's original wording. Notice how the significance of "all men are created equal" is diminished when it appears in a different part of the passage. It almost becomes an afterthought—not what Jefferson intended at all:

> We hold these truths to be self-evident, that men are endowed by their Creator with certain unalienable rights, that life, liberty, and the pursuit of happiness are among these, and that all men are created equal.

> We hold these truths to be self-evident, that life, liberty, and the pursuit of happiness are unalienable rights which the Creator has endowed men with and that all men are created equal.

Choose a piece of writing with which you are familiar—a piece of writing that you think is good—and experiment with the arrangement of the author's words and phrases. With each revision, notice how arrangement affects meaning.

5 *Sentence Fragments*

As the first two chapters indicated, a sentence, especially a written sentence, should usually be complete, which means that it should have at least a subject and a verb or, more often, a subject, a verb, and a completer. Such complete sentences make sense because they say something that has meaning for the reader. When a sentence is not complete—that is, when it is just a broken-off piece of a sentence—it is called a sentence fragment. A sentence fragment usually fails to convey a clear meaning.

Sentence fragments result from any of four causes:

The sentence has no subject.

The sentence has no verb.

The sentence has only part of a verb.

The sentence starts with a word that cannot begin a main clause.

LACK OF SUBJECT

A group of words without a subject makes little sense because no one can tell who or what the sentence is about.

Carried on like mad.	Who did?
Foamed at the mouth.	Who or what did?
Has been a long time coming.	Who or what has been?

1. No subject
2. No verb
3. Only part of a verb
4. Wrong opening word

If you have trouble picking out subjects but can pick out verbs, notice that if you put "Who?" or "What?" before the verb, the answer will be the subject!

S
Who carried on like mad? *George* carried on like mad.

S
Who or *what* foamed at the mouth? The *collie* foamed at the mouth.

S
What has been a long time coming? *His apology* has been a long time coming.

LACK OF VERB

A group of words without a verb makes little sense because no statement is made about the subject.

The girl with the red hair and sparkling blue eyes.
  Well, what about her?

The brown and white spotted pup.
  What about the pup?

Applying for the job of security guard at the local atomic plant.
  What about applying?

If you do not have a verb, you do not have a statement about the subject; therefore, you do not have a complete thought. A verb is needed to show what something *is* or *does:*

The girl with the red hair and sparkling blue eyes turned me down.

The brown and white spotted pup scampered across the porch.

Applying for the job of security guard at the local atomic plant involved three interviews.

EXERCISE 5A: RECOGNIZING THE ABSENCE OF A SUBJECT OR A VERB

Examine the following fragments and determine what is missing in each: a subject, a verb, or both. Then correct each fragment by supplying whatever is needed.

1.   Showered me with hugs and kisses when she got home from school.

_____

2.   A quaint old gentleman in the back of the room.

_____

3.   Delights in playing practical jokes on his brother.

_____

4.   In the middle of the picture.

_____

5.   Makes me laugh.

_____

6.   These kinds of experiences.

_____

7.   Inside the gates of the Hollywood mansion.

_____

8.   Three vicious Dobermans.

_____

9.   The outrageous prices on all of the "sale" items.

_____

10. Owns one of the most beautiful vineyards in California.

_____

INCOMPLETE VERB

Sometimes fragments occur because the verb is incomplete. Consider the following examples:

> Washing the dishes.
> Dad washing the dishes.

There is no subject in the first sentence, but notice that adding a subject in the second one still did not make the thought complete. "Dad washing the dishes" is not a complete thought either. A reader will be confused until the missing part of the verb is added.

> Dad *is* washing the dishes.

Your sentence sense tells you that an *ing* verb needs a helping verb. That's why *ing* verbs can't be used as main verbs.

EXERCISE 5B: FIXING FRAGMENTS CAUSED BY INCOMPLETE VERBS

Each of the following fragments begins with an *ing* verb. Complete the sentences by supplying a subject and adding a helping verb.

EXAMPLE: _____ taking the dog for a walk.

<u>Lil was</u> taking the dog for a walk.

1. _____ doing her homework.

2. _____ helping me paint my car.

3. _____ showing Vanessa his etchings.

4. _____ reading my favorite cartoon strip— "Doonesbury."

5. _____ writing a letter to my mother.

6. _____ waiting for you to apologize.

7. _____ playing his first season in the pros this year.

8. _____ listening to the radio.

9. _____ planning to open a shelter for the homeless.

10. _____ making a mountain out of a molehill.

INCORRECT OPENING WORDS

Sometimes placing a word before a subject and a verb makes a sentence a fragment. Look at a few examples:

Sentence: I went to school.
Fragment: When I went to school.

Sentence: Jack and Jill went up the hill.
Fragment: After Jack and Jill went up the hill.

Sentence: I spilled spaghetti all over my lap.
Fragment: Before I spilled spaghetti all over my lap.

Words like these, which make a sentence a fragment, are called *subordinate conjunctions.* The fragments that they make are called *dependent clauses.* Because of your sentence sense, you already know that including such words first makes the sentence incomplete. It leaves you wondering what happened *when* I went to school or *after* Jack and Jill went up the hill or *before* I spilled spaghetti all over my lap.

The following list might help you recognize incorrect opening words (subordinate conjunctions):

after	as soon as	provided	whatever
although	because	provided that	when
as	before	since	whenever
as far as	even	so that	where
as if	even though	though	wherever
as long as	if	unless	whether
as much as	in order to	until	while
	in order that		why

EXERCISE 5C: SUBORDINATE CONJUNCTIONS

Choose five of the words from the list above and place them at the beginning of the following sentence. Notice how using these words turns each sentence into an incomplete thought.

1. _____ Adam kissed Eve.

2. _____ Adam kissed Eve.

3. _____ Adam kissed Eve.

4. _____ Adam kissed Eve.

5. _____ Adam kissed Eve.

EXERCISE 5D: RECOGNIZING DEPENDENT CLAUSES AS FRAGMENTS

In the following exercise, mark the sentences *S* and the fragments *F*. If a subordinate conjunction makes the sentence a fragment, circle the conjunction.

_____ 1. When Danny went to college.

_____ 2. Driving fast is dangerous.

_____ 3. Putting rebellious kids in jail is not the answer.

_____ 4. Before I took the test.

_____ 5. Although fingerprinting is messy.

_____ 6. I love shrimp.

_____ 7. Because I thought I was a tough guy and could do anything.

_____ 8. After a freak rain storm that dropped eight inches of rain in two hours.

_____ 9. Pittsburgh was named the number one city in the country.

_____ 10. When an energetic leader is in charge.

_____ 11. Springtime is the best time.

_____ 12. Because she was blond and beautiful.

_____ 13. There are 16 million illegal aliens in America today.

_____ 14. Why President Kennedy and Martin Luther King were shot.

_____ 15. If you go away tomorrow.

EXERCISE 5E: CORRECTING FRAGMENTS

Tell which of the following groups of words are sentences and which are fragments. Mark the fragments *F,* the complete sentences *S.* Correct the fragments.

1.   Yesterday, going to the movies and losing my wallet. _____

_____

2.   Jim graduated last Tuesday. _____

3.   Taking the class helped me overcome my fear. _____

_____

4.   Is still going on long after the start of baseball, golf, and summer sports. _____

_____

5.   Was the end of the line for most of us. _____

_____

6.   Who will make the best president? _____

_____

7.   Sailing across the ocean in a twenty-seven foot boat. _____

_____

8.   The sailors, young, good-looking fellows. _____

_____

9.   Find your own way of expressing yourself. _____

_____

10.   I need to make an A in English. _____

_____

EXERCISE 5F: IDENTIFYING CAUSES OF FRAGMENTS

Tell which of the following groups of words are sentences and which are fragments. Then, tell what caused the fragment: lack of subject, lack of verb, incomplete verb, or wrong opening word.

1.   Until I met you. _____

2.   Holding your place in line. _____

3.   Between the dark and the daylight, when the night is beginning to fall.

     _____

4.   Galloped away in all directions._____

5.   Had no interest in computers._____

6.   The sound heard through the traffic noises._____

7.   Walked to work every morning._____

8.   The librarian, a tall, dark-haired young woman._____

9.   Although John had a college degree._____

10. The pleasant climate, breezy and bright._____

11. Mark driving to the stadium._____

12. If you win the lottery._____

13. Learning how to change a flat tire._____

14. For example, my next-door neighbor._____

15. Laughing at my jokes._____

WRITING FROM READING

Experimenting with Completers

Children think primarily in concrete terms—in terms of what they can see, touch, taste, feel, or smell. Thus, when first or second graders attempt to write their first sentences, their subjects and completers are usually simple and concrete: "Allison broke my crayons." "My Daddy bought a puppy." As they get older, however, their vocabulary grows, their experiences expand, and their thought processes become more complex. A six-year-old, for example, would probably complete sentences beginning with "I like . . ." with primarily one-word completers—someone or something that the child likes.

> I like *Grandma*.
> I like the *Cookie Monster*.
> I like *snowflakes* . . . I like *raindrops*.

However, the completers that would come to an adult's mind after "I like . . ." are usually more varied and specific. An adult might also like the Cookie Monster, but an adult's responses in general would probably be more specific. An adult might, for example, like "my grandmother's smile," and some of his or her favorite things might not be "raindrops" or "snowflakes," but "raindrops on roses" and "snowflakes that stay on my nose and eyelashes."

The last two completers are some of the favorite things that Maria Von Trapp (Julie Andrews) sang about in the movie *The Sound of Music*. Notice the different techniques that the lyricist used to make "My Favorite Things" specific and interesting:

Noun + a short phrase	"raindrops *on roses*"
Two descriptive words + a noun	"*warm woolen* mittens"
A noun + a "that" clause	"snowflakes *that stay on my nose and eyelashes*"

Think about some of *your* favorite things and try writing your own lyrics to the song. Follow the same pattern used in "My Favorite Things," but with your own ideas. For example, your authors produced the following lines:

Music by Gershwin and old movie classics,
A room filled with books and my worn-out green hassock,
Picnics by moonlight and birds on the wing.
These are a few of my favorite things.

Cream cheese with olives and biscuits with honey,
Cornbread with bacon, a fried egg that's sunny,
Salads of green beans and red onion rings.
These are a few of my favorite things.

6
Punctuating Simple Sentences

In order to keep from confusing your readers, you must show them where each of your thoughts begins and ends. You do this by capitalizing the first word of each sentence and by providing an appropriate punctuation mark after the last word. You capitalize the first word of every sentence, even if the sentence consists of only one word.

Hurry.
Sure.

Listen.
No.

Sentences, then, always begin with a capital letter. However, there are several ways that sentences can end. Most sentences end in periods, which show that the thought has been finished, but sometimes different punctuation marks are needed. What do the different end punctuation marks tell you in the following conversations?

"Will you marry me?"
"No." (This could mean "I can't," "I won't," or "I'm sorry, but no.")

"Will you marry me?"
"No!" (This probably means "Are you crazy? Never!")

"No!"

"Will you marry me?"
"What?" (This could mean "What did you say? I didn't hear you.")

"Will you marry me?"
"What!" (This probably means "Are you crazy? Never!")

"What!"

An exclamation point at the end of a sentence does not always mean "Are you crazy?" It usually shows urgency, alarm, fear, or sarcasm. Use it when you want to show one of these emotions:

Help me!
Watch out!
Hurry!
I was terrified!
Of course, YOU never do anything wrong!

You should also use the exclamation mark to show strong emphasis.

We will never surrender to terrorists!
For heaven's sake, don't just stand there!

The exclamation point should be used sparingly . If it is overused, it quickly loses its effectiveness, and your writing seems strained and un-natural.

A question mark indicates that the writer or speaker is seeking an answer. A writer shows this by putting a question mark at the end of the sentence.

Why did you do that?
Where is my book?
When did the accident happen?

EXERCISE 6A: END PUNCTUATION, SENTENCE LEVEL

Read the following sentences carefully. After each sentence, place either a period, a question mark, or an exclamation point, depending on which mark of end punctuation best suits the sentence.

1.   Come in and sit down

2.   Are you hungry

3.   Make yourself a peanut butter and jelly sandwich

4.   Have you made your sandwich yet

5.   You put WHAT on your sandwich

6.   Are you really going to eat that

7. YUK

8. You must have an iron stomach

9. How long have you been putting anchovies on your peanut butter and jelly sandwiches

10. You really do have some strange eating habits

EXERCISE 6B: END PUNCTUATION, PARAGRAPH LEVEL

Provide the capital letters and correct end punctuation in the following paragraph.

Malcolm X played many opposing roles in his life he was a thief and a minister, a drug addict and a strict teetotaler, a hustler and a political leader an advocate of black violence and a spokesperson for peace between the races he spent time in jail and in churches he lived in ghettos and penthouses once so uneducated that he couldn't read the mail sent to him, he became one of the nation's most powerful orators though he was once so anti-white that he told blacks to get guns to defend themselves against "the blue-eyed devils," he later led the movement for nonviolence after increasing membership in the Black Muslims by 200 percent, he turned against the group and left it he was starting a new movement for blacks when he was murdered Malcolm himself described his life as "a chronology of changes."

DIRECT AND INDIRECT QUESTIONS

Question marks are used only after direct questions.

Are you getting married?
Did you talk to your advisor yet?

Indirect questions, however, are not followed by question marks; they end with periods. An indirect question is a statement about a question.

I asked Craig if he was getting married.
I asked Gretchen if she had talked to her advisor yet.

EXERCISE 6C: PUNCTUATING DIRECT AND INDIRECT QUESTIONS

Read the following conversation. Then place a question mark after each
direct question and a period after each indirect question.

Tim:	Do you know anything about word processors
Barb:	Not much. Why don't you ask Carol
Tim:	I already asked her if she could help me
Barb:	Did she give you any useful information
Tim:	No. She asked me if I wanted to visit her Dad's computer store
Barb:	What did you say
Tim:	I asked her if she always answered a question with a question
Barb:	Did that make her angry
Tim:	No. In fact, she asked me if I would have dinner with her on Friday
Barb:	What did you tell her
Tim:	What do you think

COMMAS WITHIN SIMPLE SENTENCES

Simple sentences usually include phrases that clarify the action completed
by the subject and verb. These phrases either occur outside of the main
clause or they interrupt the internal flow of the main clause. In both cases,
commas can help clarify the meaning of the sentence. They smoothly guide
the reader through the sentence by showing where to pause. Here are a few
ways that commas are used in simple sentences.

After Introductory Details

Sometimes a sentence begins with a word or phrase that modifies either the
subject or the entire sentence.

> *Exhausted,* Professor Smedley collapsed in her easy chair.
> *Just between you and me,* I think the doctor is wrong.
> *Poised and confident,* the speaker approached the podium.
> *From a child's perspective,* school often seems dull and meaningless.
> *In the far corner of the abandoned mission,* a small child slept quietly.

If the introductory modifier is only a word or two, a comma is not always necessary. Read such a sentence aloud to see if a pause (comma) is necessary.

On Saturday my grandmother will celebrate her ninetieth birthday.
Thus her story ended.

EXERCISE 6D: COMMAS AFTER INTRODUCTORY DETAILS

Supply commas, if needed, in the following sentences. Read the sentences aloud before you make your decisions.

1. Yesterday I found a family treasure.

2. In a dusty corner of Uncle Frank's attic I found my grandmother's diary.

3. It was hidden underneath a pile of old newspapers.

4. In my enthusiasm I spilled my coffee all over my uncle's favorite childhood photograph.

5. Fortunately the picture was protected by a plastic cover.

6. In view of my near mishap I set my coffee aside.

7. I didn't want to ruin my grandmother's diary.

8. On the inside cover of the diary I found a small tintype pasted in the corner.

9. It was my grandparents' wedding picture.

10. Upon looking at the picture I suddenly saw my grandmother from a different perspective.

11. She looked young and vibrant and happy.

12. Startled by the sound of footsteps I looked up and saw my mother.

13. She suddenly looked just like my grandmother.

14. With a curious glance she let her eyes rest on the object in my hands.

15. For the next three hours we sat on the attic floor and recaptured my grandmother's youth.

Separating Items in a Series

Sometimes simple sentences contain three or more words or phrases that make a series. Each item in such a series must be set off by commas, even if the last item is connected with an *and.*

Laura is a *young*, *talented*, and *inspiring* musician.

My books were scattered all over the room—*on the bed*, *under the desk*, and *in the closet*.

The *first*, *second*, and *third* exam questions were really difficult.

EXERCISE 6E: PUNCTUATING ITEMS IN A SERIES

Supply commas, if needed, in the following sentences.

1.   My father has donated a great deal of money and energy to the project.

2.   He comes home every night nervous and exhausted.

3.   In view of his experiences with Mr. Morgan Dr. Simpson and Mrs. Leahy he has a right to be nervous.

4.   They are all short on finesse and diplomacy.

5.   Their attitudes their comments and their actions offend people.

6.   Dad finally told them to consider resigning from the board.

7.   He told them to think it over Monday Tuesday and Wednesday before the board meeting.

8.   They all agreed.

9.   Thursday's board meeting was characterized by petty threats false accusations and meaningless rhetoric.

10.   At the end of his patience my father resigned.

Setting Off Interrupters

Any word or expression that interrupts the main clause should be set off with commas. Then the reader knows that what's inside the commas is not part of the main clause but is an additional, clarifying detail.

The movie, in my opinion, was a bomb.
You, of course, already know my feelings about cheap horror flicks.
My sister, a noted physician, has just finished her third book.

EXERCISE 6F: SETTING OFF INTERRUPTERS

Supply commas, if needed, in the following sentences.

1. Dick's new car the one at the end of the driveway was built from a kit.

2. He saved himself at least $3,000.

3. The labor of course was difficult and time-consuming.

4. He asked the next-door neighbor an experienced mechanic to help him.

5. Charlie was glad to oblige.

6. Charlie a widower with no children began to look upon Dick as a son.

7. Dick in turn adopted Charlie as his second father.

8. They began their project at the end of April the day after Charlie's birthday.

9. Night after night the two of them worked until one or two in the morning.

10. By June 12th Dick's birthday Dick had gained both a new car and a new friend.

FUSED SENTENCES

At the beginning of this chapter, you learned that, in order to avoid confusing your readers, you have to show them where each of your thoughts begins and ends. Complete thoughts are usually either separated by end punctuation marks (. ? !) or joined by connecting words (conjunctions).

69

| *End punctuation:* | Mr. Van Trump was born in Pittsburgh. He is now one of the city's most respected historians. |
| *Conjunction:* | Carla majored in music, *but* she is now running the largest computer lab in the country. |

These sentences are clear, but when complete thoughts are run together, reading becomes a frustrating experience. The reader has to back up and reread passages continually to understand what the writer is saying.

Fused sentence:	Walt collects old magazines in New York he recently found a valuable set of nineteenth-century periodicals.
Corrected:	Walt collects old magazines. In New York he recently found a valuable set of nineteenth-century periodicals.
Fused sentence:	In the last twenty years, heart surgery has really advanced research and technology have combined to produce modern miracles.
Corrected:	In the last twenty years, heart surgery has really advanced. Research and technology have combined to produce modern miracles.
Fused sentence:	Time and the elements have seriously damaged the Statue of Liberty a million dollar renovation project has been initiated to save her.
Corrected:	Time and the elements have seriously damaged the Statue of Liberty, *but* a million dollar renovation project has been initiated to save her.

EXERCISE 6G: FUSED SENTENCES

In the following paragraph, correct all of the fused sentences with end punctuation or connecting words (*and, but, for, nor, or, so, yet*).

Bob loves old movies. A few months ago he bought a video cassette recorder now he watches an old film almost every night. He has seen every Alfred Hitchcock film that was ever made at least three times *Psycho* is one of his favorites. He likes to watch for Hitchcock's brief cameo appearances. He says that "Hitch" delights in surprising the viewer. He sneaks into all of his films. In one he pops up in a newspaper ad in another he slips himself into a group photograph on the wall in still another, he suddenly appears in the midst of a crowd at the corner bus stop. Tonight, Bob is going to watch *Vertigo* and *Rear Window* for the fifth time this month! His wife has suggested that he convert the living room into a movie theatre and start charging admission.

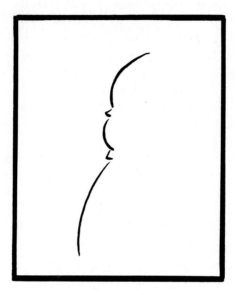

COMMA SPLICES

Comma splices can also confuse your readers. "Splice" means "join together." A film editor, for example, "splices" two pieces of film together to create one continuous strip. When you mistakenly place a comma between two complete sentences, you are running one thought into another. The readers see one continuous thought instead of two separate thoughts. For example:

Orson Welles was a great director, his best film was *Citizen Kane.*

There are *two complete sentences* here that convey *two distinct thoughts* to the reader:

1. That you admire Orson Welles
2. That you especially like his film, *Citizen Kane.*

These two sentences should be separated with a period.

Orson Welles was a great director. His best film was *Citizen Kane*.

Comma splices can be even more confusing when the readers see not just the comma splice between the sentences, but several commas within each sentence.

Orson Welles, a skilled writer and actor, was also a great director, his 1941 classic, *Citizen Kane*, is one of my favorites.

Visually, the readers see one continuous sentence broken up here and there with commas. Using their sentence sense, of course, they could eventually figure out that there are actually *two* complete thoughts here, but they shouldn't have to figure out where one sentence ends and the next one begins. Such a task is distracting, annoying, and time-consuming. It is your responsibility as a writer to punctuate your sentences clearly, so that your readers can understand what they're reading.

EXERCISE 6H: RECOGNIZING COMMA SPLICES, SENTENCE LEVEL

Eliminate any comma splices that you find in the following sentences.

1. Linda is one of the best reference librarians in the country, she is, therefore, one of our college's most valuable assets.

2. With a little help from the card catalogue and the *Readers' Guide,* she can help students find anything they're looking for.

3. Do you know what she was doing yesterday?

4. She was helping a frustrated junior, a sociology student who was searching for the name of a remote tribe in the South Pacific.

5. Day after day, the student had searched in vain for the answer.

6. He was about ready to give up, then his girlfriend made a good suggestion.

7. She told him to check with the librarian, so he did.

8. After talking to the librarian, the bewildered student realized that he had been looking in all the wrong sources.

9. Within minutes, the librarian found six sources on the South Pacific tribe.

10. She cited one book, two doctoral dissertations, and three journal articles.

EXERCISE 6I: RECOGNIZING COMMA SPLICES AND FUSED SENTENCES, PARAGRAPH LEVEL

Improve the following paragraph by eliminating comma splices and fused sentences.

Mike learned a valuable lesson today, he spent three days in the library searching for the name of a remote tribe in the South Pacific. Then he realized that he had been looking in all the wrong sources, after checking with the librarian, he discovered that he had overlooked a host of obvious references he was really embarrassed. Noticing his discomfort, the librarian asked Mike if he had attended the library orientation in a barely audible voice, Mike mumbled "No." The librarian was not pleased. When she questioned the student, she discovered that Mike had skipped English class on library day because he thought that "just going to the library" was not very important. The librarian then reminded Mike that he had just wasted three days searching for something that he could have found in fifteen minutes—*if* he had attended the library orientation, the librarian was angry, but she spent the rest of the afternoon helping Mike. She taught him essential research skills, she introduced him to the most important resources in the library Mike listened attentively. He even took notes and asked questions, he was very grateful. He now realizes the importance of knowing how to use the library.

CORRECTING COMMA SPLICES

You have already learned one way to correct a comma splice (by using a period in place of a comma), but there are three other ways to eliminate the error. If the comma splice consists of two *closely* related thoughts, you can:

1. Connect them with a conjunction.
2. Connect them with a semicolon.
3. Make one thought subordinate to the other.

These methods of correcting comma splices involve compound and complex sentences. You will learn about these types of sentences in Chapters 14 and 15, but, in the meantime, you can improve your writing by learning some other ways of correcting comma splices.

Using Conjunctions

You can correct comma splices by adding *and, but, or, for, nor, yet,* or *so* after the comma.

Comma splice:	The police arrived in five minutes, the thief had already run away.
Corrected:	The police arrived in five minutes, *but* the thief had already run away.
Comma splice:	Joey's alarm clock was broken, he was late for school.
Corrected:	Joey's alarm clock was broken, *so* he was late for school.

Using Semicolons

You can correct comma splices by replacing the comma with a semicolon. The semicolon is a stronger mark of punctuation; it can separate two closely related thoughts.

Comma splice:	He was a fine guitarist, he practiced five or six hours a day.
Corrected:	He was a fine guitarist; he practiced five or six hours a day.
Comma splice:	Six of his brothers were athletes, one played in the NBA.
Corrected:	Six of his brothers were athletes; one played in the NBA.
Comma splice:	Maria spent a lot of time working with computers, she got an A in computer science.
Corrected:	Maria spent a lot of time working with computers; she got an A in computer science.
Comma splice:	Augosto thought about proposing to Rita, he also thought about becoming a priest.
Corrected:	Augosto thought about proposing to Rita; he also thought about becoming a priest.

Using Subordination

You can correct comma splices by making one thought subordinate to the other.

Comma splice:	The police arrived in five minutes, the thief had already run away.
Corrected:	*Although the police arrived in five minutes,* the thief had already run away.
Comma splice:	Maria spent a lot of time working with computers, she got an A in computer science.
Corrected:	*Since Maria spent a lot of time working with computers,* she got an A in computer science.

EXERCISE 6J: CORRECTING COMMA SPLICES, SENTENCE LEVEL

Using your sentence sense, correct the following comma splices using any of the three methods discussed above. Try to show, by your selection, the most logical connection between the two ideas.

1.   Television bores me, I watch it a lot.

   _____

2.   *Barney Miller* used to be my favorite show, it's off the air now.

   _____

3.   I dislike most of the cop shows, I do enjoy *Hill Street Blues* and *Cagney and Lacy.*

   _____

4.   *St. Elsewhere* is probably my favorite, maybe *60 minutes* or *20/20* is.

   _____

5.   The favorites in the ratings are *Dallas, Dynasty,* and *Knots Landing,* I never could get interested in them.

   _____

6.   I like Paul Newman movies, I always watch any show that Dudley Moore or Dustin Hoffman plays in.

   _____

7.   Every night I watch the weather report, it's always wrong.

_____

8.   I lay out proper clothes for the weather predicted, they're always wrong, too.

_____

9.   Television is best for one thing, you can see sporting events better on TV than if you're actually at the game.

_____

10. I guess I like TV, I really enjoy reading books more.

_____

EXERCISE 6K: CORRECTING COMMA SPLICES, PARAGRAPH LEVEL

Using the method that you think is best, correct all of the comma splices that you find in the following paragraph.

There is only one thing that always symbolizes happy times, that is a balloon. Some people say bells are always happy, they forget that bells toll at funerals, too. Flowers are great if they're in a corsage for a dance or in a centerpiece for a dinner table, they're awful in a funeral basket. Music can signify fun, it can evoke sadness. Birthday cakes are usually a happy sight, they also signify another year of a life has passed sporting events bring happiness and excitement to many people, someone has to lose, it's not happy for the team that loses. Chocolate candy delights almost everyone, it causes cavities in teeth and pounds on the hips. Stick with balloons, they have no bad characteristics, even when they break, they're fun.

WRITING FROM READING

Group Composing

Read the following excerpt from a grown man's memory of his seventh-grade English teacher.

Miss O'Neill was dumpy, moonfaced, sallow, colorless, and we hated her. We hated her as only a pack of West Side barbarians could hate a teacher of arithmetic. She did not teach arithmetic—but that is how much we hated her. She taught English. She was a thirty-third-degree perfectionist who drilled us—constantly, endlessly, mercilessly—in spelling and grammar and diction and syntax.

Whenever one of our runny-nosed congregation made a mistake, in composition or recitation, Miss O'Neill would send the malefactor to the blackboard to "diagram" the sentence. Going to the blackboard for the public self-exposure of a grammatical tort, which in Miss O'Neill's eyes partook of at least venial sin, was the classroom torture we most resented.

Miss O'Neill's diagramming made us lay bare the solid, irreducible anatomy of a sentence. We had to separate subject from predicate, the accusative from the dative. We had to explain how each part of a sentence works, and how the parts fit together, and how they mesh and move to wheel out meaning. We had to uncover our mistakes ourselves, "naked to our enemies," then offer a correction and explain the reason for THAT—all as Miss O'Neill impassively waited. She waited as if she could sit there until Gabriel blew his kazoo, as our devastating humor had it. . . .

Some kids broke into the sweats as they floundered around at the blackboard, guessing at (and failing to pinpoint) their mistake, praying that Miss O'Neill would end the fearful ordeal either by identifying the awful error herself or, at least, by hinting, eyebrowing, murmuring a sound (positive or negative) that might guide them to the one true redeeming answer. But that Miss O'Neill would never do; instead, she shifted her inquisition from the criminal at the blackboard to the helots in the chairs. "Well, class? Who sees the mistake? . . . Jacob? No? . . . Sylvia? . . . My, my . . . Harold? . . . Annie? . . . Joseph? . . . Come, come, class; you must concentrate. There is an error—an error in grammar—on that blackboard . . ." So pitiless and unyielding was her method. . . .

But secretly, my respect for Miss O'Neill—nay, even my affection—mounted, week by week. I was exhilarated by what I can only call the incorruptibility of her instruction. I found stirring within myself a sense of excitement, of discovery, a curious quickening of the spirit that attends initiation into a new world.

Though I could not have explained it in these words, I sensed that frumpy Miss O'Neill was leading me, not through the musty labyrinth of English Composition, but into a sunlit realm of order and meaning. Her iron rules, her inflexible demands, her meticulous corrections, were not, to me, the torment or irritation they were to my companions. They were sudden flashes of light, giddying glimpses of the magic that hides within the arrangement of words, intoxicating visions of that universe that awaits understanding. It was as if a cloak of wonder had been wrapped around the barren bones of grammar.

For it was not just grammar or diction or syntax to which Miss O'Neill, whether she knew it or not, was introducing me. She was revealing language as the vehicle for thinking, grammar as the servant of logic, diction as a chariot for the imagination, the prosaic sentence as the beautiful, beating life

77

of the mind at work. She was teaching what an earlier generation called "right reason."

The most astonishing thing about Miss O'Neill was that she proceeded on the assumption that she COULD teach a pack of potential poolroom jockeys how to write clear, clean, correct paragraphs—in their native tongue.

I do not think Miss O'Neill had the slightest awareness of her influence on me, or on anyone else. She was not especially interested in me. She never betrayed an iota of preference for any of her captive and embittered flock.

. . .

And that is the point. Miss O'Neill did not try to please us. She did not try to like us. She certainly made no effort to make us like her. She valued results more than affection, and, I suspect, respect more than popularity. . . .

I do not know whether Miss O'Neill infected any other varmint in the seventh grade with a passion for, or even an abiding interest in, English. To me, she was a force of enlightenment.

Leo Rosten, *People I Have Loved, Known or Admired*
(New York: McGraw-Hill, 1970), pp. 53–58.

Do you agree with what the author says or implies about teachers?

That students respect the "tough" teacher?
That it is not important whether or not students like the teacher?
That it is less important that the teacher like the students?
That drill and discipline are good?
That children prefer competence in a teacher to friendliness?
That there may be no easy way to learn some things?

Get together with four or five of your classmates and discuss teachers you have had. Make lists of their good points and bad points. From these lists, describe an imaginary teacher—one who, like all of us, has good points and bad points. Choose from these lists some good qualities and some bad qualities and put them together to describe a teacher who, despite frailties, has become memorable to you. When each group has finished, read the paragraph to the class and discuss what makes teachers important.

7

Agreement between Subjects and Verbs

Most people recognize the basic requirement that the verb in a sentence or clause must agree with its subject in person and number. However, there are some problems in subject-verb agreement that you need to be aware of and guard against.

SUBJECT–VERB AGREEMENT

First, note this carefully:

> The *first person* is the speaker (I).
> The *second person* is the person spoken to (you).
> The *third person* is the person or thing spoken about (he, she, it).

Third Person Singular Subjects in the Present Tense

Most verbs add *s* or *es* in the *third person singular*, as in the following examples:

First person singular	I	take	go	wish	speak	possess
Second person singular	You	take	go	wish	speak	possess

Third person singular	He	takes	goes	wishes	speaks	possesses
	She	takes	goes	wishes	speaks	possesses
	It	takes	goes	wishes	speaks	possesses

If you read or hear someone say such things as "She take the bus," "He go to work," "She wish she had gone home," or "He speak the truth," you probably recognize those statements as poor English. The specific problem is that third person singular subjects require different verb forms than the first and second person subjects, *you* and *I*.

If the third person subject is *plural*, then do not add an "*s*" or "*es*."

First person plural	We	take	go	wish	speak	possess
Second person plural	You	take	go	wish	speak	possess
Third person plural	They	take	go	wish	speak	possess

EXERCISE 7A: SUBJECT–VERB AGREEMENT

In the following sentences, circle the subject and decide on the correct verb. Then cross out the incorrect verb.

1. The steel mills (is, are) closing in the eastern industrial states.

2. Because of these closings, many people (is, are) losing their jobs.

3. These production jobs (pays, pay) $14 to $20 per hour.

4. It (is, are) hard to find such a high-paying job in other areas.

5. One steel worker, George Mastellino, (says, say) that no such jobs (is, are) available today.

6. He (claims, claim) that steelworkers (has, have) to work for one-half the money they used to make.

7. Many steelworkers (has, have) been affected by the closings.

8. Ed Rable of *U.S. News* (reports, report) that 8 million Americans (has, have) dropped from the middle to the lower class.

9. Singer Bruce Springsteen (sings, sing) about the plight of working people.

10. He (does, do) still believe in the American Dream, but many out-of-work steelworkers (says, say) that it (is, are) no longer possible for a working person to make it.

Identifying the True Subject

You must identify the *true subject* and see that the verb agrees. Don't be confused by modifying words or phrases that come between the subject and the verb.

>   S   V
> The *list* of names and addresses *was* three pages long.
>
>   S   V
> The *cause* of all the noise and confusion *was* Marvin's pet snake.
>
>   S   V
> Heavy *storms* driven by a strong northwest wind *are* tearing up beaches from New Jersey to the Carolinas.
>
>   S   V
> The whole *network* of streams and rivers finally *drains* into the gulf.

EXERCISE 7B: IDENTIFYING THE TRUE SUBJECT

In the following sentences, circle the subject and decide on the correct verb. Then cross out the incorrect verb.

1. The report of a panel of scholars (claims, claim) that public schools in the United States (is, are) in trouble.

2. Now, leaders of colleges (is, are) suggesting that higher education, too, (needs, need) help.

3. The leaders of five national higher-education groups (says, say) that the campuses in America (is, are) healthy.

4. Colleges (do, does) need help, however, particularly from business, the presidents (explains, explain).

5. To achieve excellence in education, students in every college (needs, need) to take more liberal arts courses and fewer narrow, job-oriented specialties.

6. The findings of The American Council on Education (was, were) that two years of liberal arts courses (is, are) desirable for all students.

7. One member of the panel stated that "people (changes, change) jobs at least five times before they're 40."

8. Courses in the liberal arts curriculum "(provides, provide) people with a wide range of skills and attitudes."

9. "This range of skills and attitudes (helps, help) them prepare for different kinds of work situations."

10. The business world (has, have) to recognize that students (needs, need) more literature and philosophy classes along with their data processing and chemistry.

PRONOUN AGREEMENT

Indefinite pronouns—for example, *one, each, either, neither, no one, anybody, anyone, anything, everyone, everybody, nobody, somebody, someone*—require *singular* verbs.

> *Neither* of the answers *is* correct.
> *Each* of the girls *has* her own car.
> *Everyone* in the whole world *seems* to fear nuclear war.

Some pronouns always take a plural verb—for example, *all, both, many,* and *several*—as do all plural numbers—*two, three, twenty.*

EXERCISE 7C: INDEFINITE PRONOUNS
AND SUBJECT-VERB AGREEMENT

Underline the subject and circle the correct verb in each of the following sentences.

1. Everyone in the classes (was, were) prepared.

2. No one (was, were) the least bit worried about the test.

3. One of the boys (was, were) sure he had a perfect paper.

4. Each of the girls (has, have) at least 80 percent correct.

5. One of the younger students (has, have) learned more English here than in all of high school.

6. Neither of the older students (seem, seems) to have forgotten how to study.

7. Chuck said, "In this class, nobody (fail, fails)."

8.   For the first time, neither of the Hispanic students (has, have) written any of the answers in Spanish.

9.   Each of the students (have, has) a reason for studying hard.

10. Everybody (know, knows) how important writing skills are to someone who wants to move up.

PLURAL AND COORDINATE AGREEMENT

When two or more nouns or pronouns are joined by *and*, use a plural verb.

(plural verb)
My aunt and my cousin *were* in Las Vegas last week.
(plural verb)
The old lamps and the hatrack *stand* in the hallway.

The exception to this rule occurs when the two subjects joined by *and* can be thought of as a single unit.

My oldest friend and the best pal I ever had *lives* in Oakland now.

When subjects are joined by *or* or *nor*, the verb agrees with the subject that is nearest to the verb.

S   S
Either my father or my mother *has* visited the hospital every day.
S   S
Neither the cars nor the trucks *were* mechanically safe.
S   S
Neither the detectives nor the inspector *was* notified.
S   S
Neither the inspector nor the detectives *were* notified.

Nouns of amount, time, weight, and measurement are usually treated as singular.

Thirty-six dollars *is* a lot to spend for one meal.
Sixteen miles *is* a long hike.
Two and one-half hours *is* a long time to wait.

83

The exception occurs when the units are clearly separate.

Six silver dollars *were* laid out on the counter.

EXERCISE 7D: COMPOUND AND COORDINATE SUBJECTS

Cross out the incorrect verb in each of the following sentences.

1. Twenty-two dollars (is, are) my total weekly pay.

2. Either my job or my outside activities (are, is) making me tired.

3. Neither my parents nor my sister (approves, approve) of the way I live.

4. Neither my boss nor my teachers (complains, complain) about the quality of my work.

5. It's funny how five hours a day (are, is) a long time to work, but five hours a day (is, are) a short time to party.

6. Studying (take, takes) another five or six hours a day.

7. Either my mother or my father or my brothers (is, are) always telling me that I don't get enough sleep.

8. Five classes (take, takes) up a lot of the daytime hours.

9. Work or partying or both (has, have) to go.

10. Twenty-four hours (is, are) a short day.

Subjects and verbs must agree even when the subject comes after the verb.

$$\overset{V}{} \qquad \overset{S}{}$$

Behind the houses *was* a weed-filled *lot*.

$$\overset{V}{} \qquad \overset{S}{}$$

There *were* three loose *bolts* on the left rear wheel.

$$\overset{V}{} \qquad \overset{\text{—S—}}{}$$

Standing alone at the end of the pier *were* a *boy and girl* embracing in the moonlight.

EXERCISE 7E: SUBJECTS THAT COME AFTER THE VERB

In each of the following sentences, circle the subject and decide which verb is correct. Then cross out the incorrect verb.

1. In the backyard (was, were) a grove of trees.

2. Somewhere among the trees (were, was) a pair of cats fighting.

3. On the ground (was, were) multicolored maple, oak, and elm leaves.

4. On a stump near the porch (was, were) an ax and a leaf rake.

5. In front of the porch, on a cement slab, (were, was) a table and two chairs under a beach umbrella.

6. Under the table (is, are) a broken ashtray.

7. Among the scattered cigarette butts under the table (are, is) a dark brown stain.

8. Reaching from the table to the porch steps (is, are) many more dark brown spots—they grow larger and more numerous as they approach the house.

9. At the gate to the yard (stand, stands) a detective and two uniformed police officers.

10. As the cats continue to yowl and the leaves continue to drift to the ground, into the yard (step, steps) civilization in the uniform of the police officer.

AGREEMENT OF COLLECTIVE NOUNS

Collective nouns—*family, team, crew, class, gang, audience, jury, staff, flock*—usually take singular verbs.

85

The team *is* in the dugout.

The jury *is* deadlocked.

The crew *is* ready to go to work.

EXERCISE 7F: RECOGNIZING THE CORRECT SUBJECT

Circle the subject in each of the following sentences. Then write in the correct verb form to agree with the subject.

1.   A long line of ragged children _____ outside the gate.
        stand/stands

2.   Many of the older cities in the Northeast _____ to be
        deteriorating.   seems/seem

3.   All along the roadside_____ many fruit stands and flea
        markets.   was/were

4.   There _____ some things you just have to learn from
        experience.   is/are

5.   That form at the bottom of the heap of papers _____
        needed for listing the items.   are/is

6.   You _____ somewhere in that crowd.
        was/were

7.   The cows herded into the barn each night _____ ready
        to be milked at 5:00 A.M.   is/are

8.   My favorite recollections _____ the stories by Dr.
        Seuss.   is/are

9.   His greatest love _____ motorcycle races.
        are/is

10. Motorcycle races _____ his favorite pastime.
        is/are

EXERCISE 7G: RECOGNIZING FAULTY AGREEMENT

In each of the following sentences, correct the faulty agreement by drawing a line through the incorrect form and writing the correct form at the end of the sentence. If the sentence is correct, mark *C* at the end.

1. Besides, there is the students who live off campus._____

   are

2. In the restored village, each of the houses have the authentic log construction. _____

   has

3. On the chair there is a pair of pants, a jacket, and an old newspaper. _____

4. The house and the car was both bright green. _____

5. Each have plenty of money to spend. _____

6. Both has a good job. _____

7. Twelve miles is a long way for a boy to walk. _____

8. Some of the parents were delighted. _____

9. This power plant, along with all the other plants along the river, form a power
   grid that serves the needs of six cities. _____

10. Neither the other students nor the instructor were surprised at Judy Pringle's
    answer. _____

EXERCISE 7H: REVIEW OF SUBJECT–VERB AGREEMENT

In the following sentences, circle the subject and check to see if the verb
agrees with it. If the verb is correct, mark a *C* over it; if it is incorrect, write
the correct form over it.

1. Today men and women dresses more alike than at any time in history.

2. It is not surprising to see a woman in a pinstriped pants suit complete with a
   shirt and a tie.

3. One rarely see a man in a skirt, at least outside of Scotland.

4. However, there is still many differences.

5. Women has a much wider variety of clothes to choose from.

6. Look at underwear, for example.

7. Men can choose one of two types of shorts (jockey or boxer), and one of two
   types of shirts (T-shirt or undershirt) or none.

8. A woman have many choices: bloomers, briefs, bikinis, girdles, Merry
   Widows, corsets, chemises, and all sorts of bras, hose, and slips.

9. Most men owns four or five pairs of shoes: two dress (one black, one brown),
   two sport (loafers, tennis), and possibly a pair of boots.

10. Many women—not rich women but almost all women—own twenty-five to thirty pairs of shoes, and they need them.

11. A woman need high heels, medium heels, or low heels, depending on how formal the occasion is, how long she must be on her feet, and how tall her date is.

12. Her shoes also must comes in many colors and styles: red high heels for her "dressy" dress, gray pumps for her wool suit, blue flats for her navy pants suit, brown sandals for her jeans in summer, and neutral oxfords for the same in winter.

13. And the red shoes can't work with her casual red outfits because the heels is too high.

14. So she probably own two red pairs—or three!

15. Before she goes out, a woman have to decide what purse to take, what jewelry to wear, and, perhaps, what scarf or belt to choose to complete her outfit.

16. No wonder it take women so long to get ready.

17. And no wonder men get dressed so easily.

18. After she is dressed, a woman still have to make all sorts of makeup decisions: shade of eye shadow, rouge or blusher, foundation, and so on.

19. And we haven't even mentioned hair.

20. So it isn't that women is slower; they just has more choices and more decisions to make than men.

WRITING FROM READING

Writing, Reading, and Thinking

Song writers, novelists, technicians, mothers, first graders, grandparents, and college sophomores all have one thing in common: they often get their best ideas from things they have read. The image of great writers sitting alone in their studies, waiting to be inspired with profound thoughts, is a common misconception. Good writing is a process that develops *as a result of thinking* about what you have read and what you have experienced. It is no coincidence that most of the world's best writers are also avid readers. In the words of one famous writer, the man responsible for the first dictionary of the English language: "I never desire to converse with a man who has written more than he has read."

It is important, then, to think of writing and reading not as separate, isolated activities, but as complementary activities that work together to reinforce each other. The more you integrate reading skills with writing skills, the more you will improve in both areas.

The following exercises are designed to help you use reading as a means of generating ideas for writing. Remember, writing is not produced in a vacuum. You have to have something to think about before you have something to write about. Take the advice William Faulkner gave to all aspiring writers: "Read, read, read!"

In 1982 William Least Heat Moon, an American Indian, published his first book. Within weeks, it became a bestseller. *Blue Highways* is an enthralling account of the people who live on the backroads of America—people from places like Nameless, Tennessee.

> NAMELESS, Tennessee, was a town of maybe ninety people if you pushed it, a dozen houses along the road, a couple of barns, same number of churches, a general merchandise store selling Fire Chief gasoline, and a community center with a lighted volleyball court. Behind the center was an open-roof, rusting metal privy with PAINT ME on the door; in the hollow of a nearby oak lay a full pint of Jack Daniel's Black Label . . .
>
> . . . It seems the hilltop settlement went for years without a name. Then one day the Post Office Department told the people if they wanted mail up on the mountain they would have to give the place a name you could properly address a letter to. The community met; there were only a handful, but they commenced debating. Some wanted patriotic names, some names from nature, one man recommended in all seriousness his own name. They couldn't agree, and they ran out of names to argue about. Finally, a fellow tired of the talk; he didn't like the mail he received anyway. "Forget the durn Post Office," he said. "This here's a nameless place if I ever seen one, so leave it be." And that's just what they did.

From *Blue Highways: A Journey into America* by William Least Heat Moon. Copyright © 1982 by William Least Heat Moon. By permission of Little, Brown and Company, in association with Atlantic Monthly Press.

Think about the neighborhood in which you live now or the place where you grew up. Think about how it looks, about the kind of people who live there, about how you feel when you are there. Can you think of a better name for this place? Explain why you think that your name for it is more appropriate. Write a few sentences justifying each of your reasons.

We are always learning from our experiences, but one of the best things about reading is that it helps us learn from the experiences of others. Even reading books on trivia can provide useful insights. Read the following excerpts from *The Joy of Trivia* and, after each one, ask yourself, "What can I learn from this person's experience?" Write each answer in sentence form, and then compare your thoughts with those of your classmates.

John Sutter, on whose property gold was discovered in 1848, was a wealthy and happy man when the discovery occurred. But he couldn't protect his property from the horde of wild prospectors that soon tore it up. Most of those who worked for him thought it better to go hunting gold than farming or tending cattle. And Congress got into the act and grabbed most of his land through a technicality. He died bankrupt.

In the 1890s Carry Nation had little use for demon rum. Carrying a hatchet and often accompanied by a band of hymn-singing ladies, Carry would march into a Kansas saloon and proceed to reduce it to kindling. She had a list of "things to be destroyed." It included rum, tobacco, foreign foods, corsets, skirts of improper length, and barroom art works.

Michelangelo believed in glorifying the human body and he wasn't very keen on overloading his figures with clothes. His "Last Judgment" on the walls of the Sistine Chapel caused some harsh criticism by one of the Vatican's officials because of the nudity. So Michelangelo made a few changes. He painted in the face of the clergyman and added donkey's ears and a snake's tail!

Beethoven wasn't a poor man, yet he lived and worked at times in unbelievable squalor; dust was everywhere, puddles on the floor, ink pots on the bed, and chamber pots under the table, according to reports by some of his infrequent visitors.

Bernie Smith, *The Joy of Trivia* (Los Angeles: Brooke House Publishers, 1976), pp. 4, 51, 57, 71.

8
Modifiers

The most important words in a sentence are subjects and verbs and (sometimes) completers, and you can probably make yourself understood by using just these sentence parts.

> Students came late.
>
> Teacher stomped feet.
>
> Class laughed.

However, people don't talk that way, and if you write that way, using only these sentence parts, your readers will not get a very clear understanding of your written message.

Modifiers are words we use to give more information about subjects, verbs, and completers, and thus make the message clearer. A sentence such as "The girl danced" is grammatically complete, but you usually need to add modifiers to one or more of the elements to make your meaning clear. Thus, you might say the *blonde* girl, the *tall* girl, the *tiny* girl, the *Indian* girl, using modifiers to describe the subject, "girl," and make it more precise. You might also say the girl danced *slowly* or *frantically* or *sensuously* or *enthusiastically*.

MODIFIERS THAT MAKE SUBJECTS CLEARER

Notice how modifiers can help you clarify your ideas.

> The boy approached the woman.

A sentence like this doesn't tell the reader very much. How old was the boy? Was he mean or friendly? Cute or frightening? Was he smiling or snarling? Would you hug him or run from him?

You can make the *boy* clear to the reader by adding modifiers.

The smiling, freckle-faced four year old . . .
The hard-eyed, unsmiling young man . . .

93

There are two types of modifiers: adjectives and adverbs. Adjectives modify nouns (subjects and completers). They may *identify* as well as *describe.*

the *first* person	a *crimson* scarf
the *last* test	a *tart* flavor
the *only* question	a *muddy* road

A noun may take more than one modifier. Often adjectives that limit or identify are combined with adjectives that describe.

We saw *three huge* vans.
A *few wavy* lines ran through the dust.

Descriptive adjectives may also appear in a series, with each modifying the following noun.

a bright, cheerful day
a steep, slippery trail

These adjectives could be joined by *and.*

a bright and cheerful day
a steep and slippery trail

If you don't use the *and,* you should separate the adjectives with a comma. You can put modifiers before the subject, as in the above examples, or after the subject and before the verb.

The boy, a smiling, freckle-faced four year old, . . .
The young man, hard-eyed and unsmiling, . . .

EXERCISE 8A: SEEING THE EFFECT OF MODIFIERS

Change the feeling you get about the following subjects by using modifiers that are as different as possible.

EXAMPLE: the <u>huge</u> <u>snarling</u> dog

the <u>playful</u> <u>brown</u> dog

1.   a_____   _____ police officer

     a_____   _____ police officer

2. the _____ _____ car

    the _____ _____ car

3. the _____ _____ second grader

    the _____ _____ second grader

4. my _____ _____ father

    my _____ _____ father

5. the _____ _____ basketball player

    the _____ _____ basketball player

EXERCISE 8B: PLACING ADJECTIVES AFTER THE SUBJECT

In this exercise, put descriptive adjectives after the subjects. Notice that when the adjectives follow the subjects, they are set off with commas. Finish the sentences in a way that makes your adjectives appropriate.

EXAMPLE: The boxer, tired and bleeding, raised his right hand in victory.

1. The baby, _____ and _____, _____

_____.

2. My friend, _____ and _____, _____

_____.

3. The quarterback, _____ and _____, _____

_____.

4. The house, _____ and _____, _____

_____.

5. New Orleans, _____ and _____, _____

_____.

EXERCISE 8C: USING A SERIES OF ADJECTIVES

Now try writing a few sentences with three adjectives. If you are in doubt about whether you need a comma between adjectives, try inserting "and" between the adjectives. If "and" sounds natural, use a comma; otherwise don't. For example, you would never say "ten and little and old men."

EXAMPLES: My little black cat brings me good luck.

The cafeteria, noisy, cluttered, and overcrowded, is the busiest place on campus.

1. The _____ _____ _____ bird _____.

2. _____ _____ _____ tree _____.

3. _____ _____ _____ actor _____.

4. My bedroom, _____ _____ and _____, _____ _____.

5. The store, _____ _____ and _____, _____ _____.

MODIFIERS THAT MAKE VERBS CLEARER

You can also make verbs clearer to the readers by adding modifiers.

> The boy *timidly* approached.
> The boy approached *cautiously*.
> The boy approached *swiftly*.

Adverbs

Words that describe or limit verbs are called *adverbs*. In general, they show the quality of the action: *when, where, how,* or *to what degree:*

> Bill was *totally* exhausted.　(tells *to what degree* Bill was exhausted)
> The girl danced *beautifully*.　(tells *how* the girl danced)
> The bus headed *southward*.　(tells *where* the bus headed)
> They will leave *tomorrow*.　(tells *when* they will leave)

Some adverbs, usually those expressing degree or measure, can be used to modify adjectives or other adverbs.

> The pain passed *very* quickly. (*Very* modifies another adverb: *quickly*.)
> He had an *extremely* difficult job. (*Extremely* modifies an adjective: *difficult*.)
> The soup tastes *quite* salty. (*Quite* modifies a predicate adjective: *salty*.)

EXERCISE 8D: SUPPLYING ADVERBS, SENTENCE LEVEL

By the use of adverbs, show *how* the subject did something.

EXAMPLES: The old man <u>hastily</u> concealed his gun.

The old man <u>carefully</u> concealed his gun.

1. The teacher spoke _____ to the student.

2. The doctor _____ examined the boy's leg.

3. The clock ticked _____.

4. The halfback ran _____.

5. Stanley waved his hand _____.

6. The player approached the referee _____.

7. Jennifer hit the ball _____ toward second base.

8. Bill drove his car _____ down the steep trail.

9. Virginia passed the course _____.

10. The football bounced _____ on the field.

EXERCISE 8E: SUPPLYING ADVERBS, PARAGRAPH LEVEL

Make the following paragraph more interesting by supplying adverbs in the spaces provided.

_____ I took a drive to the mountains. I _____ made a few sandwiches, threw my camera into the car, and headed _____ on old Route 40. As I approached the foot of the mountains, I _____ noticed nature's patchwork of vibrant colors. Flashes of deep red and bright yellow stood out _____ against the soft, muted shades of midautumn. Towering oaks dotted the landscape, their rusty brown leaves blowing _____ in the breeze. I _____ drove to the summit of Mount Laurel where I could _____ appreciate the panoramic beauty of the Alleghenies in autumn. Retrieving my camera from the car, I _____ focused the lens and adjusted the light meter. I wanted this picture to be just like the view itself—_____

97

breathtaking. I wanted to capture the beauty of the moment as _____ as I could. Driving home from the mountains that day, I _____ realized how lucky I was to be living in an area as beautiful as western Pennsylvania.

MODIFIERS THAT MAKE COMPLETERS CLEARER

You can also make a completer clearer by adding modifiers.

The boy approached the old, feeble woman.
The boy approached the screaming, out-of-control woman.
The boy approached the sympathetic young woman.
The boy approached the frightened, but still fighting, old woman.

EXERCISE 8F: MODIFYING COMPLETERS

Supply a clear and specific completer for each of the following sentences.

1. Jean hit _____.
2. The police followed the _____.
3. The apple was _____.
4. The volunteer at the hospital forgot _____.
5. The substitute quarterback was _____.
6. My father brought _____ home.
7. Later, the president felt _____.
8. The drink tasted _____.
9. Tomorrow I'll take _____.
10. The student got _____ from the teacher.

EXERCISE 8G: SUPPLYING MODIFIERS

Add your own modifiers to the following sentences.

EXAMPLE: My friend Frieda, a school teacher, vacationed in New Jersey last August.

Joe clapped <u>loudly</u> for the performers.

Joe clapped <u>half-heartedly</u> for the performers.

1. The _____ girl lost her books.

2. The gentlemen _____ called me.

3. The halfback _____ leaped into the air.

4. A _____ Dalmatian _____ stalked out of the room.

5. Henry drove the _____ car out of the lot.

6. Playing cards with Bob and Kathy is _____.

7. _____ football is a _____ sport.

8. My favorite museum is a _____ _____ building.

9. _____ Mary _____ helps me out.

10. The _____ lottery made Sally _____.

EXERCISE 8H: USING MODIFIERS TO MAKE COMPLETERS SPECIFIC

Make these sentences send clearer messages to your readers by using more specific completers. Feel free to add a few modifiers to give your readers a clearer picture.

1. The baby swallowed *something*.

2. Bobby played a *game* all afternoon.

3. Jennie runs a *machine* at the store.

4. The house was *beautiful*.

5. The kids certainly enjoyed the *activities* at camp.

6. Michael Jackson recorded a *song*.

7. The school provided *lunch*.

8. Carlo plays an *instrument* in the college band.

9. Ken gave his wife an expensive *present*.

10. In the soccer game, Jenny sustained an *injury*.

11. The doctor prescribed *medicine* for Tony.

12. The day was *hot*.

13. My mother looked *different*.

14. The movie was *unpleasant*.

15. The _____ situation was _____ funny.

MISPLACED MODIFIERS

Modifiers can be words or phrases or even clauses; if they are clauses, however, you no longer have a simple sentence.

Words as modifiers:	the *spotted* dog (adjective)
	the dog barked *loudly* (adverb)
Phrases as modifiers:	the *sad but splendid* ceremony
	The coach ran *swiftly and silently*.
A verbal phrase as a modifier:	The girl, *cowering in the drafty corner*, was sick.
A clause as a modifier:	A man *who is fair* can easily win respect.

One rule holds for all forms of modifiers: the modifier must be as close as possible to the word it modifies—preferably next to it. If a modifier is put anyplace else, it can make your sentence unclear or even ridiculous. You make your meaning clear to your readers not only through the words you choose, but also through your placement of them in the sentence.

In the following sentences, notice how the meanings change as the placement of the modifiers changes:

Only I love you. (No one else does.)
I *only* love you. (I just love you. I don't like you, respect you, or admire you.)
I love *only* you. (I don't love anyone else.)
I love you *only*. (I love no one else.)

In a situation like this, it is best to make yourself as clear as possible.

Joe *almost* won all the games. (He *nearly* won them, but he didn't.)
Joe won *almost* all the games. (He did win the greatest number of them.)

EXERCISE 8I: MISPLACED MODIFIERS

In each of the following sentences, put the modifier where it is most suitable.

1.   *only*   We want to survive.

2.   *merely*   We think this is satisfactory.

3.   *never*   Will you promise to go?

4.   *almost*   They won all the positions in student government.

5.   *just*   She carried one.

6.   *only*   They presented comedies.

7.   *nearly*   He burned all the muffins.

8.   *almost*   The police found none of the stolen jewels.

9.   *only*   The thieves betrayed themselves.

10. *merely*   The bankers retrieved the trust funds.

DANGLING MODIFIERS

When a modifier is a verbal phrase at the beginning of a sentence, it modifies the subject of the sentence.

Incorrect:	Chiming softly, he listened to the grandfather clock. (He was not chiming. The clock was.)
Correct:	He listened to the grandfather clock chiming softly.
Incorrect:	The little girl found the violets walking in the field. (The violets were not walking. The little girl was.)
Correct:	Walking in the field, the little girl found the violets.
Incorrect:	Running frantically for the bus stop, the bus passed her. (The bus was not running. She was.)
Correct:	Running frantically for the bus stop, she was passed by the bus.
	When *she* was running frantically for the bus stop, the bus passed her.

Notice that in the incorrect examples, the modifier is not attached to anything, but it *dangles* in the sentence, thus creating confusion.

The little girl found the violets walking in the field.

EXERCISE 8J: DANGLING MODIFIERS

Correct the dangling modifiers in the following sentences.

1. Having bad study habits, my grades aren't very good.

   _____

2. Letting my work pile up, my studying spoils my entire weekend.

   _____

3. Doing it every day, the work would seem less tiresome.

   _____

4. Having some time for fun on the weekends, my work wouldn't seem such a drag.

   _____

5. Playing the radio, my attention wanders.

   _____

6. Watching television, my work takes twice as long.

   _____

7. My concentration while watching *Hill Street Blues* is ruined.

_____

8. Being in the same room with other people, my attention is distracted.

_____

9. When studying, my appetite seems to grow, and I'm always thinking of food.

_____

10. Feeling overworked, my studying is resented.

_____

EXERCISE 8K: DANGLING OR MISPLACED MODIFIERS

Correct all of the misplaced or dangling modifiers in the following sentences.

1. Walking down the hallway, the eyes of all the nurses and attendants were on Dr. Levinson.

_____

2. Having heard the testimony of the two witnesses, the trial was recessed by the judge.

_____

3. To be permitted to drive, a driver's examination must be taken.

_____

4. Worn out by the steep climb in the hot sun, the shade of the linden tree was certainly inviting.

_____

5. When selecting an apartment, the driving time to one's work should be taken into consideration.

_____

6. To see the beautiful valley from the mountain top, a half a day of hard climbing is required.

_____

7. To play the best game possible, a new carbon fiber racket is what is needed.

_____

8. Marie might have guessed what he was hiding behind his back with a little imagination.

---

9. He thought the dealer had tried to cheat him without any evidence to support his belief.

---

10. Rotting in the cellar, my brother found a bushel of apples and a half crate of pears.

WRITING FROM READING

Being Specific

Notice the difference that being specific makes as you read the same ideas expressed here in different words.

PARAGRAPH A

The department store was crowded. People were everywhere. They were looking at various items and going from place to place. Every department was crowded. People were checking items and buying things. The store was having a big sale.

PARAGRAPH B

People of all ages and types pushed through the revolving doors and wedged their way through the crowded aisles. They burst out of elevators and clawed their way to counters. They fingered suits crowded together on movable racks and tried on shoes while balancing precariously on one foot and being shoved and hassled by other eager shoppers. Kids tested footballs while their parents changed channels on floor sample TVs and snatched Sonys out of each other's arms. The cash registers clicked and hummed; I counted fifteen people ahead of me in the line at the shirt counter. The "Everything Half Off" sale was a success.

Rewrite the following general paragraph to make it livelier and more interesting by adding more specific modifiers and descriptions.

The house on the side of the hill was awful looking. It had stood there empty so long that it looked sort of broken down and beat up. A lot of old, overgrown bushes were close to it, against the windows. Some old sheds and things were in the backyard. The walk that went around the house was in poor condition. The shutters were unhinged at some of the windows and a lot of slates had come off the roof. It made the whole neighborhood look bad.

9
Pronouns

A *pronoun* is defined as a word that is used instead of a noun.

John Brown raided Harper's Ferry.
He raided Harper's Ferry.

He can take the place of *John Brown*. However, if you begin talking about the raid on Harper's Ferry without saying who *he* is, you might leave your readers confused. So, you probably wouldn't use the pronoun until after you had identified John Brown. You probably would say something like this:

John Brown raided Harper's Ferry. With this raid, *he* made a protest against slavery.

Personal pronouns always refer to an *antecedent.* An antecedent is a noun (or a group of words standing for a noun) to which the pronoun points.

(antecedent)
The man is a marine.

(pronoun)
He is in uniform.

There are five common types of pronouns: personal, relative, demonstrative, interrogative, and indefinite. Pronouns are also used as intensifiers.

PRONOUNS

Personal	Relative	Demonstrative	Interrogative	Indefinite	Intensive/Reflexive
I	who	this	who	some	myself
you	which	that	whom	any	yourself
he	that	these	which	each	himself
she		those	what	none	herself
it			whose	all	itself
				either	ourselves
				neither	yourselves
				anyone	themselves
				nobody	
				everyone	
				somebody	
				and so on	

PERSONAL PRONOUNS

Personal pronouns stand for the speaker, the one spoken to, and the one spoken about. All three of these can be singular or plural.

	Singular	Plural
First person, the speaker	I	we
Second person, the one spoken to	you	you
Third person, the one spoken about	he, she, it	they

Subject pronouns are used when the pronoun is the doer of the action: the subject.

S
I hate bugs.

S
We called an exterminator.

Object pronouns are used when the pronoun is the receiver of the action: the object.

O
Bugs bother *me*.

O
Bugs do strange things to *us*.

	First Person Singular	*First Person Plural*
To indicate a subject	I	we
To indicate an object	me	us
To indicate possession or ownership	my, mine	our, ours

	Second Person Singular	*Second Person Plural*
To indicate a subject	you	you
To indicate an object	you	you
To indicate possession	your, yours	your, yours

	Third Person Singular	*Third Person Plural*
To indicate a subject	he, she, it	they
To indicate an object	him, her, it	them
To indicate possession	his, her/hers, its	their, theirs

In the possessive for some personal pronouns, you have a choice of forms depending on whether or not a noun follows.

It is *my* book.
It is *mine.*

That is *her* Volkswagen.
That is *hers.*

This is *their* house.
It is *theirs.*

Notice also that no apostrophe is used in the possessive forms of pronouns. This is particularly troublesome with the possessive of *it.*

Its color is fading. (It's = it is. Its = possessive pronoun.)

The Use of *It*

It is usually used following an antecedent.

(antecedent)
This package is mine.

(personal pronoun)
It came late yesterday.

It has two special uses. First, it can be an expletive. This means that *it* is used as a grammatical subject even though the real subject follows the verb.

> *It* is good to win.

It can also be impersonal—for example, in describing the weather.

> *It* is snowing.
> *It's* growing cold.

EXERCISE 9A: PERSONAL PRONOUNS

Insert the correct personal pronouns in the following sentences.

1.   Mary had a little lamb. _____ fleece was white as snow.

2.   Everywhere that Mary went, _____ was sure to go.

3.   _____ followed her to school one day.

4.   The students were surprised to see the lamb in school; _____ weren't used to animals coming to school.

5.   However, one of the boys had a dog that sometimes followed him. _____ had to shout to send _____ home again.

6.   Mary was embarrassed because _____ was laughed at by the other students.

7.   _____ didn't realize _____ were hurting _____ feelings.

8.   For _____ loved the lamb and _____ loved _____.

9.   When _____ did realize _____, _____ apologized.

10.   _____ said, "_____ are sorry _____ laughed at _____ and made _____ feel bad."

RELATIVE PRONOUNS

Using *relative* pronouns allows you to make one sentence out of two—to combine two sentences for conciseness, clarity, or sentence variety.

The boxer is a champion. He has won every match in his division.

The boxer is a champion who has won every match in his division.

When you change the personal pronoun *he* to the relative pronoun *who,* you change two simple sentences into one somewhat clearer complex sentence.

Clauses that begin with relative pronouns are always dependent clauses, so they cannot stand alone.

The most important relative pronouns are *who, that,* and *which.*

who: always used of persons	The man is the photographer *who* made our home movies.
that: always used of things	This is the house *that* Jack built.
which: almost always interchangeable with *that*	This is the racehorse *which* sold for a million dollars.

Like personal pronouns, relative pronouns follow antecedents.

Photographer is the antecedent of *who.*

House is the antecedent of *that.*

Racehorse is the antecedent of *which.*

EXERCISE 9B: RELATIVE PRONOUNS

Fill in the blanks in the following sentences with the correct relative pronouns.

1.   A recent study shows that success in English classes is the way _____ leads to success in all classes.

2.   This study, _____ was made at Louisiana Tech University, surprisingly relates English grades with grades in math and science.

3.   Harold Pace, the researcher _____ conducted this study, says the English language is a good teacher of logical thinking.

4.   Students _____ deal successfully with English do well in most courses _____ they may take.

5.   An ability to communicate clearly is essential no matter _____ courses are studied or _____ career is chosen.

6.   The research focused on students _____ scored low on standardized tests.

7. The study shows a direct relationship between those students _____ scored low and those _____ had studied little English in high school.

8. This is a study _____ is changing high school English plans.

9. This is the kind of research _____ leads to improved education.

10. English teachers, _____ surely agree with this, think this is research _____ should be made public.

DEMONSTRATIVE PRONOUNS

Demonstrative pronouns point out. There are four demonstrative pronouns:

Singular	Plural
this	these
that	those

This generally refers to something nearby: *This* chair I'm sitting in . . .
That generally refers to something farther away: *That* oak tree across the meadow . . .
These refers to something nearby: *These* chairs we're sitting in . . .
Those generally refers to something farther away: *Those* oak trees across the meadow . . .

EXERCISE 9C: DEMONSTRATIVE PRONOUNS

Fill in the blanks in the following sentences with the correct demonstrative pronouns.

1. In _____ collection of short stories on my desk is one I really love.

2. _____ stories are all good, but _____ one is the best.

3. _____ anthologies on the far wall can't compare with _____ one.

4. _____ anthologies have no common theme but _____ one is tied together by the theme of the hero.

5. _____ theme points out that heroes are leaders; they are _____ characters who are willing to take a chance for the **people they** represent.

6. Unity of theme makes each story reveal more meaning in _____ that follow.

7. _____ sense of continuity makes each story clear.

8. My feelings about _____ stories in _____ collection are strong.

9. _____ kinds of feelings make reading a wonderful experience.

10. _____ kind of experience heightens readers' understanding of themselves and other people.

INTERROGATIVE PRONOUNS

Interrogative pronouns ask either direct or indirect questions. There are three interrogative pronouns: *who, which,* and *what.*

Direct question *who*	Who is that lady I saw you with?
Indirect question *who*	I asked who that lady was I saw you with.

Remember that *who* changes its form according to its use in the sentence. If it is the subject of the sentence, it is *who.* If it is the object of the verb or preposition, it is *whom.* If it shows possession, it is *whose.*

When *who* is the subject	*Who* is calling me?
When *who* is used to show possession	*Whose* voice is that?
When *who* is the object of the verb	*Whom* do you suspect?
When *who* is the object of the preposition	The woman to *whom* we spoke was the dean.
	To *whom* shall I return the book?

Which and *what,* unlike *who,* do not change form.

Direct	which	*Which* is the shortest road home?
Indirect	which	He questioned *which* is the shortest road to home.
Direct	what	*What* is the shortest distance between two points?
Indirect	what	The instructor questioned the class about *what* is the shortest distance between two points.

Remember that direct questions end with a question mark. Indirect questions end with a period.

EXERCISE 9D: INTERROGATIVE PRONOUNS

Fill in the blanks in the following sentences with the correct forms of the interrogative pronouns.

1. The dean was angry when she asked, "_____ did this dastardly deed?"

2. The student government representative was also upset because he, too, questioned _____ had put the Moped on the chapel roof.

3. "_____ one of you is responsible?" he asked.

4. "_____ was the big idea?"

5. "_____ thought was it?"

6. "_____ do you think should take it down?" the dean added.

7. She asked the student _____ she had seen hanging around

    the chapel _____ other persons he had met there.

8. "_____ Moped is it?"

9. "_____ have you injured by this silly trick?"

10. The whole meeting was made up of questions about _____,

    _____ and _____.

INDEFINITE PRONOUNS

Indefinite pronouns, like demonstratives, identify, but they do not specify precisely. Some of the more frequently used indefinite pronouns are *some, few, another, many, much, more, several, any, none, no one, somebody, one, anybody, someone, somebody, each, nobody,* and *everybody.*

Indefinite pronoun forms using *one* or *body* take the possessive form *'s.*

somebody's mother   *nobody's* business   *everybody's* welfare

anybody's money   *no one's* thoughts   *someone's* home

EXERCISE 9E: INDEFINITE PRONOUNS

Fill in the blank in each of the following sentences with the correct form of indefinite pronoun.

1. She asked _____ little girl her name.

2. _____ of our boys would do a thing like that.

3. If you want _____ to go with you, all you need to do is ask.

4. _____ of the money, even though it was only a small percentage, was squandered on lavish parties.

5. When you intend to use _____ name as a reference, always get that person's permission first.

6. If you talk to _____ at all in that department, don't mention George Salisbury.

7. _____ of the workers were angry over the concession in the new contract, but others were glad to be going back to work.

8. If he borrows _____ car, the least he should do is replace the gas he uses.

9. _____ should attend Tuesday's meeting; the issues to be discussed concern every member.

10. The way tax dollars are being spent is _____ business; after all, they are your dollars and mine.

THE USE OF SELF/SELVES PRONOUNS

Personal pronouns have special forms made with *self* or *selves* at the end. It is important to remember that these forms are used for only two purposes. The first is as an intensive; it makes the word more emphatic.

Subject:	I *myself* told him.
Object:	The article featured you *yourself*.

The second use of the self/selves form is reflective; it turns the action back on the actor.

He hurt *himself*.
I questioned *myself*.

	Singular	Plural
First person	myself	ourselves
Second person	yourself	yourselves
Third person	himself	themselves
	herself	
	itself	

Avoid the faulty use of these forms:

Faulty:	My wife and myself were invited.
Correct:	My wife and I were invited.
Faulty:	Return these forms to my secretary or myself.
Correct:	Return these forms to my secretary or *me*.

ADDITIONAL RULES ABOUT PRONOUNS

Pronouns are almost always used like nouns. When they are subjects of the sentence, they are in the subject form.

> *He* is a fine man.
> *You* and *she* were singing beautifully.

When they are objects, they are in the object form.

> They heard *us.*
> *Whom* did you see?
> They sold *me* a bunch of violets.
> The instructor paid *them* a compliment.

Be careful in choosing the correct form when a pronoun is one of several subjects or objects.

> My sister and *I* (not "me and my sister") were waiting for Grandma.
> Jim and *I* (not "Jim and me") worked well together.
> The neighbor across the street asked my wife and *me* (not "I") to join them for a barbecue.

If you are in doubt about the correct form, consider the pronouns *one at a time.* You would never say "Me went" or "Him went," and you would never say "They refused to talk to I" or "They refused to talk to he."

Also be careful with combinations of nouns and pronouns such as *we* students/*us* students or *we* consumers/*us* consumers.

> *We* students are all blamed for the antics of a few clowns. (*We* [subject] are blamed.)
> The utility company is asking *us* consumers to pay the enormous cost of construction. (. . . asking *us* [object] to pay . . .)

Be sure to use the correct form of a pronoun following a linking verb. Because what follows a linking verb is *not* the object of an action, you must use the *subject form.*

> It is *I* (not *me*) you must persuade.
> It is *we* (not *us*) who are paying the cost.

It is *they* (not *them*) who raised the question.

It may be *she* (not *her*).

Also be sure to use the correct form of the pronoun after "than" or "as in" clauses of comparison. Often the second clause is not fully stated. To determine the correct pronoun form, you may need to reconstruct the missing part.

She is almost as tall as *I* (am).

Her brother is much older than *she* (is).

I owe you as much as (I owe) *them*.

She always gave Phillip more praise than (she gave) *me*.

EXERCISE 9F: RECOGNIZING INCORRECT PRONOUN FORMS

Cross out the incorrect pronoun form in each of the following sentences.

EXAMPLE: They will be expecting Jerry and (I, me) to be there Friday.

1.   The truth is that neither Hank nor (I, me) had read the instructions.

2.   The pilot and (I, me) joked about making a soft landing in the treetops.

3.   Aunt Jennie had promised to give some candy to my younger sister and (I, me).

4.   The scholarship money from the union was to have been divided between (she, her) and (I, me).

5.   The award was intended for my brother and (myself, me).

6.   Suzy and (me, I) are going to the concert on November 13.

7.   Everything was arranged for my sister and (me, I) to go to New Orleans.

8.   The congressional committee is trying to understand the plight of the homeless so as to help (they, them).

9.   The volunteer asked my neighbor and (I, me) for a donation.

10.   The magistrate informed (we, us) that we could be charged with contempt of court.

117

EXERCISE 9G: REVIEW OF PRONOUNS

Name the classes or types of pronouns.

_____

_____

_____

_____

_____

See how many pronouns of each type you can remember without looking at the pronoun chart presented earlier in this chapter.

_____ _____ _____ _____ _____

_____ _____ _____ _____ _____

_____ _____ _____ _____ _____

_____ _____ _____ _____ _____

_____ _____ _____ _____ _____

_____ _____ _____ _____ _____

_____ _____ _____ _____ _____

Does the *form* of pronouns change as their use changes in a sentence?

EXAMPLE: *They* (third person plural personal pronoun) changes to *their* in possessive form.

Try to think of five more examples.

_____

_____

_____

_____

_____

EXERCISE 9H: CHOOSING THE RIGHT PRONOUN FORM

From the five types of pronouns we have studied, insert the correct type and form in the blanks of the following sentences.

1.   We reached the road _____ led to our camp.

2.   Before we get to camp, we must turn into a path, at the end of _____ is the lake.

3.   _____ do you think you are?

4.   She did not know _____ her instructor wanted.

5.   _____ does he want?

6.   _____ notebook is this?

7.   Friends, Romans, countrymen, lend _____   _____ ears.

8.   He only hurts _____, no one else, by his attitude.

9.   The man _____ we saw is a famous singer.

10.   I saw the President _____.

11.   _____ is _____ dog.

12.   At least, I always thought _____ was _____.

13.   My parents live in the first house, but the whole condominium is _____.

14.   _____ built _____ last year.

15.   _____ practically sold _____ into slavery to pay for _____, but _____ is finally repaying _____.

16.   _____ phoned?

17.   I do not know _____ phoned.

18.   But I think _____ was either John or _____ roommate; _____ both were making phone calls.

19.   Where did you get _____ lovely table?

20.   _____ is _____   _____ just spoke to _____?

21.   What were _____ and _____ doing?

22. "May I speak to Joan please?" "_____ is _____."

23. Seeing _____, _____ began to worry.

24. _____ are _____ plants at the end of your yard?

25. I asked _____ a question _____ had bothered me.

WRITING FROM READING

Reassessing Pronouns

Most writers take little notice of pronouns. They view pronouns merely as substitutes, words that take the place of more important words (nouns). Readers often respond to pronouns in much the same way; they skim over them on their way to the more important words in the sentence. No wonder pronouns sometimes feel like the Rodney Dangerfields of the English language. They get no respect.

But pronouns shouldn't be taken for granted. No writer or reader could get along without them, and they often have a greater impact on us than we

No respect.

realize. Mark Twain's writings provide some typical examples. Take a look at the following excerpts from two of Twain's short stories—"My Watch" and "Extract from Captain Stormfield's Visit to Heaven."

Twain begins the first story by describing his "beautiful new watch." He says that he had come to believe that the watch was "infallible in its judgments about the time of day, and its constitution and its anatomy imperishable." As the story progresses, however, the reader sees Twain's "imperishable" watch being systematically destroyed by a series of inept watchmakers who were under the impression that they were fixing the watch. The following passage describes Twain's last exasperating attempt to save his cherished possession. Notice that Twain uses feminine pronouns when referring to his watch:

> . . . my timepiece performed unexceptionally, save that now and then, after working quietly for nearly eight hours, everything would let go all of a sudden . . . *she* would reel off the next twenty-four hours in six or seven minutes, and then stop with a bang. I went with a heavy heart to one more watchmaker, and looked on while he took *her* to pieces . . . While I waited . . . I presently recognized in this watchmaker an old acquaintance—a steamboat engineer of other days, and not a good engineer either. He examined all the parts carefully . . . and then delivered his verdict . . . "*she* makes too much steam—you want to hang the monkey-wrench on the safety valve!"
> I brained him on the spot, and had him buried at my own expense.

Mark Twain, Selected Works
(New York: Harper & Brothers, 1916), p. 311.

Now look at an excerpt from Twain's short story about Captain Stormfield, who, after being dead for thirty years, began to get "a little anxious" because he had been "whizzing around space like a comet" but still hadn't seen Heaven. The following passage describes part of Captain Stormfield's journey. Notice that Twain uses masculine pronouns when referring to Stormfield's encounter with a real comet:

> Well, it was so near my course that I wouldn't throw away the chance; so I fell off a point, steadied my helm, and went for *him* . . . The comet was burning blue in the distance, like a sickly torch, when I first sighted *him*, but *he* begun to grow bigger and bigger as I crept up on *him*. I slipped up on *him* so fast that when I had gone about 15,000,000 miles I was close enough to be swallowed up in the phosphorescent glory of *his* wake, and I couldn't see anything for the glare. Thinks I, it won't do to run into *him*, so I shunted to one side and tore along. By and by I closed up abreast of *his* tail. Do you know what it was like? It was like a gnat closing up on the continent of America.

Mark Twain, Selected Works
(New York: Harper & Brothers, 1916), p. 201.

Now that you've read both passages, go back and insert masculine pronouns or neuter pronouns (it, its) in the passage about the watch and read it aloud. Then insert feminine or neuter pronouns in the passage about the comet and read it aloud. Do you like the passages better the way Twain wrote them, or do you think he should have used different pronouns? How does Twain's choice of pronouns affect your reaction to his stories? Jot down your thoughts and then compare them with those of your classmates. See where you agree and where you differ—and why.

10 *Pronoun Reference*

As you have already learned, pronouns are words used as substitutes for nouns. Properly used, pronouns eliminate a good deal of monotonous repetition in speaking and writing.

> Darlene traveled that road every day on *her* way to college. *She* knew exactly how *her* car would take each hill and curve. (To repeat "Darlene" or "Darlene's" each time would be clumsy and boring.)

AGREEMENT OF PRONOUNS AND ANTECEDENTS

The most important rule in using pronouns is that a pronoun must agree in person and number with the word to which it refers (its antecedent). Note the following examples:

> The unemployed man often thinks *he* is at fault for being out of work.
> When the students enter, ask *them* to place their chairs in a circle.
> The horse started kicking *its* stall when *it* heard the crack of thunder.

If the antecedent is singular, the pronoun should be singular; if it is plural, the pronoun should be plural.

EXERCISE 10A: PRONOUN-ANTECEDENT AGREEMENT

Underline the antecedent and insert the correct pronoun in each of the following sentences.

1.   Many people from the northeastern United States think _____ want to retire to Florida or somewhere else where it is warm all the time.

2.   Others, like me, feel that _____ would be bored by a one-season temperature.

3.   A friend of mine who lived in Hawaii for two years said _____ got disgusted with the weather.

4.   He said _____ was sunny and warm and beautiful every day.

5.   Many things change with the seasons; _____ are clothes, food, sports, and activities.

6.   Fall brings football, which makes _____ special to me.

7.   Shorts and T-shirts are replaced by corduroy pants and knit sweaters; _____ are a welcome change when the weather becomes nippy.

8.   Hearty soups and stews replace salads and tuna fish sandwiches; _____ taste and smell terrific when the snow flies.

9. Bowling replaces golf; _____ uses different muscles and is played inside where it's warm.

10. I wouldn't ever give up winter, for _____ makes spring special.

Agreement with Indefinite Antecedents

Many errors in pronoun agreement result from confusion about the *number* of the antecedent. Here are some guidelines that will help you avoid such errors.

Anybody, anyone, someone, somebody, everybody, everyone, nobody, no one, each, either, and *neither* are singular and require singular pronouns.

> *Everybody* has a right to *his* opinion.
>
> If *anyone* disagrees, let *him* speak up.

It has been conventional to use a masculine pronoun (he/him/his) to refer to male or female or to an unspecified gender. The use of the masculine form is seen by some people as sexist, so frequently the pronouns are doubled: *he or she, him or her, his or hers.* But to repeatedly use these *he or she* forms can become awkward. Often, the problem can be avoided by using a plural rather than an indefinite pronoun.

> *People* have a right to express *their* opinions.
>
> If the *listeners* disagree, let *them* speak up.

EXERCISE 10B: PRONOUN AGREEMENT WITH INDEFINITE ANTECEDENT

Underline the antecedent and insert the correct pronoun in each of the following sentences.

1. Stephen King is the most widely read author in the United States today.

2. Everyone who reads one of his stories is likely to feel _____ hair stand on end because _____ are really scary.

3. No one seems to be able to read King's books and retain _____ objectivity.

125

4. *Salem's Lot* and *The Shining* are two of King's earliest books; both had _____ moments of complete terror.

5. Someone said _____ was so frightened in the movie *The Shining* that _____ left before _____ was over.

6. Anyone who bought *Pet Sematary* got _____ money's worth if _____ wanted to be frightened.

7. People of all ages like to have _____ emotions aroused by a book or a movie.

8. Nobody likes to have _____ dreams turned into nightmares, though.

9. Therefore, not everyone likes to read _____ books.

10. Each must decide whether or not _____ should indulge in such reading.

Agreement with Collective Nouns

A collective noun—for example, *group, class, team, jury, committee, family, gang, flock*—usually requires a singular pronoun.

> The *committee* should make *its* decision by Tuesday.
> The *class* will have an opportunity to plan for *its* next field trip.

In these sentences it is clear that the committee and the class are each acting *as a unit*. However, when it is clear that the members of a group are acting *individually*, then a plural pronoun is needed.

> The *gang* broke up and went *their* separate ways. (The group obviously acted as individuals.)

**EXERCISE 10C: PRONOUN AGREEMENT
WITH COLLECTIVE NOUNS**

Underline the antecedents and insert the correct pronouns in the following sentences.

1. The Mortuary Madcaps had a rocky start in _____ 1986 season.

2. The team had lost _____ all-pro quarterback Planter Mc-Soon.

3. Either Graves or Moldy would have to make _____ debut as the starting quarterback.

4. A group of offensive linemen said that _____ various injuries kept them from playing.

5. The whole gang of tight ends had _____ troubles, too.

6. At one point, the entire group of tight ends was on the bench and not because of _____ attitude.

7. The jury (made up of coaches) finally made _____ decision on the starting quarterback, Graves.

8. After one game, the team added Graves to _____ list of injured.

9. The fans were still expecting _____ team to be a champion.

10. The team showed _____ character by winning despite _____ bad luck in having so many players injured.

Agreement with Antecedents Joined by *and*

Antecedents joined by *and* are referred to by a plural pronoun.

> *Vivian and Shirl* said *they* share the rent.
>
> *Her mother and father* finally gave up in *their* attempt to persuade Evelyn to live at home.

Agreement of Antecedents Joined by *or/nor* and *either/or*

Singular antecedents joined by *or/nor* and *either/or* are referred to by singular pronouns. When one of the antecedents joined by *or* or *nor* is singular and one plural, the pronoun always agrees with the *nearer* of the two antecedents.

> *Incorrect:*   Neither the general manager nor the coach would state *their* opinion.
>
> *Correct:*   Neither the general manager nor the coach would state *his* opinion.
>
> *Incorrect:*   Neither the general manager nor the coaches would state his opinion.
>
> *Correct:*   Neither the general manager nor the coaches would state their opinion. (Coaches is the nearer of the two subjects.)

**EXERCISE 10D: PRONOUN AGREEMENT
                  WITH TWO ANTECEDENTS**

Underline the antecedent and insert the correct pronouns in each of the following sentences.

1.   During the 1984 campaign, Mondale and Reagan took _____ messages to voters across the United States.

2.   Geraldine Ferraro, the first woman ever to be a major party Vice-Presidential candidate, and George Bush, Republican Party Vice-Presidential candidate, gave _____ views on a nationwide debate.

3.   Republicans and Democrats said that _____ candidate won.

4.   Walter "Fritz" Mondale said that _____ won the first debate.

5. Most of the commentators and all of the Democrats expressed _____ agreement.

6. Neither Mondale nor the Republicans could claim that _____ side won the second debate decisively.

7. Neither my sisters nor my mother would say for whom _____ was going to vote.

8. Neither Reagan nor the Republicans had much to fear about the outcome of the election according to _____ polls.

9. Both Republicans and Democrats turned out at the election to support _____ respective candidates.

10. I don't think either Reagan or his supporters expected that _____ would win in forty-nine states.

Avoiding the Vague Use of *You, It,* or *They*

Faults in pronoun agreement are often carried over from casual conversation. But in your written work, you need to be especially careful when using *you, it,* or *they.* Be sure your sentences include clear antecedents, or your writing will be vague.

> *Faulty:* In the newspaper it says that China has signed a new treaty about Hong Kong. (*It* is unnecessary here.)
>
> *Improved:* The newspaper says that China has signed a new treaty about Hong Kong.
>
> *Faulty:* They say that Mexico is the ideal place to go for a vacation. (*They* is unclear because it has no antecedent.)
>
> *Improved:* Many people (or travel agents) say that Mexico is the ideal place to go for a vacation.

EXERCISE 10E: FAULTY PRONOUN REFERENCES

What is wrong with the following sentences? How would you correct the faults in pronoun reference?

1. In San Francisco they have lots of fog. _____

_____

2. In Argentina, you didn't dare to say anything against Eva Peron. _____

   _____

3. In a recent article in *Fortune,* it says that Gordon Getty was worth more than
   $4 billion. _____

4. Mrs. Peebles told her daughter that her car had a flat. _____

   _____

5. Neither Turk nor Dave was willing to give up their weekend. _____

   _____

6. Somebody has forgotten their keys. _____

   _____

7. The jury had reached their verdict in less than 20 minutes. _____

   _____

8. Neither the girls nor Jack should have their wishes ignored. _____

   _____

9. They say you've never lived until you've seen Naples. _____

   _____

10. In the movie it showed how to surf. _____

    _____

EXERCISE 10F: ELIMINATING REPETITION BY USING PRONOUNS

Rewrite each of the following sentences or groups of sentences using the correct pronoun forms to replace the repetitious nouns.

EXAMPLE: When the candidate promised to cut taxes, the candidate was telling the people what the people wanted to hear.

When the candidate promised to cut taxes, *he* was telling the people what *they* wanted to hear.

1. There are catfish in Florida that can crawl long distances out of water. These

   catfish have been known to attack household pets. _____

   _____

2. When Margaret talks about Tennessee walking horses, Margaret really knows what Margaret is talking about. _____

_____

3. Junior smashed a dozen eggs in the back of his mother's station wagon. Junior's mother was furious with Junior. _____

_____

4. When I visited my home town last month, I found that the old soda fountain had not changed. The old soda fountain was exactly the same as when I left there in the 60s. _____

_____

5. Children who had attended kindergarten usually did better later in life. Those children were more likely to finish high school and go on to college. _____

_____

6. On TV last night, there was a country music awards special. The country music awards special lasted for more than three hours. _____

_____

7. Mr. Pottle believed that the house had cement termites. Mr. Pottle said he would have to exterminate the cement termites. _____

_____

8. Most prime-time television shows are silly and boring. These programs waste the viewers' time. _____

_____

9. Fast-food restaurants can be found in every American city. These restaurants spend millions of dollars a year on advertising. _____

_____

10. Children of alcoholics often develop serious social and emotional problems. Children of alcoholics need programs that build their self-esteem and teach them how to cope with their problems. _____

_____

EXERCISE 10G: REVIEW OF PRONOUN REFERENCE

In each of the following sentences, fill in the correct pronoun and underline its antecedent.

1. A person should have _____ choice of optional equipment on a new car.

2. Each of the girls wanted to have _____ own bedroom.

3. Either of these models will do the job if you properly maintain _____.

4. The company decided to move _____ main office to Austin.

5. Each of the men had _____ own reasons for wanting to leave the company.

6. No one should be surprised to learn that _____ house has increased in value.

7. A merry group was gathered in the village square for _____ traditional Halloween parade.

8. Neither the Australians nor the American had succeeded in _____ attempt to find oil.

9. The chief executive would have welcomed anyone who cared to offer _____ solution to the company's financial problems.

10. Either the main library or one of the branches ought to have that book in _____ collection.

11. This year Congress decided to postpone _____ annual orientation program for new members.

12. Everyone who attended the meeting was asked to volunteer _____ services to the local food drive.

13. The oldest members of the McCavitt clan have transferred _____ stock options over to the twins, Iris and Ichabod.

14. Each of the songwriters is going to donate _____ royalties to the Big Brothers and Sisters of America.

15. Dr. Coffee always has a kind word for _____ patients.

16. Either the owner or the manager will send the Grumpkes_____ security deposit.

17. Part of Mark's problem is _____ inability to say no.

18. Even an animal needs _____ ego stroked once in a while.

19. The Director of Environmental Resources promised that everyone would have _____ tap water analyzed by the end of the week.

20. You can't tell a book by _____ cover.

WRITING FROM READING

Using Your Imagination

Writing is a creative process. Through the medium of language, you can solve problems, build friendships, shape reality, or even escape from reality for a while. You can conquer fear or create fear. You can discover things about yourself that you never would have learned in any other way.

One of the ways that people express themselves best is through story telling. Following is the beginning of a story and three possible endings. Choose one of the endings and write a story that you think your classmates would enjoy reading. After you're finished, find those students who chose the same ending and compare your story with theirs. Did they write the same kind of story? Did they describe the characters differently? How did your own experiences shape the direction of your story?

Beginning: Once upon a time, in a long forgotten ghost town, lived the only inhabitants of Goldrush Flats—an old man and his dog.

133

Ending 1:	To this day, no one has ever been able to solve the mystery of Goldrush Flats.
Ending 2:	The old woman never looked back.
Ending 3:	The stranger would never return, but he left Goldrush Flats a richer man, for he had found something there that he had been searching for all of his life.

Now break into small groups, choose another ending, and write a story together. After you have finished, ask yourself some questions:

1. Which type of writing experience did you enjoy most—writing alone or writing with other people? Why?
2. In which type of writing experience did you learn more about yourself— writing your own story or contributing to a group story?
3. Which story do you think turned out better?
4. What are the advantages of writing alone?
5. What are the advantages of writing with others?

Writing on the Job

Almost all jobs require some sort of writing. A great deal of on-the-job writing today requires an ability to condense information so that someone else can solve a problem or make an intelligent decision. Managers' summary reports, nurses' care plans, police officers' accident reports, and computer analysts' problem statements are just a few examples. Being able to pinpoint important information and to eliminate irrelevant information become invaluable skills in the working world.

Suppose that you work in the Marketing Department of Computer Research Associates. You have just been asked to present a brief written report on the marketability of a new concept in video games—less violence and more creativity. In "Save the Sap," two players compete to save Sam the Sap from his own insecurities. The object of the game is to build up Sam's self-confidence so that he can move on to the next challenge. The winner is the first person to put a full smile on Sam's face.

After checking with the Manufacturing Department and your own Marketing Department, you have collected the following information. Evaluate the information, and then write up a brief, one-page report.

MEMO FROM MICHAEL SCANLON, MANUFACTURING DEPARTMENT

"Save the Sap" could be manufactured at a cost of $1,000 per unit, 15 percent less than any video game we now produce and 5 percent less than any video game on the market today. If "Save the Sap" were to sell as well as our "Attack Zack" game, CRA could show a 25 percent profit within six months of production. Production, however, could not begin for at least six weeks because of backlogs and vacation schedules. I'll be gone for the next three weeks—taking the family to Florida for some R & R. The kids are just dying to see Disney World.

By the way, congratulations on your promotion to marketing Supervisor.

Mike

MEMO FROM JANE WALKER, MARKETING DEPARTMENT

I have some good news and some bad news. According to our educational psychologists and advertising analysts, "Save the Sap" has great potential. The latest survey conducted by our Department showed that over 63 percent of the 1,500 adult respondents were greatly concerned about the violent nature of today's video games, and even 42 percent of the adolescent respondents said that they were tired of war games and space battles.

However, the same survey indicated that the majority of video-game users fall between the ages of 8 and 13, and "Save the Sap" appeals to an older audience, perhaps 12 to 16. The "life challenges" are too sophisticated. They have to be modified to appeal to a younger audience.

I hope the game can be saved. I'd like to see us market the product. It would be good for our image, and, besides, I love the name, "Save the *Sap*"—sounds like my life story.

Congratulations on your promotion!

Jane

11 *Consistent Tense*

As you already know, a verb is a word or group of words that shows action or indicates a state of being. Verb *tense* shows the *time* the action of the verb takes place or a particular condition exists.

1. *Present tense* is used to show that the action or condition is going on or exists now.

    Suzy *is playing* in the backyard.

2. *Future tense* indicates that an action will take place, or a certain condition will exist, in the future.

    She *will run* to the house when her daddy comes home.

3. *Past tense* indicates that an action or condition took place or existed at some definite time in the past.

    Suzy *played* in the backyard yesterday afternoon.

4. *Past perfect tense* indicates that an action or condition was completed at a time prior to some other incident in the past.

    She *had played* in the sandbox until noon, when her mother called her in.

English is a very flexible language, and there are many variations in verb form to indicate time precisely. Note how the verb forms in the following sentences indicate variations in *time:*

He *plays* baseball.
He *is playing* in Montreal.
He *has played* in every major city.
He *has been playing* with the Expos.

He *played* baseball.

He *was playing* when he was only seven.

He *had been playing* for fourteen years before he tried out for the majors.

He *will play* for Montreal next year.

He *will be playing* in almost every game.

He *will have played* every team in the league by next fall.

He *will have been playing* in the majors for three years by the end of this season.

It is *not* necessary for you to learn the names of all the verb tenses. What *is* important is that you develop your awareness of the verb phrases used to express differences in time. If you want your readers to understand you, you need to present your ideas in a clear and logical sequence.

IRREGULAR VERBS

Most verbs in English are *regular*—that is, their past and past perfect forms end in *ed*.

I smell gasoline. (present tense)

I smell*ed* gasoline. (past tense)

I had smell*ed* gasoline. (past perfect)

But English also contains a large number of *irregular* verbs—verbs whose forms change as their tenses change. Following is a list of some common irregular verbs:

Present	Past	Perfect
hold	held	held
ride	rode	ridden
shake	shook	shaken
drink	drank	drunk
choose	chose	chosen
sit	sat	sat
spring	sprang/sprung	sprung
write	wrote	written
shrink	shrank	shrunk
freeze	froze	frozen
swim	swam	swum
speak	spoke	spoken

There are many other irregular verbs; when you use these verbs in your writing, check your dictionary carefully for their principal forms and variations.

Here are some especially troublesome verbs that you need to watch out for:

lie (recline)	lay	lain
lay (place)	laid	laid
rise (get up)	rose	risen
raise (lift up)	raised	raised

Notice how these verbs are used correctly:

I *lie* on the couch to take a nap. (present)
I *lay* awake all last night. (past)
I *have lain* ill for days on end. (perfect)
I *lay* the book on the table. (present)
I *laid* the tile in the bathroom. (past)
I *have laid* ceramic tile. (perfect)
They *rise* to give the performer a standing ovation. (present)
They *rose* early to catch the 5:15 A.M. bus. (past)
They *have risen* early throughout their military service. (perfect)
They *raise* corn and oats. (present)
They *raised* Black Angus cattle. (past)
They *have raised* some award-winning steers. (perfect)

CONSISTENT USE OF TENSE

Selecting the precise verb tense and being consistent in your choice can be complicated and demanding. You need to know how the various tenses are formed, and you need to think carefully about the *time* expressed by your ideas.

In Main Clauses in a Sentence

Inconsistent: There *was* a period of dead silence; then he *orders* the men to march.

Consistent:	There *was* a period of dead silence; then he *ordered* the men to march.
Inconsistent:	For several years now I *have been attending* Public Theatre performances, and I *enjoyed* every one of them.
Consistent:	For several years now I *have been attending* Public Theatre performances, and I *have enjoyed* every one of them.
Inconsistent:	Jane *stood* on the edge of the bank and *stared* into the dark water below; she *is determined* to leave Pottsville forever.
Consistent:	Jane *stood* on the edge of the bank and *stared* into the dark water below; she *was determined* to leave Pottsville forever.

In the Main Clause and in a Dependent Clause

Inconsistent:	Until that day, I *had* never *seen* Butch when he *hasn't* a wad of tobacco in his cheeks.
Consistent:	Until that day, I *had* never *seen* Butch when he *didn't have* a wad of tobacco in his cheeks.
Inconsistent:	The fleeing bank robber *dashed* around the corner into the alley, where he *runs* right into the arms of the detective.
Consistent:	The fleeing bank robber *dashed* around the corner into the alley, where he *ran* right into the arms of the detective.

139

Inconsistent:	They gradually *began* to understand what the old wood-cutter *has* done to prepare them for survival in the wilderness.
Consistent:	They gradually *began* to understand what the old wood-cutter *had done* to prepare them for survival in the wilderness.

In a Paragraph

Do not shift from present to past or back and forth between any two tenses without a good reason.

EXERCISE 11A: USING CONSISTENT TENSE

Note the unnecessary and inconsistent tense shifts in the following bit of narrative. Rewrite the passage to make the tenses logical and consistent.

> She walks out on the street and begins walking slowly down the hill toward the minimarket. Suddenly a car came over the crest of the hill at high speed. The driver was not in control because the car is weaving crazily across both lanes, sometimes almost sideways. I thought she would get hit for sure, but she jumped into the ditch just before the car skids in the gravel on the shoulder of the road—right on the spot where she is standing just a moment before. Then the car straightened up a little and disappears over the next hill. I keep waiting for a big bang, but maybe some fools are lucky—some of the time.

EXERCISE 11B: CHOOSING THE CORRECT TENSE

Choose the correct tense and verb form for each of the following sentences. Cross out the incorrect verb.

EXAMPLE: After watching the news and sports, I began studying again, but someone (~~comes~~/came) knocking at the door.

1.   For years I have been going to Bruce Springsteen concerts and I (enjoyed/have enjoyed) every one of them.

2. It is estimated that 10,000 caribou (drowned/drownded) at two flooded river crossings in Quebec.

3. I would consider moving to Austin if I (know/knew) I could get a job.

4. The great white shark that had (bit/bitten) the swimmer was finally caught.

5. The bodies of the two sailors were perfectly preserved because they had been (frozen/froze) in the Arctic ice.

6. By the time we got there, the boys had (drank/drunk) more than their share of the beer.

7. After the sun had (rose/risen), it quickly burned away the mist.

8. The construction gang had (raised/risen) the steel skeleton of the building in three days.

9. He (lay/laid) down to rest after he (finished/had finished) trimming the hedge.

10. After I had (rode/ridden) home with Harry, I was a wreck.

EXERCISE 11C: RECOGNIZING INCONSISTENT TENSE

Make any changes necessary to correct the tense in each of the following sentences.

1. A great many years pass before the public became aware that he was a financial wizard.

2. Fabric-covered furniture should not be placed by sunny windows because sunlight will have faded the fabric in just a few months.

3. Since many people have believed that vitamin C helps prevent colds, they say you must either have plenty of vitamin C in your diet or take vitamin supplements.

4. Although people have often thought of Borneo as being filled with primitive headhunters, the Sultan of Brunei is just completing work on a fabulous palace with hundreds of lavishly furnished rooms.

5. She wants everything, even though she didn't want to work more than an hour or two a day.

6. As soon as it started to rain, he runs in and gets his jacket.

7. By the time we got there, the horses had drank from the brackish water.

8. Marigolds are hardy little flowers that grew in almost any soil.

9. The hurricane had passed Cape Canaveral and is heading out to sea.

10. We should be kept informed when they reached a decision.

11. The soldiers seldom listened when he had spoken to them about duty and honor.

12. Mr. Twaddle got up, gets in his car, and goes to the office every day.

13. Jimmy had been ready to start running if the dog shows the slightest sign of being unfriendly.

14. Did you see where I lay my jacket?

15. The population of the Sunbelt states has raised dramatically since the 1960s.

16. Jody tried to remember the number and then begun to flip through the yellow pages.

17. It was the house where she was suppose to live.

18. After that big truck drove down the street, the water main busted.

19. They tried to do things that no one has tried to do before.

20. She uses *Roget's Thesaurus* and *Bartlett's Quotations* and had found them both to be very useful in her writing.

WRITING FROM READING

The Importance of Tense

If a writer is consistent in the use of tense, you probably will not even be aware of the tenses used—unless you are assigned to identify them for an English class. However, it is often the correct use of tense that enables you to understand a particular piece of writing. In the following excerpt from *People I Have Loved, Known or Admired*, Leo Rosten discusses his father, a man he obviously both loved and admired. Note how Rosten shows, through the use of tense, how his father was, how he was before that, and how he now lives in his son's memory.

My father had been a stocking-maker in Poland and became a sweater-maker in America. He came to Ellis Island in his early twenties, alone, and later brought over my mother and me, and in Chicago he spent sixty hours a week at work pulling the heavy carriage of a knitting machine back and forth across the inverted-V bed of needles.

He would get up before dawn, during the ferocious Chicago winters, and take a streetcar for an hour or more to be at work by eight. When he returned from his long workday, he would eat his dinner (we called it "supper" in those days) and then start working on a secondhand knitting machine in our front room—to make sweaters on his own. My mother was determined to start "a business of our own," so they would never be at the mercy of a "boss." She had gone to work as a girl in a textile plant in Lodz and had been so swift and skillful that they made her a foreman at fifteen.

My father was always full of talk about great wealth, which I do not think he ever really believed he would acquire. But the thought and talk of being rich warmed his hopes. My mother never denied us anything really important, but the memory of great hardships left my father forever uneasy, even frightened, about spending money. Even when he would concede that he was "well-off," he would add "—but not THAT well-off." For instance, he considered airmail stamps an unneeded luxury, and he would enter a taxi, even one he knew I would never let him pay for, only after obligatory protestations. "Who NEEDS it? We can take a bus."

Leo Rosten, *People I Have Loved, Known or Admired*
(New York: McGraw-Hill, 1970), p. 25.

Think about some person that you have known for years. Has the person changed? Has the person changed in the way he or she acts toward you now that you're older? Write a paragraph about this person, contrasting how he or she is now to how he or she used to be, and (if you remember) how he or she was even before that. Use present tense to describe how the person is now, past tense to describe how the person used to be, and past perfect tense to describe how the person was before that.

Think about some aspect of your own life that has changed. Did you make the change consciously because there was a part of your life you were unhappy with? Did some important person in your life influence you to change? Was the change for the better? Did you change after your sister or brother was born? When you got your first job? When you met your girlfriend or boyfriend? When you decided to go to college? When you landed your first job? When you discovered a new talent in yourself? When you made the team?

Write a letter to a friend you haven't seen for years. Describe a change in yourself, along with the cause of the change and its effect on your relationships.

Or explain to your parents or your teacher or your friend that you understand how you have been acting and that you have decided to change. Then explain to them how you expect to behave in the future.

12 Consistent Person

One of the hallmarks of good writers is their ability to see themselves as both writer *and reader*. If writers don't view their words from the readers' perspective, they can thoroughly confuse their readers. Writers may think that they have put across their points effectively, but some readers may never be quite sure what the writer is trying to say. As you learned in the last chapter, for example, unnecessary shifts in tense force the readers to jump from one time period to another without any logical explanation.

Just as it is important for the readers to know *when* things happen in relation to each other, so it is important for them to know *who* is speaking. This is what is known as *person*. Person has to remain the same, unless there is some logical reason to move the point of view from one person to another.

If you were being consistent in person, you would not say, "*I* want to go to the movies. *We* have been waiting for this movie to come to town. *You* can't beat this movie for excitement." Your poor, frustrated readers will not know who is speaking or from what point of view they, the readers, must look.

Of course, if you have a logical reason to shift person, then you must shift in order to keep the readers clearly informed—for example, "*I* must tell you this. Otherwise, *you* might go to the meeting unprepared."

In order to avoid frustrating your readers, you have to maintain a consistent point of view. If you are writing a story about your happiest childhood memory, don't suddenly shift to your future career plans, or from a personal narrative (first person) to a formal report (third person) as if someone else were the main character of the story. For example, writing about your childhood memory, you wouldn't say, "The little boy opened his eyes and saw his mother." You would say, "*I* opened *my* eyes and saw *my* mother."

Being consistent in person, therefore, is one way of keeping your readers with you. You can write in first person, second person, or third person, depending on how you approach your topic and on your purpose. The pronouns that you use will let your readers know in which person you are writing.

Person	Relationship to Audience	Pronouns
First person	The writer is *speaking*.	I, we
Second person	Someone is being *spoken to*.	you, your (or *you* understood)
Third person	The writer is *speaking about* something or somebody.	he, she, one, it, they

Most writing is written in the third person. Your textbooks, for example, as well as the newspaper and magazine articles you read, are usually written *about* something or somebody. An autobiography or a letter from your sweetheart, on the other hand, would most likely be written in first person, and a set of directions or an interoffice memo might be written in second person—speaking directly to a specific audience.

THE DIRECT *YOU* VERSUS THE INDIRECT *YOU*

Language is one of the finest products of the human mind. It is one of the attributes that make us human. With language, we can conquer both time and space. Homer, the Greek poet, still speaks to us across more than 3,000 years. We can write to people on the other side of the world.

The English language is one of the greatest languages in the world. But, since language is man-made, it is not perfect. One of its imperfections concerns the second person, *you*. You will probably find that it is most difficult to avoid shifting point of view when you are writing in the second person.

Most languages have an "impersonal" person, a point of view that really means "people in general." But English does not have a satisfactory impersonal person. "People" doesn't quite say what is meant, and "one" quickly begins to sound affected. ("Is *one* allowed to eat *one's* lettuce with *one's* fingers?") Therefore, writers are faced with the problems of expressing the sense of "one" or "people" without having quite the right English word for it.

You in Direct Address

When you use *you* correctly, it is in *direct address.* "Will *you* (John) come to dinner tonight?" Or, "Class, *you* (all) have twenty minutes to finish this exam." *You* in direct address, thus, can be either singular or plural.

You in Indirect Address

Difficulties arise when you want to remark about people in general. If you make such a statement as "You can't have more fun than watching the Browns play," you may get a denial from a cranky reader. "I certainly can! I hate the Browns."

You can usually solve this particular dilemma by recasting your sentence to change the second person *you* to *third person:* "*Most people* have a marvelous time watching the Browns play." Or you can change to *first person:* "*I* can't have more fun than watching the Browns play."

Sometimes, however, that strategy won't work. In that case, you have no choice but to stick with the misapplied second person. This, nevertheless, may still be a less-than-perfect solution because it is sometimes difficult to tell whether *you* is being used in direct address or indirect.

Example:	You have to be crazy to want to be President of the United States.
Recast:	Anyone who wants to be President of the United States has to be crazy.
	A person would have to be crazy to want to be President of the United States.
Example:	You can't win 'em all.
Recast:	No one can win 'em all.
Example:	You can't make a silk purse out of a sow's ear.
Recast:	One can't make a silk purse out of a sow's ear.
Example:	You never know when you're well off.
Recast:	One never knows when one is well off.
	People never know when they are well off.

EXERCISE 12A: RECOGNIZING FIRST, SECOND, AND THIRD PERSON

Think about the various types of writing listed below. Indicate whether you would expect each item to be written in first person, second person, or third person.

PERSON

1. A recipe _____

2. A biography of Martin Luther King _____

3. Your high school yearbook _____

4. A cover letter accompanying your job application _____

5. An editorial in your local newspaper _____

6. The owner's manual for your car _____

7. Your biology textbook _____

8. Your narrative paragraph for English class _____

9. An essay question about the Civil War _____

10. A letter from your utility company explaining the latest rate hikes _____

11. An entry in your diary or private journal _____

12. An article in a medical journal _____

13. An advertisement for designer jeans _____

14. Your aunt's eye-witness account of the Johnstown flood _____

15. A newspaper story about the Johnstown flood _____

EXERCISE 12B: SHIFTS IN PERSON, SENTENCE LEVEL

Read the following sentences carefully and see if they are consistent in person. Circling the pronouns in each sentence should help you determine whether the sentence shifts in person. Note your conclusions on the lines provided after each sentence. Then compare your answers with those of your classmates. See if you have identified the same shifts for the same reasons.

1. One should not be afraid to criticize, but you shouldn't focus solely on a person's weaknesses either.

    _____

2. Everyone needs a little positive reinforcement once in a while.

    _____

3. We all know that some of the best teachers and business managers use strategies that build your self-confidence.

    _____

4. Some of your best programs in drug and alcohol rehabilitation are also based on improving one's self-esteem.

    _____

5. Don't take my word for it. One can find plenty of research that supports your basic positive approach.

    _____

6. When one hears an encouraging word now and then, he finds it easier to approach a task with enthusiasm.

    _____

7. Of course, I am not saying that criticism, in itself, is bad.

    _____

8. Our experience shows us that accepting constructive criticism is often your key to success.

    _____

9. One's ability to accept constructive criticism helps you in both your private life and your public life.

    _____

10. One should always remember Samuel Johnson's comment that ''Criticism, as it was first instituted by Aristotle, was meant as a standard of judging well.''

    _____

    _____

    _____

EXERCISE 12C: SHIFTS IN PERSON, PARAGRAPH LEVEL

Improve the following paragraph by making it consistent in person.

I always thought that after you had a root canal done on a tooth, you could no longer feel pain in that tooth, but, BOY, was I wrong! After having a root canal done, you learn that there is no such thing as a "dead" tooth. My dentist informed me that the only things you can't feel after a root canal are electrical stimulation and the sensations of hot and cold. With these exceptions, he explained, the tooth is still capable of experiencing the sense of touch. When he started gently probing with one of his favorite little instruments, I understood instantly what Dr. Lauver meant. My tooth was still very much alive!

WRITING FROM READING

Problem Solving

In the many worlds you live in—your private world, your working world, and your academic world—you have to solve problems. Some problems, however, never get solved because you don't take the time to think through them: to define them clearly, to clarify positions, and to formulate workable solutions.

The following passage depicts the type of problem that a working adult is often faced with. Read Frank's story and see if you can help him solve his problem.

Frank is 22 years old. He graduated from high school with a C average, but he never really applied himself—except in biology and chemistry classes; he was fascinated with science. When he graduated from high school, Frank had no great desire to go on to college. He just wanted to get a job and make some money. He often thought that he'd like to someday become a medical lab technician like his cousin Gene, so he tried to get some sort of job in a hospital. Unfortunately, however, there was nothing available. Frank finally decided to take a job with a local tire company. When he took the job, though, he learned that the manager was fed up with employees who worked for a few months and then quit because "they didn't like lugging around 100 pound truck tires." Frank therefore promised the manager that he would stay for at least a year. Then, two months later, Rochester General Hospital offered Frank a job in the Pediatrics Ward with an opportunity to take advantage of the hospital's evening education program whereby employees could become qualified for various other jobs—lab assistant, emergency care, and so on. Frank really wanted the job, but he didn't want to renege on his promise. He prided himself on being a man of his word.

If you were Frank, what would you do? Could you handle the problem in a way that would be fair both to the manager and to yourself? Think about possible solutions to Frank's dilemma. Brainstorm with your classmates and record your thoughts on paper. Before you begin, however, make sure that you all have a clear understanding of Frank's problem. Write a sentence defining the problem.

Statement of the Problem:

Then write a sentence or two clarifying Frank's position and the manager's position.

What Frank Wants:

What the Manager Wants:

Finally, see if you can think of at least one fair, workable solution to Frank's dilemma.

Possible Solutions:

13 *Parallel Wording*

As thousands of common expressions in our language illustrate, parallel structure is a natural part of speaking and writing:

> the beautiful and the damned
>
> to have and to hold
>
> of the people, by the people, and for the people
>
> blood, sweat, and tears
>
> take it or leave it
>
> different strokes for different folks

All of these statements have one thing in common: they are all examples of parallel wording. Parallel means that two or more things have similar corresponding parts. They resemble each other. In sports, for example, parallel bars are two bars of the same dimensions placed in the same horizontal position equidistant from each other. In writing, parallelism refers to a group of words, phrases, or clauses that resemble each other, both in meaning and in structure. Writers use parallel wording for emphasis. Through the process of repetition and the rhythmic structure of the thought, the writer can call the readers' attention to what is being expressed.

Without your realizing it, in fact, parallel wording has probably already had an impact on those expressions you remember, as opposed to those you have long forgotten. For example, you would probably have little trouble supplying the missing parts of the following sayings, largely because their parallel structure makes them easy to remember:

Buy now, _____ _____.

The bigger they come, _____ _____ _____

_____.

What you see is _____ _____ _____.

I came, I saw, _____ _____.

When you complete these sayings, you are using parallel wording. In "Buy now, pay later," for example, "pay later" is the parallel counterpart to "buy now." The slogan gets a short, succinct message across to the listener. Advertisers could get the same message across in different words, but it wouldn't have the same direct impact. The business world has long known the value of simple repetition of verb-adverb combinations.

Verb	Adverb
Buy	now,
pay	later.

Such wording is far more effective than a lengthy nonparallel statement such as "You may purchase the item now, and, at a later date, pay for it."

When used properly, parallel wording can be one of your most effective tools as a writer. Whether you're dashing off a witty note on a birthday card or carefully constructing a thirty-page term paper, parallel thoughts are best expressed in parallel form—in a series of words, phrases, or clauses.

Words	*faith, hope,* and *charity*
Phrases	*the thrill of victory* and *the agony of defeat*
Clauses	*To err is human; to forgive, divine.*

Notice that, in addition to expressing similar ideas (the virtues of *faith, hope,* and *charity*), parallel wording is also very effective in expressing *contrasting* ideas (*the thrill of victory* versus *the agony of defeat*).

Properly handled, parallel construction is an important aid to *clarity* and *emphasis*. To convey ideas to your readers precisely and effectively, you need to express ideas of equal importance in parallel form. A coordinate series of words, phrases, or clauses should always be parallel in form.

Words	She is *rich, charming,* and *beautiful.*
	The flag of France is *red, white,* and *blue.*
Phrases	The troops were ordered *to pack their gear, to march to the highway,* and *to wait for the convoy.*

Clauses	He firmly believed *that no one was willing to work, that almost everyone was overpaid,* and *that anyone who joined a union was a troublemaker.*

When the signs of parallelism (*to, by, for, with, that,* and so on) are not repeated, the sentence often lacks clarity. Repeating a preposition or conjunction with a series tends to emphasize the parallelism.

Knowledge of the latest developments is vital *to* the President, *to* the Joint Chiefs of Staff, and *to* the National Security Council.

Doubtful:	The agent told us home prices were increasing and we should buy the house today.
Clearer:	The agent told us *that* home prices were increasing and *that* we should buy the house today.

Faulty:	The guide gave us tips on hunting, fishing, and how to cook.
Correct:	The guide gave us tips on hunting, fishing, and cooking.

Faulty:	Marie is pleasant, intelligent, and works hard.
Correct:	Marie is pleasant, intelligent, and hard working.
	Marie is pleasant and intelligent, and she works hard.

Faulty:	The company is looking for a person with a college degree, a good scholastic record, and who has some interest in computer science.
Correct:	The company is looking for a person with a college degree, a good scholastic record, and some interest in computer science.

EXERCISE 13A: RECOGNIZING PARALLEL WORDING, SENTENCE LEVEL

See if you can recognize the parallel thoughts in the following sentences. Underline any series of words, phrases, or clauses worded in parallel form. Not all of these sentences exhibit parallel construction.

1. Dr. Lafferty is a kind, generous, compassionate woman.

2. She is not only a good doctor; she is a good person.

3. No matter how busy she is, she always has time for her patients.

4. Once I called her at 2:00 in the morning, desperate for her advice and needful of her reassurance.

5. I thought I was having a heart attack.

6. Dr. Lafferty listened patiently, questioned me thoroughly, and instructed me calmly.

7. She said that my pains were probably being caused by a combination of nerves and indigestion, but she offered to meet me at the hospital and check me over.

8. I left immediately, my heart pounding, my hands trembling, and my knees shaking.

9. I was still convinced that there was something wrong with me.

10. When I arrived at the emergency room, Dr. Lafferty met me at the door and greeted me with a smile.

11. Just seeing her calmed me down considerably.

12. My heart stopped pounding, my hands stopped trembling, and my voice stopped quivering.

13. She didn't appear worried, so I stopped worrying.

14. Of course, Dr. Lafferty was right . . . as usual.

15. I was simply overreacting to a typical flareup of nerves and a bad case of indigestion.

16. I apologized profusely and thanked her repeatedly.

17. But she was not the least bit upset about being dragged out of bed, summoned to the emergency room, and plagued with an hysterical patient.

18. She was just happy that I was O.K.

19. I will never forget her kindness, her concern, and her professionalism.

20. Dr. Lafferty is not only a doctor; she is a friend.

EXERCISE 13B: COMPLETING PARALLEL THOUGHTS

In each of the following sentences, supply a word, phrase, or clause to complete the parallel thoughts.

WORDS

1. Professor Cluceau's course examined the *social, economic,* and _____ aspects of the French labor movement.

2. He *cried, begged,* and _____, but the judge showed no mercy.

3. Helen is a *bright, energetic,* _____ young woman.

4. Milk is good for you; it contains *vitamins, calcium,* and _____.

5. Charlie's house looks like a zoo; it is filled with *cats, dogs,* and _____.

PHRASES

1. I came here *to rest, to read,* and _____ _____.

2. Susan likes to jog *in the spring, in the summer,* and _____ _____ _____.

3. I can still feel his presence, both *in my mind* and _____ _____ _____.

4. *Walking quietly* and *humming* _____, the old woman approached the baby.

5. *A fine dinner, a rousing speech,* and _____ _____ _____ helped make the evening enjoyable.

CLAUSES

1. You have to let Maria know *that you love her* and _____ _____ _____ _____.

2. *Mr. Who is on first, Mr. What is on second,* and *Mr. Why* _____ _____ _____.

3. Lou taught me *how to plant tomatoes* and *when* _____ _____ _____.

4. I *ran into the house, locked the door,* and _____ _____ _____.

5. The film *that we watched* and the speech _____ _____ _____ made us think twice about drinking and driving.

EXERCISE 13C: COMPLETING PARALLEL CONSTRUCTIONS

In each of the following sentences, add words or phrases that are parallel to the italicized constructions.

1. She was *young, pretty,* and _____.

2. His favorite subjects are *biology,* _____, and _____.

3. The old man was *rich* but _____.

4. We were happy that the day of the picnic turned out to be neither *too hot* nor

   _____.

5. When Sally's purse was stolen, she lost *her driver's license*, _____,

   and _____.

6. He is remembered today not only *for his genius* but also _____.

7. Jack loved *to hunt, to fish,* and _____.

8. The chimpanzee displays *a high degree of intelligence, a good deal of*

   curiosity, and _____.

9. He was in trouble *with his parents, with school authorities,* and _____

   _____.

10. Crowds began to gather *in the central square,* _____,

    and _____.

Sentence elements that are joined by *correlative conjunctions* (*either/or; neither/nor; both/and; not only/but also*) should be parallel in structure. You should treat each of these correlative pairs as a frame, so that what falls to the right of each is parallel in form to what falls to the left.

either _____	or _____
neither _____	nor _____
both _____	and _____
not only _____	but also _____

Joe should either *go back to school* or *go out to look for a job.*

Neither *his life at home* nor *his experience in the army* had prepared him for a police officer's life.

He should resign immediately, both *for his own good* and *for the good of the company.*

We truly believed not only *that he was honest,* but also *that he was concerned about the child's welfare.*

Sentence elements linked with *than* or *as* should also be parallel in form.

Operating a motorcycle is less expensive than *operating a car.*

The style of his work was as surprising as the *subject matter of his books.*

Coordinate elements in a series are most often joined by *and, or, but*. The elements (words or groups of words) that they join must be parallel: noun with noun, adjective with adjective, prepositional phrase with prepositional phrase, and so on. Remember that correlative conjunctions demand parallel structure.

Faulty:	They either arrived late or I missed them at the airport.
Correct:	Either *they arrived late* or *I missed them* at the airport.
Faulty:	Not only did they refuse to pay but also demanded that they see the manager.
Correct:	They not only *refused to pay* but also *demanded to see the manager.*
Faulty:	She was both attractively dressed and knew how to apply makeup well.
Correct:	She was both *attractively dressed* and *attractively made up.*
	She knew both *how to dress attractively* and *how to apply makeup well.*

EXERCISE 13D: FAULTY PARALLELISM

Using parallelism to achieve greater clarity and emphasis, revise each of the following sentences.

1. You are either wrong or I am crazy.

    _____

2. We couldn't decide whether we should leave or to wait for Helen.

    _____

3. She had silver hair, pale blue eyes, and her skin had deep wrinkles.

    _____

4. She was rich, charming, and knew a great deal about the world.

    _____

5. They met in Casablanca, traveled to Italy together, and it was Switzerland where they parted company.

    _____

159

6. The programmers were praised for their loyalty to the company and because they were willing to work long hours.

_____

7. Maybe he will get a student loan, might even win a scholarship, or working after school to pay for his tuition.

_____

8. Delbert is honest, intelligent, and works hard.

_____

9. I hope either to graduate in May or September.

_____

10. He wanted not only to be outstanding on the playing field but in the classroom.

_____

WHEN TO USE PARALLEL WORDING

You should not use parallel wording too frequently. Too much repetition can be boring. After all, emphasizing everything is like emphasizing nothing. Watch out for these two types of problems in particular:

1. Including too many parallel thoughts in a short piece of writing.
2. Using parallel wording for *nonparallel* thoughts.

If you concentrate too hard on using parallel wording and forget about what you want to say to the readers, your writing will lose its honest, natural quality. As soon as the readers suspect that you are more concerned with using a specific technique than you are with communicating your thoughts, they will lose interest in what you have to say. In other words, don't use parallel wording just for the sake of using parallel wording.

For example, don't force parallel wording onto thoughts that are not parallel. The following sentence illustrates this point.

Ken is *a reader, a thinker,* and *middle-aged.*

The first two items in the series tell the reader what kind of a person Ken is, but the last detail has nothing to do with Ken's character or personality. It simply refers to Ken's age. If Ken's age is an important detail, then it can be subordinated in another part of the sentence or else included in a different sentence, but it should not be made parallel to characteristics of Ken's personality. A more logical completion of this parallel construction would read something like this:

> Ken is *a reader, a thinker,* and *a doer.*
> Ken is *a reader, a thinker,* and *a fighter.*

In these examples, notice that all the items in the series are the same part of speech; "reader," "thinker," and "fighter," for example, are all nouns. The sentences would not be parallel if you included a modifier or a phrase at the end of the series instead of just one word. The following sentences would be poor examples of parallel wording:

> Noun Noun Adj.
> Ken was a *reader,* a *thinker,* and *angry.*

> Noun Noun Phrase
> Ken was a *reader,* a *thinker,* and *ready to fight.*

Make sure that you keep your parallel wording consistent in structure. Avoid the error of putting a series of items in parallel form when the items are not parallel.

EXERCISE 13E: INAPPROPRIATE USE OF PARALLEL WORDING

Underline any parallel wording you find in the following sentences. Make any revisions necessary to eliminate poor examples of parallel wording.

1. The television comedy "Barney Miller" had some memorable characters.

2. Deitrich was one of my favorites—a philosopher, a cynic, and curly haired.

3. With his sly smile and his dry wit, Deitrich had a way of charming everyone in the twelfth precinct.

4. Another of my favorites was Inspector Luger, an obnoxious, tactless, almost someone to be pitied character, but he was such a buffoon that just the sight of him made me laugh.

5. Lieutenant Scanlon, another interesting character, played the typical tough guy; he liked to taunt, to harass, and embarrassing the detectives.

6. Like many tough guys, however, Scanlon was really just an insecure, incompetent wimp.

7. Each character portrayed a distinct personality type: Detective Harris, the cool dude; Detective Wojohowitz, the overzealous idealist; Little Levit, the perennial pest; and the calm, rational leadership of Captain Miller.

8. Many of the minor characters in ''Barney Miller'' were also outstanding.

9. I remember three in particular: the friendly bum, the macho storekeeper, and the laid-back atmosphere of the twelfth precinct.

10. I always enjoyed watching ''Barney Miller'' because it was consistently funny, realistic, and humane.

EXERCISE 13F: USING PARALLEL WORDING, SENTENCE LEVEL

Rewrite the following sentences. Whenever possible, use parallel structure to express parallel ideas. Avoid forcing elements into parallel form if they are not really parallel in meaning.

1. The prisoner escaped by pretending to have a heart attack and that he was on his way to the prison hospital. _____

_____

2. My mother thinks that young women should never call young men on the phone, refuse to get into a car with a young man, and a lot of other silly notions. _____

_____

_____

3. What those children really lack is the feeling of belonging and that somebody does care. _____

_____

4. He was under investigation because he was suspected of engaging in mail fraud and for failure to report his illegal earnings to the IRS._____

_____

_____

5. Their trip through Cajun Country gave them opportunities to sample Cajun cooking, getting photographs of alligators, and for seeing the fantastic flowers and trees of the swamps. _____

_____

_____

6. Nick is a football player with tremendous strength and who is very fast.

_____

_____

7. It is as difficult getting a good apartment as paying the rent in this place.

_____

_____

8. The old house was brick, with arched windows, a turret on the right front corner, and had hand-split shingles on the roof._____

_____

9. The old man was mean, ignorant, and a bigot._____

_____

10. She is a successful businessperson, a civic leader, and has a magnificent home._____

_____

EXERCISE 13G: FAULTY PARALLELISM, PARAGRAPH LEVEL

Improve the following paragraph by revising the bad examples of parallel wording.

According to the authors of *Gone Hollywood,* a book about the golden age of the movie industry, Hollywood pets were often pampered as much as the stars themselves. They had their own training schools, beauty parlors, and custom-manufactured beds. These pets even had their own special funeral services, complete with touching eulogies, expensive caskets, and the flowers that were also present. At the Los Angeles Pet Cemetery, dogs and cats would be buried with their favorite toy. From cat motels to dude ranches for dogs, many Hollywood pets enjoyed a better life than large numbers of American children. Joan Crawford's poodle had a custom-made wardrobe which included monogrammed jackets, rhinestone collars (for evening wear, of course), and a daily diet of chicken and ground sirloin. Some of the stars preferred less conventional pets: John Barrymore's king vulture, Rudolph Valentino's pet snake, and Fanny Brice, who owned a white rat, were some of Hollywood's more unusual pets. From cats and dogs to lizards and lions, Hollywood pets were often much like some of the stars themselves: They were spoiled; they were neurotic, and they were buried in the Los Angeles Pet Cemetery.

Based upon Christopher Finch and Linda Rosenkrantz,
Gone Hollywood (New York: Doubleday, 1979).

WRITING FROM READING

Arranging Your Thoughts

Writing is a very personal activity. Each individual processes thoughts in a different way. Some writers work best from outlines. They want to set their thoughts in order before they begin to write. Others prefer to sit down and begin writing immediately, organizing and revising their thoughts as they go along. There is no single "right" or "wrong" way to compose or arrange your thoughts. Any type of information can be logically organized in more than one way. The important thing is that you arrange your thoughts in a way that makes sense to your readers.

Put yourself in the role of a teacher who has been asked to write a letter of reference for a student. Melanie, a junior at Fairview High, is applying for a job as counselor at a summer camp for underprivileged children. She has asked you, her biology teacher, to write her a letter of reference. You want to jot down some thoughts before you begin writing, and, upon reflection, this is what comes to mind when you think of Melanie:

Melanie is a good student. She works hard for her grades and shows a genuine interest in learning. When she was in my biology class, her enthusiasm was contagious. Sometimes, she would get so excited about a topic that she would entice her classmates into a heated debate, and they'd still be arguing ten minutes after the bell rang. As I watched Melanie on those occasions, I often thought to myself, "What a great teacher Melanie would make."

Melanie has a good heart. She is always helping someone out. She is especially kind to those students that the rest of us, both students and teachers, too often neglect—the quiet, troubled students who hide in the back row agonizing over personal problems that no one seems to care about. Melanie has a way of drawing those students out. She's a good listener, and, sometimes, that's all those students need—just someone to listen.

Melanie loves kids. She comes from a large, close-knit family herself (six brothers and sisters) and she's used to being around children. She was very active in the Big Sister Program during her first and second years of high school. Last year, she organized the "Rent a Kid" program to help young kids from the poorer neighborhoods get part-time summer jobs in the suburban areas—doing yard work, painting, cleaning, whatever the families wanted done. The program was a great success. The children kept themselves busy, made some money, and learned responsibility, while the suburbanites received needed services at a fair price and, in the process, developed a deeper understanding of some of the problems of the disadvantaged.

Melanie wants to major in social work in college. This counseling position would provide her with some good on-the-job experience.

All of the information just presented could be used effectively in a letter of reference. How would *you* arrange those points? Is any one point more important than the others, or are they all equally important? Try arranging these points in a number of different ways and see if one is more effective than the other. Keep your audience in mind. What part of the information would be most important to the camp director who has to decide whether to hire Melanie?

165

14 Coordination: The Compound Sentence

Coordinate means of equal importance. Coordination in language means combining two ideas of equal importance. These ideas may be words, phrases, or sentences.

Words: I like bacon and eggs.
              (Obviously, the writer likes both bacon and eggs equally.)

Phrases: Joan decided to study for a degree but also to keep her job.
              (Both opportunities are equally important to Joan.)

Sentences: Harry liked warm weather, so he moved to Florida.
              (Both ideas are equally important to Harry.)

SHOWING RELATIONSHIPS BETWEEN IDEAS

In this chapter, we will look at the compound sentence, which is made by combining two simple sentences. As you may remember, one of the limitations of using all simple sentences is that you cannot show relationships between two ideas. If you can connect the two ideas, you can show how they relate to each other.

Here are four pairs of simple sentences without any relationships shown. Might a reader misunderstand your message?

My son makes a lot of money. He lives in the fast lane.

I like football. It is a violent sport.

I like football, *for* it is a violent sport.   I like football, *but* it is a violent sport.

Mary seemed happy. She was watching her mother.

She cried into her pillow at night. Her children were all successful.

Your writing can be much clearer to your readers if you show the relationship between two ideas. Notice that the use of a connecting word can change the meaning of the sentence completely. Discuss the differences in the following messages:

My son makes a lot of money, *so* he lives in the fast lane.

My son makes a lot of money, *but* he lives in the fast lane.

I like football, *for* it is a violent sport.

I like football, *but* it is a violent sport.

Mary seemed happy, *for* she was watching her mother.

Mary seemed happy, *but* she was watching her mother.

She cried into her pillow at night, *for* her children were all successful.

Her children were all successful, *but* she cried into her pillow at night.

Using Coordinating Conjunctions

For your meaning to be clear, you must purposefully show your readers the relationships between ideas. Sentence combining helps you work out these relationships.

Usually you will connect your simple sentences with a coordinating

    167

conjunction. Because there are only seven coordinating conjunctions, it isn't difficult to remember them.

and	means simply an addition: John loved Mary, *and* Mary responded.
but	means an opposite: John was bashful, *but* Mary popped the question.
or	means a choice: Mary will sell her sports car, *or* John will sell his station wagon.
nor	means deciding against two things: Mary doesn't want to sell her sports car, *nor* does John want to give up his station wagon.
for	means a reason or cause: John loves Mary, *for* she has a great personality.
so	means a result: Mary loves John, *so* she is happy when they are together.
yet	means on the other hand: John and Mary love each other, *yet* they often quarrel.

Keep in mind that coordinate means equal, so you should use coordinate conjunctions only when the ideas in your sentences are *equally important.* Using a coordinate conjunction when one idea is much more important than the other is incorrect.

I was walking home from school, and a man fell dead in front of me.

EXERCISE 14A: WRITING COMPOUND SENTENCES

Write seven good compound sentences, each illustrating the correct use of the coordinating conjunction given.

SIMPLE SENTENCE		SIMPLE SENTENCE
1. _____	, and	_____ .
2. _____	, but	_____ .
3. _____	, or	_____ .
4. _____	, nor	_____ .
5. _____	, for	_____ .
6. _____	, yet	_____ .
7. _____	, so	_____ .

EXERCISE 14B: SELECTING COORDINATE CONJUNCTIONS

Select one of the seven coordinate conjunctions (*and, but, or, nor, for, yet, so*) to link each pair of independent clauses below.

1. The whole crew was late, _____ the boss was grumbling all morning about falling behind schedule.

2. We ran across the boulevard, _____ the tour bus had already pulled out.

3. He could go to work for his uncle, _____ he could go back to college.

4. No one wanted to say anything, _____ everyone was afraid of losing his job.

5. Marion Spencer had been teaching in one-rooom schools for thirty years, _____ she was no country bumpkin.

6. We were in a hurry to get home, _____ we decided to take a shortcut across the frozen river.

7. Beth knew she could go with Richard, _____ any one of a half dozen other students would be glad to take her.

8. We must reduce production costs, _____ we will soon be out of business like the other steel fabricators.

9. Julie was obviously getting more and more embarrassed, _____ Frank finally stopped teasing her about Jimmy.

10. It rained hard all morning, _____ it cleared up for the picnic.

EXERCISE 14C: EFFECTIVE COORDINATION, SENTENCE LEVEL

Each of the following sentences contains two ideas of equal weight. In some of the sentences, the ideas are not logically connected. Examine each sentence carefully and rewrite those which contain inappropriate coordinate conjunctions.

1. Five doctors and four nurses told Richard that his new medication had no dangerous side effects, *so* he was still reluctant to try it.

    _____

    _____

2. Ken loves to fish, *and* he hates to touch fishing worms.

    _____

    _____

3. I am really proud of my grandfather, *but* I have never told him how much I admire him.

    _____

    _____

4. Few people remember the Pittsburgh Crawfords baseball team, *and* it had one of the best pitchers who ever lived—Satchel Paige.

    _____

    _____

5. I know a great deal about elephants, *so* I didn't know that they are the only four-legged creatures that can't jump.

    _____

    _____

6. Suzanne was raised in San Antonio, *and* it's hard for her to get used to Pennsylvania's long, cold winters.

    _____

    _____

7. Brenda is allergic to bee stings, *so* she will be interested in Dr. Griffith's new vaccine.

    _____

    _____

8. Uncle Mickey loved his weeping willow tree, *and* the borough officials ordered him to cut it down.

    _____

    _____

9. Either Dominic bleached his hair, *or* these fluorescent lights are playing tricks on my eyes.

   _____

   _____

10. My dogs are afraid of thunderstorms, *and,* at the first sight of rain, they head for the barn.

   _____

   _____

11. Jeanette would love to order a hot fudge sundae, *for* she is allergic to chocolate.

   _____

   _____

12. Bob wanted a new truck, *and* he couldn't afford it.

   _____

   _____

13. You know your mother doesn't like animals in the house, *so* why do you insist on keeping Marmaduke in your bedroom?

   _____

   _____

14. I called the manager of the store six times, *and* six times I got the same phony excuse.

   _____

   _____

15. Steve loves to cook, *and* he hates to clean up his messes.

   _____

   _____

OVERUSE OF COORDINATION

Avoid just stringing a series of simple sentences together with coordinating conjunctions so that they seem patched together without purpose.

Faulty:	Saturday we went over to Renfew to watch the final game of the season, *and* this game was supposed to decide the Osceola Valley championship, *but* in the third inning the rain began to come down in blinding sheets, *and so* the game was finally called, *and* the huge crowd scattered, grumbling in the downpour.
Improved:	Saturday we went over to Renfew to watch the final game of the season. This game was supposed to decide the Osceola Valley championship, but in the third inning the rain began to come down in blinding sheets. The game was finally called, so the huge crowd scattered, grumbling in the downpour.

There are many ways to revise this passage, including some methods we have not yet discussed.

EXERCISE 14D: EFFECTIVE COORDINATION, PARAGRAPH LEVEL

Because the following paragraph is composed entirely of simple sentences, it is choppy and the relationships are unclear. Improve the paragraph by combining some of the sentences. In each case, be sure to use the coordinating conjunction that shows the correct relationship between the two or three sentences you connect.

I thought I knew what a whiteout was. Now I really know what it is. On my way home from class last January 25, I ran headlong into one—-a real whiteout. I had left school at 3:00. I was driving along a relatively clear road at about 40 mph. All of a sudden, I couldn't see anything. I was in a world of white. I couldn't see 10 feet in front of the car. I could not see the car in front of me. As I saw it, I had two choices. I could stop. I could go on. If I stopped, I would surely get rear-ended by the car behind me. If I went on, I had a good chance of hitting someone ahead of me or of going off the road. I decided to compromise. I reduced my speed to 10 mph.

I watched mailboxes on the side of the road to keep myself at least close to the road. The guy behind me was no idiot. He slowed down and followed me. I made it home. I was thankful. I now know what a whiteout is. I'm glad I know. I hope I don't experience one again.

EXERCISE 14E: COORDINATION, PARAGRAPH LEVEL

Connect the following sentences with the correct coordinating conjunctions. You need not connect all sentences—just those sentences where relationships are necessary for clarity and smoothness. Don't forget to put a comma *before* the conjunction.

Everyone seems to have forgotten that we had a social revolution in the 1960s. The young people of the United States decided that many things that the country valued were worthless. They thought that the war in Vietnam was wrong. They refused to go. They thought that colleges were teaching courses that were irrelevant. They took over college presidents' offices. They rebelled against working hard all their lives for things they didn't need. They rebelled against discrimination. They lived in communes. They could live cheaper that way. They worked only enough for necessities. They didn't have to work many hours. They gave up cars and dishwashers and beautiful houses. They had more time for their children. Maybe they had a good idea. It didn't work.

EXERCISE 14F: COORDINATION, SENTENCE COMBINING

Combine each of the following groups of sentences into one or two more precise compound sentences.

1.   Mary was happy.

      John had asked her to the prom.

      He had asked her yesterday.

      She had been happy ever since.

      _____

      _____

2.   John had earned money over the summer.

      He had earned it for tuition.

      He had earned more than he needed.

      He hoped to buy a car with the extra money.

      _____

      _____

173

3. The zoo was enlarged.

   It was also renovated.

   It bought new animals.

   The animals can now live in natural habitats.

   _____

   _____

4. The tropical storm was ferocious.

   The islanders fled to the mainland.

   Several boats capsized.

   Fourteen people were drowned.

   _____

   _____

5. The house was said to be haunted.

   The neighborhood children were afraid of it.

   They never went into its overgrown yard.

   They even ran when they went past it.

   _____

   _____

6. An old man lived in it.

   He lived there all alone.

   He had lived there for many years.

   He had grown odd with loneliness.

   _____

   _____

7. He remembered playing in that overgrown yard.

   He had played there when he was a boy.

   He hoped the children would come into his yard.

   He hoped they would play as he had.

   _____

   _____

8. He peered out of the windows endlessly.

His face looked sad.

The children were frightened by his sad, white face.

They screamed and ran from the sight.

_____

_____

9. Once one little boy realized that the old man looked sad.

He screwed up his courage.

He decided to wave to the old man.

He decided to go close enough to the window to say hello.

_____

_____

10. The little boy went close to the window.

He was nervous.

The old man beamed.

He had found a friend.

_____

_____

175

PUNCTUATING SENTENCES CONTAINING TWO IDEAS

You have already learned that a sentence containing two equally important ideas (coordination) always has a comma *before* the conjunction that connects the two ideas. You have also learned that there are only seven coordinate conjunctions: *and, but, or, for, nor, yet, so*. However, you *only* use the comma when the coordinating conjunction connects *two* sentences or two complete thoughts. Do *not* use a comma every time you use *and, but, or, for, nor, yet,* or *so*. Look at these examples:

> She screamed and reached for the telephone.

The phrase "reached for the telephone" is *not* a complete thought; it has no subject. The sentence is simple; it merely has a compound verb. (Remember compound subjects and verbs? See page 21.)

> She screamed, and he reached for the telephone.

Here you do have two complete thoughts. "She screamed" is a complete thought; "he reached for the telephone" is another complete thought. In this sentence, then, you *do* need a comma because the comma shows where one complete thought ends and the other begins.

**EXERCISE 14G: USING COMMAS
WITH COORDINATE ELEMENTS**

Examine the following sentences and insert a comma where needed to separate complete thoughts.

1. Ninety-five percent of Egypt's 45 million people live on 5 percent of the land for 95 percent of the land is desert.

2. The population is settled along the Nile River and the Mediterranean coast.

3. The Suez Canal, which runs along Egypt's eastern border, connects the Red Sea with the Mediterranean Sea so it is one of the most important waterways in the world.

4. Boats coming from Asia must use the canal or travel around the southern tip of Africa to get to Europe.

5. The trip around the Cape of Good Hope in Africa takes about two weeks but the trip through the canal can be completed in nine hours.

6. Egypt is a strange mixture of the ancient and modern worlds.

7. There are multi-story apartment buildings and skyscrapers but there are also one-room shacks made of corrugated iron or metal panels or mud bricks with dried vegetation for roofs.

8. In the streets, modern trucks and buses share the road with people riding burros and horses pulling carts.

9. High-rise apartment buildings in various stages of construction surround Cairo yet these could not begin to solve the housing problem.

10. Twelve million people live in Cairo and many of them live and die in the streets, sidewalks, medial strips, and cemeteries for there are no houses, apartments, or huts available for them.

EXERCISE 14H: SENTENCE COMBINING

Make one or two good compound sentences from each of the following groups of sentences.

1. The first time I had a real beau I was in high school.

   He was a senior.

   I was a junior.

   I was pleased but shy.

   _____

   _____

2. Our lockers were side by side.

   I saw him in the mornings before school.

   I saw him at lunch time.

   I saw him after school.

   I never saw him during school hours.

   _____

   _____

3. He used to come to school just before the last bell.

I usually came early.

He started to come early.

I started to come late.

_____

_____

4. It took us a while to realize what was happening.

We laughed when we realized it.

We were trying to meet each other.

We tried so hard we defeated ourselves.

_____

_____

5. I decided not to be shy any more.

He liked me.

We could agree on that.

_____

_____

6. I'll never forget my Junior Prom.

I had a beautiful dress.

I had a lovely corsage.

Best of all, I had *him*.

_____

_____

7. I wanted to dance every dance with him.

I had promised my mother I'd dance at least once with my droopy cousin.

Once with the droop was enough.

I was back with John for the rest.

_____

_____

8. The dance was over at midnight.

John and I went out for a snack.

My great night finally ended at 1:30.

I still have golden memories.

_____

_____

9.   That was our first date.

It was not our last.

Our last was four years later.

It was for my college Junior Prom.

_____

_____

10.   We don't have dates now.

We don't have to have them.

We are married now.

Our whole lives are shared.

_____

_____

WRITING FROM READING

Distinguishing Main Ideas from Subordinate Ideas

Young children are great fans of the word *and*. They attach equal importance to so many things that, sometimes, they connect even the most
unrelated thoughts with *and:*

> My Daddy drives a red truck, and I'm goin' to Grandma's.
> Jamie has the chicken pox, and I'm 4 years old.

Adding one thought to another is such a natural part of using language
that, even after we get older, we often have a tendency to rely too much on
the conjunction *and* to connect one thought to another. As a result, we end
up with run-on sentences.

> Melanie worked at the firm for three years and then her father became ill and
> she took a leave of absence and she lost contact with her friends at work
> and . . .

Or we end up with compound sentences that don't make sense because *and* doesn't adequately explain the relationship between the first and second thought.

Michael always made good grades, and he never seemed happy with himself.

instead of

Michael always made good grades, *but* he never seemed happy with himself.

The following somewhat disjointed bits of information represent a seven-year-old's thoughts about his new teacher. Help Eric condense the information into a coherent description of Mrs. Malone. Decide what ideas are of equal importance, and then choose coordinate conjunctions (*and, but, for, nor, or, yet, so*) that connect those ideas logically.

My new teacher is a lot different from my old teacher.
I like my new teacher.
My old teacher's name was Miss Crabtree.
Miss Crabtree was a crab.
She was kind of pretty.
She had lots of nice clothes.
She never smiled.
My new teacher is Mrs. Malone.
Mrs. Malone never yells at us.
She smiles a lot.
Sometimes she makes us laugh.
She knows a lot of funny riddles.
She doesn't tell us riddles all the time.
Sometimes she helps us with our math and spelling.
Sometimes she reads us interesting stories.
We ask Mrs. Malone lots of questions.
She never gets tired of answering them.
She tells us that we're all special.
One day she gave me a big hug.
That was the same day I offered Kevin part of my lunch.
Sometimes Kevin's mom forgets to pack his lunch.
Mrs. Malone said that Kevin's mom is sick.
I really like Mrs. Malone.
I wish that all my teachers could be like her.

15
Subordination: The Complex Sentence

As we discussed in Chapter 2, one of the limitations of the simple sentence is its inability to show that one thought or idea is more important than another. Every simple sentence shows one thought, and all thoughts are given equal importance. Sometimes that is exactly what a writer wants, but sometimes one thought is far more important than another. Consider the following pair of sentences:

> The moon rose over the mountain.
> Captain Lancy died in my arms.

Obviously the second sentence is far more important than the first, which merely tells *when* the dramatic event happened.

Now consider the following pairs of sentences. Is one idea more important than the other?

1. I lay down to sleep.
   An explosion rocked the neighborhood.

2. I watched from my window.
   The youth raced after the fleeing mugger and, with a bone-jarring tackle, brought him down.

In these sentences, the more important ideas are obvious. No one would consider passive actions more important than an explosion or the brave actions of the youth.

The point is that simple sentences *cannot* show the relative importance of ideas. A reader can sometimes tell which sentence is important by its content; at other times, however, it is impossible, even from the content. Which idea is more important in the following pairs of sentences? Or are they of equal importance?

Message A:	Jan excels in tennis. She prefers basketball.
Message B:	We are having a really heavy rain right now. It should clear up soon.
Message C:	Mr. Meyer has been checking papers for six hours. He has not finished them.

Unless the writer shows you which idea is more important, you can only guess, and, if you have to guess, the writer is not communicating well. *It is the writer's job to be clear.*

Put yourself in the position of receiver of the following messages. Suppose you are the tennis coach at a small college where relatively few scholarships are available for female tennis players. Jan is a top contender for one of the scholarships. You receive Message A from a trusted scout sent to evaluate Jan. Would you give her the scholarship?

Message A:	Although Jan excels in tennis, she prefers basketball. (Don't give her the scholarship.)
	Although Jan prefers basketball, she excels in tennis. (Give her the scholarship.)

Suppose you have been invited to a picnic at your cousin's, thirty miles away. If you receive Message B, would you start driving out there?

Message B:	Although it should clear up soon, we are having heavy rain right now. (Wait a while; don't come now.)
	Although we are having a heavy rain now, it should clear up soon. (Come on out.)

Suppose you are the principal of the high school where Mr. Meyer works. After receiving Message C, would you think Mr. Meyer is slow or just overworked?

Message C: Although Mr. Meyer has been correcting papers for six hours, he has not finished them.
(Mr. Meyer is a real slowpoke.)

Although he has not finished them, Mr. Meyer has been correcting papers for six hours.
(Pity the poor, overworked teacher.)

The writers of the first messages know what they want to say, but they are not saying it clearly to their readers. The messages are not clear because the writers have not shown the readers which of their ideas is more important. How much easier it would be for the receivers of the messages to make the right decision if the writers had done their job.

THE PURPOSE OF SUBORDINATION

A sentence that contains one main independent clause and one or more subordinate (or less important) clauses is called a complex sentence. Since one of two ideas is usually more important than the other, most sentences you write probably are complex.

Not all ideas are of equal value or deserve equal emphasis. Subordination enables you to line up your ideas in terms of the value and emphasis you intend. If you want to express the relationship between your ideas precisely, you must be careful to choose the right subordinating conjunction.

To indicate time: before, after, as, just as, when, whenever, until, once

To indicate cause: because, since

To indicate purpose: in order that, so that

To indicate condition: if, provided that, although, unless, once, though, as soon as

To indicate concession: though, although, even though, except that

To indicate place: where, wherever

In addition, you can use the subordinate conjunctions *who, which,* or *that* to refer to something mentioned in the main sentence:

The man *who works in the book store* is Mary's uncle.

There are too many things *that can go wrong.*

His voice, *which is powerful and vibrant,* rings out in eloquent phrases.

Never use *which* to refer to a person; use *who* or *that.*

Here are some of the common words and phrases that signal subordinate ideas. Watch for them in your reading, and try to use a variety of them in your writing.

if	even though	once	whereas
as	so that	until	whenever
as if	because	as soon as	where
as though	since	when	wherever
although	as long as	while	provided that
though	before	after	unless

EXERCISE 15A: SUBORDINATE IDEAS

In each of the following sentences, draw a line under the *subordinate* idea and draw a circle around the word or phrase that shows it is dependent.

EXAMPLES: ⟨So that⟩ he could go to college in the fall, he had to work all summer on construction jobs.

He was able to pay his own tuition ⟨because⟩ he had worked to earn the money.

1. We ran over to Martha's house as soon as we heard the news.

2. Even though he had been badly treated as a child, he felt more sorrow than anger toward his parents.

3. She left just as we arrived.

4. After he had carried Jimmy home, he wrapped him in a woolen blanket.

5. Although he was very tired, he kept on driving until they reached El Paso.

6. As soon as the weather turns cooler, you'll find woolly caterpillars in the garage.

7. While I was trying to read, Jerry kept pounding a pot with a spoon.

8. If you take time to read the ads carefully, you will see that there is always a gimmick.

9. He carried a Canadian silver dollar wherever he went.

10. She munched on a chocolate bar as she watched her favorite soap opera.

11. After only four performances on Broadway, the play folded.

12. Whenever those two get together, you can expect some fireworks.

13. Gerald would be my first choice because he is not afraid to say what he thinks.

14. When the movie first came out, the critics panned it unmercifully.

15. Janie refused to go unless Billy would take her.

16. Though she may not be a genius, she is a whiz at math.

17. After her knee began to swell, Louise took her to the emergency room.

18. They will wait until you come.

19. Her family made many sacrifices so that Juanita could go to college.

20. Whenever he got frustrated, he would find a quiet corner somewhere and read.

EXERCISE 15B: EFFECTIVE SUBORDINATION

In each of the following sets of ideas, one thought is more important than the other. Each set contains two thoughts which can be logically connected if one thought is *subordinated* to the other. Place the main idea in an independent clause and the subordinate idea in a dependent clause. First, figure out exactly *how* the dependent thought is related to the main thought. Does it show *when* something happened, *where* something happened, *why* something happened, or *under what conditions* something happened? Then choose a subordinating word that expresses that relationship and form an appropriate dependent clause. Notice that each set of thoughts can be expressed in two different ways.

EXAMPLES: The magician turned the lady's purse into a chicken.
The children laughed.

When the magician turned the lady's purse into a chicken, the children laughed.

or

The children laughed *when* the magician turned the lady's purse into a chicken.

1.   I won't prepare dinner _____ you promise to wash the dishes.

_____ you promise to wash the dishes, I won't prepare dinner.

2.   I will prepare dinner _____ you promise to wash the dishes.

_____ you promise to wash the dishes, I will prepare dinner.

3.   _____ you refused to prepare dinner, I still washed the dishes.

I still washed the dishes _____ you refused to prepare dinner.

4.   The convention delegates cheered _____ Jessie Jackson walked to the podium.

_____ Jessie Jackson walked to the podium, the convention delegates cheered.

5.   _____ you said you loved me, I began to look forward to getting up in the mornings.

I began to look forward to getting up in the mornings _____ you said you loved me.

6.   Thanksgiving dinner didn't seem the same this year _____ you weren't home.

_____ you weren't home, Thanksgiving dinner didn't seem the same this year.

7. _____ he had a head-on collision with a herd of sheep, Larry really enjoyed his trip to Ireland.

Larry really enjoyed his trip to Ireland _____ he had a head-on collision with a herd of sheep.

8. She cried _____ she found her missing child.

_____ she found her missing child, she cried.

9. _____ you start saving now, you'll have enough money for a down payment by spring.

You'll have enough money for a down payment by spring _____ you start saving your money now.

10. You can't eat that bacon _____ you're supposed to be on a low cholesterol diet.

_____ you're supposed to be on a low cholesterol diet, you can't eat that bacon.

EXERCISE 15C: SENTENCE COMBINING

Each of the following items contains a set of two simple sentences. Combine the two sentences by changing one of the simple sentences into a *subordinate* clause.

EXAMPLE: Dues had to be increased. There was no money left in the treasury.

Dues had to be increased because there was no money left in the treasury.

or

Since there was no money left in the treasury, dues had to be increased.

1. I wrote her almost every week. I only received a letter from her once in four months.

2. The tomatoes were still green. The birds picked holes in most of them.

3. He came striding down the street. He looked handsome in his new uniform.

4. He works in a hardware store. He doesn't know much about tools.

5. She was riding in the back seat. The car slid off the road and rolled over twice.

6. I was quite small. I never tried out for football.

7. Salmon fishing is considered a great sport in Scotland. Not many Scottish people can afford to go salmon fishing.

8. I am only a first-year student. I'm not worried about choosing a major yet.

9. My father went into business for himself. He started out using half of the basement for his office.

10. His salary seemed quite high. He had little money left after paying his expenses.

PUNCTUATING COMPLEX SENTENCES

Punctuating clauses that are *not* equal in importance is simple if you remember just two rules:

> *Rule 1:* If the less important idea (subordinate clause) comes first, put a comma after it. If the subordinate clause follows the main clause, no comma is needed.

> Because they are warm and friendly, I love to visit Velda and Mandy.
> I love to visit Velda and Mandy because they are warm and friendly.

In the second sentence, no comma is needed because the dependent clause *follows* the main clause.

> *Rule 2:* If the subordinate clause is placed in the middle of the sentence (embedded), put commas around it. This shows the readers that that idea is not as important as the main sentence.

> *Henry Ford*, who at his death left a personal fortune estimated at about $700 million, *once said that no man was worth more than $5 a day.*

This sentence shows that the writer wants to emphasize Mr. Ford's assessment of the worth of a workingman and has included the facts about Mr. Ford's fortune to add information (also to point up the irony, no doubt). Notice that you could change the emphasis by embedding the other idea:

> *Henry Ford*, who once said that no man was worth more than $5 a day, *at his death left a personal fortune estimated at about $700 million.*

In this sentence, the emphasis is on Mr. Ford's amassed wealth, and what he thought of the workingman's pay is of lesser importance. Sometimes it is hard for readers to tell which idea is more important. That's why the writer must show, by punctuation or placement, which idea is dominant.

Each of the preceding sentences about Henry Ford contains an embedded clause: "who at his death left a personal fortune estimated at about $700 million" and "who once said that no man was worth more than $5 a day." If you read the sentences again, you will notice that each of these clauses is set off with commas (a comma before the clause and a comma after the clause). These are called *nonrestrictive clauses* because they do not restrict or limit the subject. Each adds an interesting detail about Henry Ford, but these details are not essential. Each sentence would make a point without them.

> Henry Ford once said that no man was worth more than $5 a day.
>
> At his death, Henry Ford left a personal fortune estimated at about $700 million.

In other words, if you remove the embedded clauses, you have not drastically changed the meaning of either sentence. Setting off this type of embedded clause with commas helps the reader recognize the purpose of the clause—to add descriptive details rather than to qualify the subject in any way.

Not all embedded clauses, however, should be set off with commas. If a clause sets important limitations on the subject, it is called a *restrictive clause*. Such a clause contains essential information.

> The man *who sold me the jeep* was found guilty of fraud.
> (Not just any man was found guilty of fraud. The man who sold you the jeep was found guilty of fraud.)
> The gloves *that I bought at that boutique* have lasted longer than all of my other gloves.
> (Which gloves have lasted longest? The ones that you bought at that boutique.)

Notice that removing a restrictive clause changes the meaning of the sentence. "The man was found guilty of fraud." says something much less specific than "The man *who sold me the jeep* was found guilty of **fraud**." The first sentence does not identify "the man"; the second sentence contains a clause that tells the reader who "the man" is. When a clause contains such essential information, it should not be set off with commas because it, in effect, becomes part of the subject.

Extended subject	Verb	Completer
The man who sold me the jeep	was found	guilty.

EXERCISE 15D: PUNCTUATING THE COMPLEX SENTENCE

Place a comma where needed in the following sentences

1.   Although many people think Henry Ford originated the assembly line he did not.

2.   The success of his technique which he started at Ford Motor Company in 1913 did make the assembly-line process popular.

3.   As more and more manufacturers started to use this process American industry doubled and tripled its output.

4.   As a result Americans enjoyed a standard of living far above that of any other nation in history.

5.   Because the assembly-line work was monotonous and boring Ford's monthly turnover rate for workers was about 50 percent.

6.   Ford who realized this was hurting productivity and therefore the profit doubled the daily rate for his workers.

7.   While workers in the other automobile plants were making $2.50 per day Ford workers were earning $5.

8.   Ford's profits doubled in two years after he made this move.

9.   After war was declared in 1941 Ford began building airplanes for the United States government.

10. Although in many ways Henry Ford was progressive and innovative he remained the only major automobile manufacturer to deny union representation of his workers until forced to.

EFFECTIVE COORDINATION AND SUBORDINATION

A series of short, simple sentences (often referred to as "primer style" of writing) does not always express the relationship between the various facts and ideas stated because it fails to show the relative *value, stress,* or *emphasis* of one thing compared to another. Even joining some short, choppy sentences with an *and, but,* or *so* often fails to express the precise relationship you intend. Note the following two accounts of the same incident:

He lit a cigarette, and he lay back on the couch and fell asleep, and so the cigarette started a fire. His mother came home about an hour later, and the room was filled with smoke.

About an hour after he had fallen asleep on the couch with a lit cigarette, his mother came home and found the room filled with smoke.

The first version is an example of *faulty coordination* in which independent clauses are just strung together with *and* or *and so.* The second version illustrates a clearer style of writing in which everything else is clearly subordinated to the one main idea: "she found the room filled with smoke."

It is the writer who decides what he or she wants to stress. Thus, the writer must decide whether his or her ideas are equally important or whether some are less important. If the ideas are equally important, the writer will use a compound sentence; if one idea is more important than the other, he or she will use a complex sentence.

EXERCISE 15E: RECOGNIZING COORDINATE AND SUBORDINATE RELATIONSHIPS

In the following two exercises, decide whether the ideas in each of the phrases are equally important or not. If they are, write in the coordinate conjunction that best shows the relationship between them. If they are not, choose the subordinate conjunction that best shows the relationship.

1. Elephants are the largest land mammals _____ they are popular with zoo visitors.

2. There are two basic kinds of elephants _____ it is easy to tell them apart.

3. _____ at birth an elephant weighs only 200 pounds, _____ it is 9 months old, it may weigh 800 pounds.

4. _____ elephants are so big and heavy, they are very careful when they move.

5. _____ elephants are very heavy, they walk on their toes.

6. _____ the bottoms of elephants' feet are covered with thick, elastic pads, they are very surefooted _____ they can walk very quietly.

7. Many keepers say that elephants are the most dangerous animals _____ their moods change rapidly.

8. _____ elephants can be useful to people, _____ they are in captivity they require much care and caution.

9. Elephants make a lot of different sounds, like screaming, trumpeting, grunting, rumbling, and purring _____ their trunks magnify these sounds.

10. _____ there are only two kinds of elephants in the world today, more than 600 kinds have lived on Earth.

11. Wild elephants are in serious trouble _____ in Africa they are being killed for their tusks.

12. _____ there are laws against killing elephants, the price of ivory is so high that some people break the laws.

13. _____ a single pair of tusks may sell for more than $20,000, some people are willing to take the risk of breaking the law.

14. An even worse problem is the growing population in Africa and Asia _____ more and more people require more and more land _____ this takes land away from the elephants.

15. There is much empty land now _____ it is rapidly diminishing.

16. Elephants need a lot of land _____ they eat a lot of food.

17. _____ an elephant's digestive system is not very good, it digests only about half of what it eats _____ the elephant must eat twice as much food.

18. In some way, we must keep hunters from killing elephants _____ we must leave them enough room.

19. _____ this world is theirs as much as ours, we must share it with them.

20. Human beings tend to think that only their existence is important _____ _____ they should protect the creatures who share the world with them.

EXERCISE 15F: SENTENCE COMBINING

Combine each of the following groups of sentences to make one or two good complex sentences.

1. The morning was warm and sunny.

   I decided to go for a walk.

   I made up my mind to go through the woods.

   _____

   _____

2. I talked to my brother about taking the walk.

   He loves walking.

   He especially loves walking through the woods.

   He agreed to go.

   _____

   _____

3. We agreed to spend the whole morning walking.

   We thought it would be nice to take a picnic.

   We could walk to Pulpit Rock in three hours.

Pulpit Rock is a nifty place for a picnic.

_____

_____

4. We had to decide on what food to take with us.

    We had to decide whether to build a fire to cook over.

    We had to decide if we just wanted cold food.

    We thought maybe we should take both.

    _____

    _____

5. It is a nuisance to carry wood to make a fire.

    We would have to carry it.

    All the wood around Pulpit Rock would be wet from winter snows.

    We thought we'd just get along with sandwiches and fruit.

    _____

    _____

6. The paths through the woods were cluttered.

    Dead branches had fallen across them.

    Puddles were everywhere.

    The walking was hard.

    _____

    _____

7. We began the long climb to Pulpit Rock.

    The puddles had drained from the path.

    We picked up the dead branches.

    We threw them off the path.

    _____

    _____

8. We stopped complaining about how difficult the path was.

    We noticed the first wildflowers.

    They were beside the path.

They were peeking out from under the dead leaves.

_____

_____

9. The wildflowers were trillium.

The wildflowers were violets.

There was also Colt's foot.

Colt's foot is probably the earliest of all flowers.

_____

_____

10. We reached Pulpit Rock.

We were tired.

We were happy, too.

We ate our lunch.

We enjoyed the lovely spring sun.

We liked looking at the view.

_____

_____

_____

EXERCISE 15G: SENTENCE COMBINING

Combine each of the following groups of sentences into one or two precise complex sentences or compound-complex sentences.

1. Shirley Jackson wrote a famous short story.

It was called "The Lottery."

It was made into a movie.

It was then made into a ballet.

_____

_____

2. The plot is strange.

The lottery isn't really to win a prize.

The prize is not something anyone would want.

The prize is death.

_____

_____

3. The setting seems real.

The story takes place in an ordinary little country town.

The time isn't too long ago.

The characters have cars and worry about taxes.

"The Lottery" is puzzling but haunting.

_____

_____

4. The meaning just isn't clear.

It might be clearer in an ancient setting.

It might be clearer in a remote setting.

_____

_____

5. I read lots of stories.

I like most stories.

"The Lottery" leaves me puzzled.

I need someone to explain it to me.

_____

_____

6. *My Brilliant Career* is a good movie.

It is Australian.

It is based on a novel by Joan Miles Franklin.

The novel was written fifteen years before the movie was made.

_____

_____

7.   The plot tells about the heroine's decision.

   The story is autobiographical.

   Franklin thinks she must choose between a career and marriage.

   At first she doesn't think this will be hard.

   _____

   _____

8.   She falls in love.

   The man's name is Harry.

   He is everything she admires in a man.

   He loves her.

   _____

   _____

9.   She wants to be a writer.

   She wants to be a writer above all else.

   She loves Harry.

   She thinks she can't write and be married.

   _____

   _____

10.   The audience wants her to marry Harry.

   The audience can't bear to see her lose Harry.

   The audience doesn't like Harry to be unhappy either.

   The audience doesn't care about her career.

   _____

   _____

11.   The heroine chooses a career.

   She lets Harry go.

   Her heart is almost broken.

   _____

   _____

12. The movie indicates she made the right choice.

At the end, she rejects Harry.

The final scene shows her mailing off her first manuscript.

She stands by the post box and the rising sun is reflected on her face.

_____

_____

WRITING FROM READING

Making Comparisons

In the early 1800s, a visiting French citizen, Alexis de Tocqueville, made a journey through America and recorded his observations about the effects of democracy on almost every aspect of American society. In 1840, he published his impressions in a massive two-volume work called *Democracy in America*. Included in his observations was a chapter on "How the Americans Understand the Equality of the Sexes." Read the following excerpt:

> In no country has such constant care been taken as in America to trace two clearly distinct lines of action for the two sexes . . . American women never manage the outward concerns of the family, or conduct a business, or take a part in political life; nor are they, on the other hand, ever compelled to perform the rough labor of the fields, or to make any of those laborious exertions which demand the exertion of physical strength . . .
>
> Nor have Americans ever supposed that one consequence of democratic principles is the subversion of marital power . . . They hold that every association must have a head in order to accomplish its object, and that that natural head of the conjugal association is man.
>
> Alexis de Tocqueville, *Democracy in America*, Vol. II, 6th ed., trans. Henry Reeve (New York: Schocken Books, 1974), pp. 252–253.

How much do you think American society has changed since de Tocqueville recorded his observations nearly 150 years ago? Are his remarks strictly part of America's past? If de Tocqueville were observing America today, what sorts of thoughts do you think he would be jotting down in his notebook under "How Americans Understand Equality of the Sexes"?

Imagine that you are a modern-day Alexis de Tocqueville making observations about sexual equality in American society. Based on the people in your life (your friends, your family, your coworkers), what conclusions would you reach about the division of the sexes? What notations would you make in your journal? Record your thoughts, and then compare them with those of the other students in your class. See if they differ in any way, and try to find out why. Did a classmate's sex or home environment or working environment affect his or her perception of sexual roles? Does that tell you anything about your own observations? About de Tocqueville's observations? After you are finished comparing notes and sharing differences of opinion, list your conclusions under two categories: (1) those on which most students agreed, and (2) those on which few students agreed. For example:

Areas of Strong Agreement	*Areas of Least Agreement*
Things have changed quite a bit since de Tocqueville's time.	In American homes, the man is the boss.
Being a mother and home-maker is hard work.	Alexis de Tocqueville was a male chauvinist.

Review your lists, and then write a series of sentences in which you state your conclusions. Place areas of strong agreement in main clauses and areas of least agreement in dependent clauses. For example:

Dependent clause:	Although the husband is still boss in many American homes
Main clause:	things have definitely changed since 1840
Sentence:	Although the husband is still boss in many American homes, things have definitely changed since 1840.

Writing Reports

Many jobs available in fields such as health care and law enforcement often involve a great deal of report writing—patient care plans, progress reports, accident reports, and so on. This type of writing requires clear, concise language and a neutral, objective tone. The writer's main purpose is to inform. Nurses and law-enforcement officers are writing for audiences whose main concern is obtaining accurate information on which they can base their decisions. An essential ingredient in this kind of writing, then, is the effective placement of information—emphasizing the most important information and subordinating the less important information—in other words, effective coordination and subordination. For example, in a patient progress report, a nurse might write:

Although vital signs are stable, the patient is extremely weak and disoriented.

199

Upon reading this sentence, a doctor or another nurse would understand that the nurse who observed the patient is saying that despite "normal" pulse and blood pressure readings, the patient is not in good condition. Both items of information are important, but the second is more important than the first.

The nurse gets the message across with effective *subordination*, placing the information about the patient's vital signs in a dependent clause ("*Although* vital signs are stable . . ."), and the information referring to the patient's general weakness and confused state of mind in a main clause (". . . patient is extremely weak and disoriented.").

Read the following information about a patient's condition before medication and after medication. Then put yourself in the role of the nurse who has to describe the patient's condition *after* medication has been administered. Write a patient progress report using effective coordination and subordination to get your message across.

Before Medication (2:30 A.M.)

Blood pressure: subnormal $\frac{80}{60}$ —going into shock

Temperature: subnormal—97°

Pulse: weak, rapid pulse—120 beats per minute

Severe chest pains

Patient lapsing in and out of consciousness

After Medication (3:05 A.M.)

Blood pressure: returning to normal— $\frac{100}{70}$ —beginning to stabilize

Temperature: still below normal—97.5°

Pulse: stronger, less rapid pulse—100 beats per minute

Chest pains somewhat less severe

Patient in conscious state for last 20 minutes

Answering questions coherently

16
The Comma

Read the following paragraph:

Getting up in the morning is a real chore for me and my dogs Mandy and Zelda don't help much when I'm groping around in the dark looking for the light switch they always manage to place themselves directly under my feet trying to maintain my dignity in the dark is difficult enough when I'm only half-awake without the added challenge of trying to sidestep two dogs both of whom seem to take special delight in seeing me sprawled face-down on the floor halfway between the bedroom and the bathroom then of course once I am on the floor I am trapped dutifully Mandy and Zelda take it upon themselves to wake me up believe me there are better ways of waking up than being licked to death by one dog and having another one barking in your ear but of course there is a method to their madness the sooner I wake up the quicker they get fed they know that the more they lick and the louder they bark the faster I will get up as much as I dislike being awakened in such an un-conventional manner I should be grateful to Mandy and Zelda because without them I would probably never make it to work on time.

Did you find yourself rereading parts of the passage in order to figure out exactly what the author was saying? Imagine how frustrating it would be if everything were written like this—with no punctuation. If your text-books were written like this, you probably would have dropped out of school long ago just from sheer frustration.

Punctuation, then, is essential. Neither the writer nor the reader can do without it. Without punctuation marks as guideposts, the reader is lost. So don't think of punctuation as a set of rules that have to be learned just to get through English class. Think of punctuation as something you can use to help you get your points across to your readers.

In this chapter, you will learn more about the comma, one of the most useful punctuation marks in the English language. It can serve you in many ways. You already know how to use it to separate coordinate and subordinate thoughts. In the last two chapters, you learned two important uses of the comma.

1.   Use a comma to separate two main ideas connected with a coordinate conjunction (a compound sentence):

   Main Idea   Main Idea
Adam hated apples, but *he ate one anyway.*

2.   Use a comma to separate a subordinate thought from a main idea (a complex sentence):

      Subordinate Idea   Main Idea
Although Adam hated apples, he ate one for Eve's sake.

Here are some other ways that you can use the comma:

To separate items in a series
To separate introductory details from the main idea
To set off interrupting words
To set off names in direct address
To punctuate dates and addresses
To set off direct quotations

SEPARATING ITEMS IN A SERIES

When you talk to someone, your natural speech rhythms are characterized by stops and pauses. For example:

John (*short pause*) you are the most thoughtful (*short pause*) generous (*short pause*) compassionate person I have ever met (*full pause*) I think I am falling in love with you (STOP)

When you write, you are actually talking to someone on paper. Your writing, then, also has natural rhythms. Punctuation helps you to create the natural sound of speech on paper. The comma, for example, may indicate a short pause; the period indicates a full stop.

John₉ you are the most thoughtful₉ generous₉ compassionate person I have ever met. I think I am falling in love with you.

Talking or writing about *items in a series* (the most thoughtful, generous, compassionate person) requires brief pauses—commas. Whenever you write a sentence with three or more items in a series, use commas to separate those items, whether those items are words, phrases, or clauses.

Words in a series:	Pittsburgh is a *lovely, friendly, fascinating* city.
Phrases in a series:	I love Pittsburgh for *its beauty, its people,* and *its cultural heritage.*
Clauses in a series:	*When you see Pittsburgh's rivers and valleys, when you meet its people,* and *when you discover its rich cultural heritage,* you will understand why I love it.

Notice that the last two items in a series are usually connected by the coordinate conjunction *and.*

. . . its beauty, its people, *and* its cultural heritage.

As soon as the reader sees the word *and* (or another coordinate conjunction such as *or* or *nor*), he or she knows that the next item in the series will be the last.

Next semester, Ginny is going to take calculus, physics, psychology, French, *and* computer science.

Neither his mother, his father, *nor* his sister have seen him since he moved to California.

Notice that you don't need a comma after the coordinate conjunction that connects the last two items in a series. The following sentence would not be punctuated correctly because there is no reason to pause after the *and.*

Next semester, Ginny is going to take calculus, physics, psychology, French, and₉ computer science.

EXERCISE 16A: PUNCTUATING ITEMS IN A SERIES

Insert commas, where necessary, in the following sentences.

1. Pittsburgh is lovely friendly and fascinating.

2. My chocolate frosting recipe consists of the following ingredients: cocoa powdered sugar milk butter and vanilla.

3. Madeline Hunter is an educator who writes books about motivation reinforcement and retention.

4. I want to know what you read how you read and why you read.

5. The burglar was wearing a red tassel cap a blue shirt and a green army jacket.

6. Stuffed crab baked scrod trout almondine and lobster Newburg are the most expensive items on the menu.

7. Everything in his house is made of wicker, including the picture frames the wastebaskets and the kleenex boxes.

8. You've got to "know when to hold them know when to fold them know when to walk away and know when to run."

9. Neither his money nor his fame nor his power could buy him happiness.

10. Our birdfeeder attracts bluejays cardinals sparrows thrushes and chickadees.

All of the sentences in the exercise above contained three or more items in a series, so each sentence required commas. However, if you have only two items, then you can simply connect the items with *and*. *Two* coordinate words or phrases should *not* be set off with commas.

Words:	Pittsburgh is *friendly and fascinating.*
Phrases:	*Her flaming red hair and her dark green eyes* were impossible to ignore.
Clauses:	I want to know *what you read and how you read.*

EXERCISE 16B: DISTINGUISHING COORDINATION FROM ITEMS IN A SERIES

Supply commas where necessary in the following sentences:

1. Getting a job and buying a car are Jim's two major concerns right now.

2. When Ray went to the convention, he met Jessie Jackson Ray Charles and Coretta Scott King.

3. The pollution control board is supposed to monitor the air we breathe and the water we drink.

4. *Dark Victory Of Human Bondage* and *Jezebel* are three of my favorite Bette Davis movies.

5. Peter Lorre and Sydney Greenstreet are at their best in *The Verdict* and *The Maltese Falcon.*

6. She cleared the room washed the rug and moved all the furniture back while I went grocery shopping.

7. Pam ordered a large pan pizza with pepperoni extra cheese onions and anchovies.

8. Vic couldn't decide whether he wanted a pan pizza or a regular pizza.

9. Knowing that I studied hard for the final and that I handed in a good paper made me feel confident about my grade.

10. Since I aced my first three tests I studied hard for the final and I handed in a good paper, I expect to get a good grade in Math 101.

SEPARATING INTRODUCTORY DETAILS
FROM THE MAIN IDEA

In Chapters 14 and 15, you learned that when a sentence begins with a dependent clause, you place a comma at the end of the dependent clause to set it off from the main idea. For example:

> *When a sentence begins with a dependent clause*, place a comma at the end of the dependent clause.

If you were reading this sentence aloud, you would probably pause briefly at the end of the opening clause, and your voice would probably change in pitch. The same thing will occur if you read the following sentences aloud:

> Undoubtedly, Mark is a persistent suitor.
> Last summer, Mark gave Julie an engagement ring.
> By the middle of July, Julie had returned the ring.
> Stunned but undaunted, Mark tried again.
> At 7:00 P.M. last evening, Mark and Julie were married.
> With a warm glance and a sly grin, Julie promised "to love, honor," but *not* to "obey."

All of these sentences begin with introductory details that help to clarify the main idea.

> *When* did Mark give Julie an engagement ring? "Last summer."
> *How* did Julie make her vows? "With a warm glance and sly grin."

This kind of sentence adds variety to your writing style. (If you began every sentence with a main clause, you would soon bore your readers to death.) But remember, when you use this kind of sentence, separate your introductory details from your main idea with a comma.

EXERCISE 16C: USING COMMAS
AFTER INTRODUCTORY DETAILS

Insert commas where needed after introductory words, phrases, or clauses.

1. Proud and tall stood the courageous "Daffy Dozen."

2. On the coldest day of the year the Polar Bear Club dives into the icy waters of the Monongahela.

3. Winter after winter the same ritual takes place.

4. From the youngest to the oldest they all brave the subfreezing temperatures.

5. The oldest member of the Polar Bear Club is 79.

6. Believe it or not he is usually the first one in and the last one out.

7. Of course the press is always fully represented on Polar Bear Day.

8. With temperatures dipping down to 5° above zero this year's spectators also included a paramedic team.

9. Fortunately they were not needed.

10. None of the Polar Bears developed hypothermia but none of them stayed in the water more than a few minutes either.

11. When the "Daffy Dozen" came out of the water this year they didn't look too lively.

12. Breathing hard and quaking in their flippers they all looked very much relieved.

13. I don't know how they do it.

14. Just watching them chills me to the bone.

15. Since I freeze when the temperature drops below 80° I'm afraid I wouldn't last long in the Polar Bear Club.

SETTING OFF INTERRUPTING WORDS

Every sentence has a basic core, a main idea usually expressed in a *subject-verb-object* unit.

      S   V   O
Suzanne loves cats.

No matter what details you add to this sentence, the main idea will still be "Suzanne loves cats." For example:

> *Suzanne,* undoubtedly, *loves cats.*
> *Suzanne,* my sister-in-law, *loves cats.*
> *Suzanne,* who is afraid of dogs, *loves cats.*

In each of these sentences, the main idea is *interrupted* by a word, a phrase, or a clause. If you read these sentences aloud, you can *hear* the main flow of thought being broken. Commas enable you to *see* the break in the main flow of thought. When you're writing, then, you should set off interrupting expressions for your readers so that they can easily separate minor details from the most important part of the sentence. Remember, the reader has to see

207

where the interruption begins and ends, so don't forget to place a comma both *before and after* an interrupting expression.

EXERCISE 16D: SETTING OFF INTERRUPTING WORDS

Supply commas where necessary in the following sentences.

1.   Calvin Coolidge the thirtieth president of the United States once said that "The business of America is business."
2.   Coolidge of course was no intellectual giant.
3.   There is however a great deal of truth in this seemingly lackluster statement.
4.   For many Americans the business of America is indeed business.
5.   The stock market for example has become the focal point of countless lives.
6.   For some in fact it is an obsession.
7.   Understandably predicting what the stock market will do is quite a difficult task.
8.   As a result economists for the most part are a rather serious lot.
9.   Some of them quite frankly have forgotten how to smile.
10.   But yesterday as I was listening to the news I discovered that even economists have a sense of humor.
11.   The news segment dealt with theories that predicted changes in the stock market.
12.   One economist a sedate looking fellow uses women's fashions to predict stock market behavior.
13.   When hemlines go up he explains the stock market goes up too.
14.   Another economist uses of all things men's ties to predict stock market behavior.
15.   This theory equally unscientific claims that narrow ties indicate a drop in the stock market.
16.   One of the more popular theories at least among football fans is the Super Bowl theory.
17.   This theory as implausible as the rest claims that a healthy stock market depends on an NFL victory in the Super Bowl.

18. None of the economists by the way claimed that his theory was 100 percent correct.

19. They were just having a little fun.

20. They pointed out however that historical coincidences often provide the basis for some unusual economic theories.

SETTING OFF NAMES IN DIRECT ADDRESS

When your writing refers to a person spoken to directly, set off that person's name (or title) with commas. If the name appears as the first or last word in the sentence, you will need only one comma.

Neil, hand me that dictionary.
When should I change the bandage, Doctor Garrison?"
You, Regina, have just won $50,000.

EXERCISE 16E: USING COMMAS IN DIRECT ADDRESS

Supply commas where necessary in the following sentences.

1. We've got to make a plan Stan.
2. Don't try to be coy Roy.
3. You sir have gone one step too far.
4. Fortunately ladies and gentlemen my speech will be brief.
5. Mrs. Keibler you make the best orange cookies I've ever tasted.
6. Can you drive me to the airport Bob?
7. Ricardo do you know anything about computers?
8. In conclusion fellow farmers it is time to stand up for your rights.
9. John have you ever read *The Lazlo Letters*?
10. I feel certain Mr. Thompson that Lisa will qualify for the scholarship.
11. Tell me Matthew how did you learn so much about snakes?
12. The land is everything Katy Scarlett O'Hara.
13. I'm glad you're moving Laura; the change will do you good.
14. You Mr. Know-it-all are wrong again.
15. Buddy can you spare a dime?

209

PUNCTUATING DATES AND ADDRESSES

Without commas, dates and addresses can be confusing. Suppose that Sam, your best friend, has just moved to California to get a job. He needs some papers that he left with you, and he drops you a line to give you his new address: "I'm renting an efficiency at 3735 Pearson Apartment Complex 10 Southwest Oxnard California 10732." Where would you send Sam's papers?

3735 Pearson Apartments		3735 Pearson Street
Complex 10 Southwest	or	Apartment Complex 10
Oxnard, California 10732		Southwest Oxnard, California 10732

When you are addressing an envelope, you can separate major parts of an address by placing each part on a different line. But when you are referring to an address in a sentence, you have to rely on commas to separate the major items of information. In dates, as well, the reader wants to see one piece of information at a time: the day of the week, the day of the month, and the year—for example, Friday, October 19, 1929.

When a date occurs in the middle of a sentence, make sure that all items are set off by commas, including the final item, which requires a comma after it.

On Friday, October 19, 1929, the great crash occurred.

EXERCISE 16F: USING COMMAS IN DATES AND ADDRESSES

Supply commas where necessary in the following sentences.

1. The armistice ending World War I was signed at the eleventh hour of the eleventh day of the eleventh month: 11 A.M. November 11 1918.

2. My contract was extended to May 30.

3. Please forward my mail to 15411 McCann Road Southgate Michigan 17802 because I have moved.

4. On Saturday September 30 1926 my parents took their wedding vows.

5. Chris moved to 110 Downing Street.

6. In May 1948 Israel became a nation.

7. Donations should be sent to the following address: Hunger Relief 2038 Pennsylvania Avenue Washington D.C. 10532.

8. On December 1 Aunt Jessica will be 90 years old.

9. Mr. Liedecker works somewhere near 42nd Street in New York City.

10. She met him in Hot Springs Arkansas and married him in Fargo North Dakota on a cold and wintry day.

SETTING OFF DIRECT QUOTATIONS

When you write down on paper exactly what someone else has said, you are quoting that person directly: Ann said, "My husband is an incurable romantic." Whenever readers see a group of words enclosed in quotation marks (" "), they know that those words represent a special part of the sentence. Commas help to set off a direct quotation from the rest of the sentence; they also allow readers to pause briefly before the quotation, just as one would in conversation.

For example, if you read the following two sentences aloud, you will notice that you pause in the first but not in the second, in which the statement is not quoted directly:

The woman shouted angrily, "Leave my husband alone."
The woman told the protestors to leave her husband alone.

Usually, you need only one comma to set off a direct quotation, but if the quotation is broken at any point, you need two commas.

"I'm exhausted," he said. "Jim, we're all tired," the boss said.
He said, "I'm exhausted." The boss said, "Jim, we're all tired."

"Whew," he said, "I'm exhausted." "Jim," the boss said, "we're all tired." (broken quotations)

EXERCISE 16G: SETTING OFF DIRECT QUOTATIONS

Supply commas where necessary in the following sentences.

1. "Bernie" I asked "did you see my *National Geographic* anywhere?"

2. "Which one?" he inquired.

3. I said "The January issue."

4. "What did the cover look like?" he asked.

5. I said "There was a picture of an adorable little freckled-faced boy sitting on the banks of Dingle Bay."

6. "Oh, that one" he mumbled sheepishly.

7. Then he added "I'm afraid I spilled coffee all over it."

8. "I thought you were finished reading it anyway" he continued.

9. "How could I be through with it" I exclaimed "when we just got it in this afternoon's mail?"

10. "Well, I thought you were a speed reader" he chuckled.

THE MISUSE AND OVERUSE OF THE COMMA

You may sometimes have seen papers written by your friends (never by you, of course) in which the commas seem to have been randomly sprinkled on with a pepper shaker. Needless to say, such overuse of commas is incorrect. As was pointed out in the beginning of this chapter, commas, like all punctuation, should be used only to make writing clearer. If there isn't a reason for using a comma, don't use one. Look at the third sentence in this paragraph:

> As was pointed out in the beginning of this chapter,[1] commas,[2] like all punctuation,[3] should be used only to make writing clearer.

In the sentence above, the reasons for using the three commas are, first, to set off introductory material and, second, to set off interrupters. Why, in the preceding sentence of explanation, are the five commas used?

1. _____

2. _____

3. _____

4. _____

5. _____

One misuse of the comma that leads to great confusion is using it to separate the subject and verb.

The bells, rang softly through the summer night.

Bill, and Denny skated on the frozen river.

Bill and Denny skated, and sailed on the frozen river.

A second and similar misuse is to separate the verb and completer with a comma.

The horse kicked, the fence.

The horse kicked the fence, and the rider.

One of the few rules of punctuation that *never* varies is the rule that a subject and a verb or a verb and an object are not to be separated by a comma. Subject and verb, of course, can be separated by two or more commas, as can verb and object, if the commas set off parenthetical expressions.

The mouse, nevertheless, ran up the clock.

The mouse ran, with unusual speed, up the clock.

If you use the comma, which is the signal to pause, when there is no reason for readers to pause, they may easily miss the point of your communication.

EXERCISE 16H: UNNECESSARY AND MISUSED COMMAS

In the following paragraph, there are a number of misused and overused commas. Which ones do you think should be taken out?

The funny papers, really aren't funny, but they strongly influence American society. They, are one of the most influential methods, of mass communication. Surveys of readers, consistently, reveal that the funnies are among the best read features of American newspapers. Regularly, between 75 percent, and 90 percent of readers, are in the age brackets from 30 to 40. A majority of comic strip readers, are from the middle, and upper-middle class. Advertisers want to reach, these young, free-spending readers. And, editors want to please the advertisers. Therefore, more and more comic strips reach more and more American readers, to reflect on contemporary life. And by reflecting that life, the comics help to shape it.

EXERCISE 16I: UNNECESSARY AND MISUSED COMMAS

Here is a much more difficult paragraph from which to remove the commas, but you might like to give it a try. When Thoreau wrote this, he used only seven commas. The pepper shaker style of punctuation put in eighteen. Which would you keep and why?

> I have heard of a man, lost in the woods, and dying of famine, and exhaustion, at the foot of a tree, whose loneliness was relieved by the grotesque visions, with which, owing to bodily weakness, his diseased imagination surrounded him, and which he believed to be, real. So, also, owing to bodily, and mental health, and strength, we may be continually cheered by a like, but more normal and natural society, and come to know that we are never, alone.

EXERCISE 16J: REVIEW OF COMMAS

Supply commas where necessary in the following sentences.

1. Bert and Ernie live at The Children's Television Workshop 123 Sesame Street New York New York.
2. As most American children know both Bert and Ernie love oatmeal cookies.
3. Unfortunately so does the Cookie Monster.
4. As a result Bert and Ernie are constantly being tricked out of their cookies.
5. Yesterday for example Ernie brought out a huge plate of oatmeal cookies.
6. As soon as he set them on the table in walked the Cookie Monster.
7. Ernie said "Don't try to trick me Cookie Monster."
8. The Cookie Monster promised to be good but then he asked Ernie a question.
9. "Ernie do you know the *right* way to eat cookies?"
10. Looking very puzzled Ernie said that he wasn't aware of any special rules regarding cookie eating.
11. The Cookie Monster then explained that there are two ways to eat cookies: the slow way and the fast way.
12. He said "Let me demonstrate."
13. Then he ate one cookie the slow way.

14. As he nibbled on the cookie the Cookie Monster explained that one has to hold up one's pinky finger when eating a cookie the slow way.

15. Ernie watched closely listened carefully and waited patiently.

16. As Ernie watched he grew more and more suspicious.

17. He decided however to give the Cookie Monster the benefit of the doubt.

18. Finally the Cookie Monster finished his first demonstration.

19. Then he began to demonstrate how to eat cookies the fast way.

20. "Ern" he said "this is the *right* way to eat cookies."

21. Before Ernie realized what was happening the Cookie Monster had gobbled up the whole plate of cookies.

22. Poor Ernie had been fooled again.

23. The Cookie Monster couldn't stop laughing and Ernie couldn't stop staring at his empty plate.

24. Then before he left the Cookie Monster got in one last shot.

25. He said "Anytime you need help in cookie eating, just call Cookie Monster."

WRITING FROM READING

Role Playing

Creative writing instructors often find that students produce some of their best work when they are placed in situations in which they have to really use their imaginations: pretending to be a grain of sand on the ocean floor, describing what it feels like to be a French fry, or a stick of gum, or the last leaf to be raked from the autumn lawn.

The imagination is a great learning device. In fact, through role playing, you can even expand your understanding of punctuation. Here is a real challenge for your creative energies. Imagine for the moment that you are a comma. Think about what it feels like to be a comma. Do you have a good self-image? What do you do for a living? How do people treat you? What kind of personality do you have? What kind of people do you hang around with? What do you do for fun? Describe a typical day in the life of a comma.

Here is how one student felt as a stick of gum:

My life is a short one. The hope of remaining unchewed and dying of old age is, alas, just a fantasy. I have to face the inevitable: I am destined to end up in some stranger's mouth with saliva gushing about me in all directions. Oh . . . the utter shame of it all! Even worse, I'll probably die in disgrace. I'll get stuck underneath a table or thrown onto the ground where someone can step on me, or . . . horror of horrors . . . I'll be swallowed! Even a stick of gum deserves a more fitting burial. All I ask is to be placed back into my own wrapper so that I can go out in style.

David Kasunic

Social science teachers employ a similar technique when they have their students engage in role playing. Sociology students, for example, learn something about the dynamics of street crime when they view the problem from different perspectives: through the eyes of the victim, the police, the criminal, and the families of each.

Viewing a problem from different perspectives can help you develop your thinking skills. Consider the issue of drinking and driving. Suppose that you have been asked to testify before a statewide conference on DUI (Driving Under the Influence). The governor's commission is investigating various ways of dealing with the problem. Some of the proposals being considered include the following:

Imposing automatic jail sentences
Imposing heavy fines

Taking away the individual's license for two years after the first offense

Embarrassing those who have been arrested for drunk driving by placing DUI bumper stickers on their cars

Making bartenders subject to arrest for selling alcoholic beverages to a person who is already intoxicated

Raising the drinking age to 21

Raising the driving age to 18

Prohibiting the beer industry from advertising on TV

Break the class up into groups of three, and consider these proposals from three different perspectives. Each of you pretend that you are one of these people:

1. A mother whose son was killed by a drunk driver
2. A bartender who works at the most popular night spot in town
3. A man who was recently arrested for driving under the influence (This was his first offense, and he was not involved in an accident.)

After you have discussed the problem with each other, jot down some notes in preparation for the hearing. In your role as mother, bartender, or DUI offender, what points would you make to the commission?

17 *The Colon and the Semicolon*

If you need something stronger than a comma, but not as strong as a period, you can use a colon (:) or a semicolon (;). Both of these punctuation marks can be used to connect two complete thoughts.

> I noticed a big change in Ryan; the experience has taught him a great deal.
> I noticed a big change in Ryan: he is much more mature than he used to be.

At this point, you might be wondering how the colon and the semicolon differ from the period, which is also used after a complete thought. A period

separates two complete thoughts, but a colon or a semicolon *connects* two complete and *closely related* thoughts. For example, the second thought might explain the first, or it might provide a specific example of an idea introduced in the first thought. In any case, there is a definite relationship between the two thoughts: cause to effect, general to specific, and so on. A period, on the other hand, indicates the completion of one thought and the beginning of a *new* thought.

Notice the difference in these two sets of sentences:

Set A

You're overlooking an important point; you have to consider the Senator's background.

You're overlooking an important point: the Senator grew up on a dairy farm in the Midwest.

Set B

Senator Dowd doesn't seem to understand what life in the city is really like. Growing up on a farm can distort one's perception of crime in America.

Senator Dowd's background might be influencing his views on urban crime. After all, people who have been raised on a farm often find it difficult to understand the city dweller's fear of crime.

In the first set of sentences (Set A), the author is using two complete clauses to make one point. Notice that the second clause does not begin with a capital letter because it is still part of the same sentence. The author leads up to something in the first clause and delivers it in the second.

First clause:	Something is being overlooked. (What is being overlooked?)
Second clause:	The Senator's background is being overlooked.

In the second set of sentences (Set B), however, each sentence stands alone. Each makes a point without being connected to another thought.

THE COLON

The important thing to remember about both the colon and the semicolon is that they are much stronger than a comma. They have almost the same force as a period, so you should use them only after an independent clause, not after a phrase or an incomplete thought. The following sentence illustrates one way in which the colon is commonly misused:

The categories in Trivial Pursuit are: History, Entertainment, Science and Nature, Geography, Arts and Literature, and Sports and Leisure.

It is proper to use a colon to introduce a list of items, but only after a complete statement has been made about the list. "The categories in Trivial Pursuit are" is not a complete thought. It can be completed in a number of ways. For example:

The categories in Trivial Pursuit are challenging.
The categories in Trivial Pursuit are boring.

In other words, the reader has not yet been told to *expect* a list, so the colon is inappropriate. The following sentences illustrate a more logical use of the colon:

Trivial Pursuit questions fall under the following categories: History, Entertainment . . .
Trivial Pursuit focuses on six categories: History, Entertainment . . .

Notice that, in each sentence, the colon is preceded by an independent clause. Whether you are using a colon to introduce a list of items or to connect two closely related thoughts, make sure that what comes *before* the colon is a complete thought—an independent clause.

EXERCISE 17A: RECOGNIZING IMPROPER USE OF COLONS

Mark *R* (for "revise") before any sentence in which the colon is not used sensibly. Then either eliminate the colon or revise the sentence.

_____ 1. This semester, Mrs. Merriman is taking: chemistry, physics, and abnormal psychology.

_____ 2. I told my math teacher that I liked his new bumper sticker: "If you think education is expensive, try ignorance."

_____ 3. Mary Claire's favorite colors are: yellow, lavender, and mint green.

_____ 4. In order to make a good picture frame, you need several important tools: a router, a miter box, and a hammer.

_____ 5. This election will determine whether young people are willing to take a stand on arms control: I think Joyce Farrell will make a fine candidate for governor.

_____ 6. In the back row of the auditorium: I found the missing tape recorder.

_____ 7. The answer to your problem is simple: stop eating fried foods.

_____ 8. Coming from you: that is a real compliment.

_____ 9. My dog is: friendly, loyal, and intelligent.

_____ 10. Remember this: don't use a colon unless you need one.

EXERCISE 17B: USING COLONS

Revise any sentences that contain inappropriate punctuation and insert colons wherever you think they are necessary.

1. In his later years, the billionaire, Howard Hughes, led a bizarre, secretive life.

2. His living circumstances were certainly unusual he secluded himself in a hotel room in Nevada and never ventured outside the room.

3. Except for his contact with a small group of aides, Hughes completely isolated himself from the outside world.

4. His daily routine included the following watching television, writing memos, and negotiating multimillion dollar business deals by phone.

5. Howard Hughes made most of his money in the aircraft business.

6. His private life also attracted a lot of attention Hughes dated some glamorous women, and, at one point, he was married to a famous movie star.

7. Hughes has been called many things—some good, some bad.

8. Journalists have characterized him in the following ways ''a megalo-maniac,'' ''a pathetic old man,'' ''a financial genius,'' and ''a king-maker.''

9. One writer even claims that, if it had not been for Howard Hughes, there would have been no Watergate scandal during the Nixon administration.

10. It seems that in death, as well as in life, Howard Hughes will always be associated with three things: money, fame, and power.

THE SEMICOLON

At least two types of sentences require something stronger than a comma but not as strong as a period:

1.   Sentences connecting two closely related main clauses
2.   Sentences separating two-part items in a series

For both of these constructions, the semicolon will serve you well.

Connecting Two Closely Related Main Clauses

You already know several ways to connect two main clauses. In Chapter 14, for example, you learned about the compound sentence, in which two main clauses are connected with a coordinate conjunction.

> David never had a voice lesson in his life, but he can really belt out a tune.

The semicolon provides you with another way of connecting these types of clauses.

> David never had a voice lesson in his life; however, he can really belt out a tune.

Both of these sentences use the same two clauses to make the same point. They just do it in slightly different ways.

Coordinate Conjunction
_____, but _____.
Conjunctive Adverb
_____; however, _____.

The content of the sentences remains the same; only the structure of the sentences changes. Other writers might express the same thought by subordinating one clause to the other.

> Although David has never had a voice lesson in his life, he can really belt out a tune.

The point is that none of these sentence constructions is "right" or "wrong." They are just different. Knowing how to use a semicolon, then, is not a matter of studying a neat little set of rules about when *not* to use a semicolon.

Rather, it is a matter of knowing when a semicolon *can best be used* and when it is being illogically used.

One of the most frequent uses of the semicolon is between clauses joined with a connector or a modifier called a *conjunctive adverb*.

Conjunctive Adverbs

however	nevertheless
therefore	thus
consequently	in fact
moreover	still
furthermore	indeed
granted	then

The semicolon is used when the conjunctive adverb is used as a connecting word.

> David never took a voice lesson in his life; *however*, he can really belt out a tune.
>
> David has a superb singing voice; *furthermore*, he is a fine pianist and an excellent composer.

Notice how the conjunctive adverbs in these sentences relate the second clauses back to the first. In fact, if you examine these connectors closely, you'll see that they don't make sense unless they are related to a previous thought. Imagine reading a story that began:

> Furthermore, . . .
>
> or
>
> Consequently, . . .

Neither would make any sense to you. "Furthermore" doesn't make sense because there is nothing to add on to, and "consequently" doesn't make sense because there is no cause-effect relationship established. In other words, whenever you see a conjunctive adverb between two main clauses, you know that the clauses must be closely related. A semicolon, then, is an appropriate form of punctuation to use in such cases because it indicates a close relationship between two main clauses.

Remember that you need both a semicolon and a comma in these sentences:

> Joy is a real whiz in math; *however*, she wants to major in history.

If you read this sentence aloud, you will hear the need for a pause after "however." Some conjunctive adverbs, though, don't always need to be set off with commas when joining two complete clauses—"thus" and "then," for example.

First I ripped the package open; *then* I read your letter.

In this sentence, there is no need to pause after *then*, so there is no reason to use a comma. Let your ear help you decide whether to omit the comma in such cases.

As mentioned earlier, conjunctive adverbs can also be used as modifiers, and, as such, they can be placed in various parts of the sentence. However, when you use a conjunctive adverb as a modifier, you don't need a semicolon. You simply set off the modifier with commas, just as you would do with any other interrupting word or expression.

Joy is a real whiz in math. She has decided, *however*, to major in history.

The semicolon is commonly misused in sentences such as the following:

Clara's car has some unusual features; for example, the built-in refrigerator in the back seat.

Notice that the second half of the sentence is not a complete thought. A semicolon, however, is used to connect two main clauses, just as a comma and a coordinate conjunction are used in a compound sentence. When readers see this:

> Main clause   , and

or this:

> Main clause   ;

they expect to see another main clause. Make sure, then, that you have a complete thought on *both* sides of the semicolon. Also, remember that the semicolon performs the same connecting function as the comma plus a coordinate conjunction:

> comma + coordinate conjunction = semicolon

Therefore, if you use both a coordinate conjunction *and* a semicolon, you are connecting the clauses twice. In other words, don't write a sentence like this:

> Cliff loved law school; *but* he hated the New England winters.

EXERCISE 17C: USING SEMICOLONS

Supply appropriate punctuation for the following sentences

1. Marriage is still a thriving institution however the traditional marriage ceremony is really changing.

2. The weather forecaster predicted subfreezing temperatures consequently the inaugural festivities had to be moved indoors.

3. The new department store was doing a booming business the manager therefore decided to give each of her employees a raise.

4. Mr. Holbright's credentials are impeccable furthermore he is just the sort of person we need in this department.

5. I have never seen an American bald eagle in its natural habitat in fact I've never really seen an eagle in any habitat.

6. The basketball team lost only one game this season granted they should have won that last game, but I'm not complaining.

7. Stephan has made remarkable progress he is indeed one of the hardest working students I have ever had.

8. Learning how to administer CPR is an invaluable skill therefore all employees will be required to attend a workshop on Cardio-Pulmonary Resuscitation.

9. Harry's fund raising dinner was a huge success however he is still over $1,000 in debt.

10. Harry's fund raising dinner was a huge success he is however still over $1,000 in debt.

11. Larkin went from rags to riches but he never forgot his family and friends back home.

12. Professor Koppel believes that American history textbooks present a distorted view of Indian culture therefore she has chosen a new textbook written by an American Indian.

13. I didn't expect the phone rates to go up and I certainly didn't expect to be charged a fortune for long distance calls.

14. I didn't expect the phone rates to go up furthermore I did not expect to be charged a fortune for long distance calls.

15. Ralph is a real sucker for all the latest diet fads however he hasn't shed a pound in ten years.

EXERCISE 17D: RECOGNIZING INAPPROPRIATE USE OF SEMICOLONS

Improve the following sentences by revising the wording or punctuation or both.

1. The American Indians were talented artisans: for example, the Pueblos.

2. The Pueblo Indians were highly skilled basketmakers, in fact, their baskets are now worth thousands of dollars.

3. Today, the Pueblo tribe is not heavily involved in the art of basketmaking; however, it now produces some of the most beautiful pottery in the country.

4. The Apaches were a more aggressive tribe; so they tended to focus their skills on the art of hunting.

5. For example; they made technical improvements in the bow and arrow.

6. The Navaho Indians have always made finely crafted baskets and jewelry; but they are also known for their exquisite rugs and blankets.

7. Their woven goods have several distinguishing characteristics; natural fibers, soft, earth-tone colors, and intricate designs.

8. Smaller, less well-known tribes like the Palouse tribe, had a great deal of expertise in the art of horse breeding.

9. The Appaloosa; for example, was named after this tribe.

10. American Indians continue to take much pride in their work, consequently, they continue to create products of the highest quality.

Separating Two-Part Items in a Series

In Chapter 16, you learned that commas are used to separate items in a series. However, if each item contains several points of information, you need something stronger than a comma to separate the items. For example:

> Margaret's resume revealed substantial experience in restaurant management: *Assistant Manager, Burger King; Manager, King's Family Restaurant; District Manager, Bob Evans;* and *Regional Manager, Bob Evans.*

Each of these items consists of two parts separated by a comma. Therefore, in order for the readers to see that they have reached the end of an item, they need to see a stronger mark of punctuation at the end of an item. A semicolon works perfectly.

EXERCISE 17E: USING SEMICOLONS TO PUNCTUATE ITEMS IN A SERIES

Supply appropriate punctuation for the following sentences.

1. Food distribution centers are opening in the following areas: Penn's Manor Indiana County McKees Rocks Allegheny County and New Sewickley Township Beaver County.

2. Brock was elated with the new slate of officers: Donna Cole President Vic Taylor Vice-President Tom Walker Secretary and Lynn Heinz Treasurer.

3. Macy's is having a sale on men's clothing: dress shirts cardigan sweaters and wool suits.

4. The interior decorator recommended several color changes: blue for the living room beige for the dining room and off-white for the kitchen.

5. We purchased a number of interesting items at the auction: an old fruit press an Edison victrola and an oak pie cupboard.

6. Ann's vacation took her to the following cities: Paris France London England and Rome Italy.

7. William Manchester has written several interesting biographies of significant historical figures: John F. Kennedy *Portrait of a President* Douglas MacArthur *American Caesar* and Winston Churchill *The Last Lion*.

8. The menu included some expensive items: fresh lobster filet mignon and veal cordon bleu.

9. Raquel has three favorite stuffed animals: Snuffy her puppy Wee Willie her walrus and Murphy her teddy bear.

10. Richard ate the same meals for two weeks: breakfast French toast lunch spinach salad and dinner chicken pot pie.

WRITING FROM READING

Making Facts Meaningful

Many times we read statistics that are so large—or so small—that we really can't comprehend them. In such cases it is the writer's duty to break the numbers down, to make them more meaningful to the reader. For example, look at these facts about the population of India:

> The huge population of India, numbering some 730 million, is inhibiting government attempts to reduce the number of people living below the poverty line. India's population continues to grow at the rate of about 2 percent per year.

The reader sees two facts:

India's population is approximately 730 million.
India's population is growing at a rate of 2 percent per year.

Just stating isolated facts, however, is not the best way to get your points across, especially if you are dealing with statistics—numerical facts. You are more likely to reach your readers if you make the facts more meaningful. You can do this by breaking the numbers down and relating them to something. The following information is more specific, more meaningful, and, therefore, more likely to leave an impression on the readers:

The huge population of India, numbering some 730 million, is inhibiting government attempts to reduce the number of people living below the poverty line. *Every minute, day and night, forty infants are born in India.* India's population continues to grow at a rate of about 2 percent per year. *This rate of growth means that every year, India's population increases by about 15 million people*, which is equal to the entire population of Australia!

Break into small groups and examine the facts listed below. See if you can think of some ways to make these facts more meaningful. When you are finished, try out your ideas on the rest of your class. Find out which of your strategies is most effective.

Facts

According to the Christian Bookseller's Association, Bible sales in this country total some $197 million annually.
The Los Angeles Olympics created 25 million pounds of trash.
Americans spend over $4 billion a year on pet food.

18 Capitalization

If you looked up the word *capital* in a dictionary, you would learn that capital means "important," "chief," "notable." A capital offense, for example, is not just a minor transgression: it is a serious crime such as murder or treason. On the more positive side, a "capital" dinner is not just a can of cold beans: it is something special—perhaps a sumptuous seven-course meal consisting of your favorite foods, cooked to perfection.

The word *capital*, then, suggests something different, something out of the ordinary. That's why capital letters are larger than lower-case letters. They are used to call attention to something special—your name, for example. Knowing that you are "Rosie O'Grady" or "Samuel B. Spade" sets you apart from other people. Think of how you would feel if no one ever addressed you by your proper name, if all you ever heard was "Hey, you," or if all of your personal letters were addressed "Dear Occupant." You would be insulted, and rightly so, because you would lose your identity.

In the same sense, capitalization enables readers to *identify* important types of information, namely:

1.   Where a sentence begins
2.   The names of specific people, places, and things

CAPITALIZING THE BEGINNING OF A SENTENCE

You already know a great deal about sentence boundaries. You no doubt remember, for instance, that the first word of a sentence should always be capitalized. As soon as readers see a period, they realize that a sentence has been completed. They then expect a new sentence to follow. However, if the first word of the new sentence does not begin with a capital letter, readers can become distracted and confused. For example:

> Dolphins are very intelligent creatures. endowed with an acute sense of hearing, they respond immediately to the sound of a human voice.

What does the writer mean?

> Dolphins are very intelligent creatures endowed with an acute sense of hearing. They respond immediately to the sound of a human voice.
> or
> Dolphins are very intelligent creatures. Endowed with an acute sense of hearing, they respond immediately to the sound of a human voice.

Be particularly careful when writing sentences that begin with little words that might not look as important as other words: *a, an, the, in, on,* and so on. If you misunderstand the purpose of capitalization, you might write something like this:

> Not all birds can fly. the Ostrich is a perfect example.

instead of this:

> Not all birds can fly. The ostrich is a perfect example.

EXERCISE 18A: CAPITALIZATION, SENTENCE BOUNDARIES

Improve the following paragraph by eliminating faulty capitalization.

> The ostrich is an interesting bird. it can't fly, but it can run faster than any animal on two legs. it is not a particularly graceful runner. In fact, an ostrich looks pretty awkward even when it is standing still. nevertheless, No other two-legged animal can outrun the ostrich. these rather comic looking creatures have been clocked at thirty-five miles an hour. the Ostrich is also the world's largest living bird. It reaches close to nine feet in height. its height, coupled with its superb vision, gives the ostrich an excellent view of the terrain. thus, Through speed and an enlarged field of vision, the ostrich can usually manage to outwit its predators.

CAPITALIZING SPECIFIC PEOPLE, PLACES, AND THINGS

Names are not limited to individuals. Specific *groups* of people also have names: races, religious sects, unions, business organizations, baseball teams, and so on. Streets, towns, stores, restaurants, cities, states, countries, and planets also have names. So do months, days of the week, holidays, and historical events. Sometimes names are thought of as titles—for books, newspapers, magazines, headlines, movies, songs, paintings, college courses, television programs, and radio shows, for example. Brand names are also specific and therefore require capitalization.

In short, when you are referring to a general class of things (actors, cars, cities), you have no reason to capitalize. But when you are referring to a *specific* person, place, or thing *by name*, then you should begin those words with a capital letter (Paul Newman, a Plymouth Horizon, Peoria, Illinois). Look at the following examples:

Identifying without Naming	*Identifying by Name or Title*
the doctor	Dr. Spock
a coal mine	Rabina Mine #3
potato chips	Wise Potato Chips
my research paper	"Tests That Don't Teach"
a river	the Missouri River

Identifying without naming: A secretary.

Identifying by name or title: Mrs. Hines, Secretary of the Department of Humanities.

a peace treaty	the Treaty of Versailles
the third chapter	"Visions of Glory"
your mother	Mrs. Fletcher
toothpaste	Crest
my physics course	Technical Physics 101
the highway	Garden State Parkway
the president	President Roosevelt
your religion	Methodist
a church	St. Patrick's Cathedral
communism	the Communist Party
an island	Madagascar
an organization	Common Cause
a moth	the South American Migrant Moth
my mother	Mother

Some Rules of Capitalization

1. *Not all words in titles need to be capitalized.* In the previous list of terms, notice that the "of" in "Visions of Glory" is not capitalized. When they appear in titles, neither articles (*a, an, the*) nor prepositions (*from, between, on, to, of,* and so on) need to be capitalized, unless *they appear first in the title.*

2. *The personal pronoun "I" should always be capitalized.* Most pronouns (*he, she, it . . .*) are not capitalized *unless* they appear at the beginning of a sentence because they do not identify anyone by name. However, the personal pronoun "I" must always be capitalized because the readers know that it refers specifically to one person—you, the writer.

3. *Nicknames and fictional names need to be capitalized.* Although nicknames are not proper names, they are still specific designations. "Froggy," "Doc," and "Babs" are all substitute names and therefore require capitalization. Names of fictional characters, those names created by a writer, should also be capitalized. The words "pink" and "panther," for example, would not normally be capitalized, but when you are referring to the character portrayed in the movies by Peter Sellers, then you should write "the Pink Panther."

4. *A person's occupation does not need to be capitalized, but a person's title does.*

the queen	Queen Victoria
a personnel director	Director of Personnel
the police officer	Officer Krumpky

5. *Seasons of the year are not normally capitalized.* The words *spring, summer, fall* (or *autumn*), and *winter* do not need to be capitalized unless they are part of a title:

the painting, "Winter Wonderland"

the song, "Autumn in New York"

the film, *The Long, Hot Summer*

the book, *Silent Spring*

6. *Sometimes the words Mom and Dad are capitalized: sometimes they are not.* The words *Mom* and *Dad* are capitalized if they are used instead of someone's given name: I went to the movie with Dad. They are not capitalized if a possessive pronoun precedes them: I went to the movie with my dad.

7. *Errors in capitalization can be reduced through practice in writing.* Writers who have good sentence sense can still make mistakes in capitalization. Studies show that some writers mistakenly use capitalization for emphasis (We lost the game Because . . .) while others have irregular handwriting habits that lead to errors in capitalization. Regardless of the cause, however, *the more you write*, the quicker you will eliminate problems in capitalization.

EXERCISE 18B: CAPITALIZING NAMES REFERRING TO PEOPLE

Supply capitalization where necessary in the following sentences.

1. According to lieutenant columbo, basset hounds make great police dogs.

2. The reporter scheduled two interviews with jimmy the greek.

3. The president of the company is a former psychiatric nurse.

4. Before i met president hartmann, i was ready to request a transfer.

5. The former secretary of state, henry kissinger, is a good friend of ted koppel's.

6. My best friend has an unusual nickname—"fodpod."

7. Your secretary is extremely efficient.

8. Yesterday, I saw aunt alyce and uncle frank doing wheelies on their new bikes.

9. If you want to be promoted to chief supervisor, you have to be able to communicate with your employees.

10. The iroquois indians had quite an advanced political structure.

11. My favorite character in the story was ludlow kissel.

12. Joy's sister has just been made a vice-president in the company.

13. The professor's paper focuses on the lithuanians and yugoslavians who settled the remote mountain villages.

14. On the immigration form, malaysians and eskimos were listed as part of the mongoloid race.

15. In greek mythology, athena is the goddess of wisdom.

EXERCISE 18C: CAPITALIZING NAMES REFERRING TO PLACES

Supply capitalization where necessary in the following sentences.

1. Mark's mother has moved to sherwood estates.

2. Dad loves to shop at station square and stop for lunch at houlihan's.

3. We ended our trip to rome with a visit to the sistine chapel.

4. David and Ernie enjoyed their tour of universal studios.

5. Gloria has enrolled in the harvard school of medicine.

6. The Kramers have invested a fortune in hartwood acres.

7. Which of the restaurants do you prefer?

8. Julia's cousin has been appointed rabbi at the new synagogue.

9. Driving across ouray pass in colorado is one of life's most terrifying adventures.

10. The peace treaty ending the Civil War was signed at appomattox court house in virginia.

11. Our local high school is sponsoring a refugee family from cambodia.

12. My eye doctor has purchased space in the catlin medical center.

13. The space satellites have produced some incredible photographs of jupiter and mars.

14. Carol is renting a charming two-room flat on melrose avenue.

15. My home town, freedom, pennsylvania, is noted for its brick streets and steep hills.

EXERCISE 18D: CAPITALIZING NAMES REFERRING TO THINGS

Supply capitalization where necessary in the following sentences.

1. My neighbor just bought a new car—a cadillac seville.

2. Margaret prefers herbal tea, but I like the brand called constant comment.

3. John and Jan's new company sells both business computers and educational computers.

4. Robert Pirsig's book, *zen and the art of motorcycle maintenance,* changed my life.

5. Ray practices every day on his new steinway piano.

6. My mother said that she was going to book a seat on the next space shuttle.

7. The orient express is a famous passenger train in Europe.

8. Did you see my renewal form for *u.s. news and world report?*

9. I prefer news magazines to sports magazines.

10. Last year's new year's party was a total disaster.

11. Craig likes the kaypro word processor because it is portable.

12. My grandmother loves tea roses, so I ordered her three Jackson & Perkins "sweetheart" hybrids.

13. The eagle paper corporation makes good quality typing paper.

14. Dad's old zenith radio that he bought in 1952 is still working.

15. Norman Thomas was one of the American socialist party's most interesting candidates.

EXERCISE 18E: REVIEW OF CAPITALIZATION

Read the following sentences carefully. Supply capitalization where necessary; delete any unnecessary capitalization.

1. rhoda morganstern was Dan's favorite character from the mary tyler moore show.

2. You can't run for President in this country unless you are an american citizen.

3. I love philadelphia cream cheese.

4. The only disney picture to be nominated for an academy award was *mary poppins.*

5. scrabble is one of the best Word Games on the market.

6. Doug and Marianne are moving to delancey street.

7. Anita is reading a book about the famous russian Czar, ivan the terrible.

8. Brett wants to get a head start on Spring cleaning.

9. My most interesting classes are Psychology and Genetics.

10. This semester, i am taking abnormal psychology I and genetics II.

11. Jenny bought an old maxwell house coffee poster at the new Antique Shop on fifth avenue.

12. The head of the forestry department is known as smokey the bear.

13. My brother reminds me of ralph kramden, the star of "the honeymooners."

14. Next sunday, my best friends are getting married.

15. Richard is hooked on Soap Operas.

16. May i borrow your Dictionary?

17. Do you want the american heritage dictionary or the webster's new twentieth century dictionary?

18. Carrie looks forward to november because she loves the thanksgiving holiday.

19. I will meet you at market square.

20. Tom always pays his bills on the last day of the Month.

21. do you think I need a checkup, dr. peterson?

22. The name of the book is *arnie, the darling starling.*

23. Next Winter, we are going to invest in a good woodburning Stove.

24. Our school Newspaper, Trailblazer, has received several awards.

25. mr. kowalski is an expert on the polish labor union, solidarity.

WRITING FROM READING

How What You See Affects What You Get

The beauty of the written word can be strongly affected by the reader's visual perception. In other words, the emotional impact of a sentence depends partly on the way the sentence is presented to the reader—the way it looks on the page. That's why a poem can sometimes say more than a paragraph, even if both contain the same sentences in the same order. When reading a poem, the reader often becomes more aware of how well chosen the phrases are and how aptly placed the details are. The following seven-sentence paragraph originally appeared in the form of a poem. Read the paragraph carefully.

> Luther Miller was a moron who walked the nursing home hill every morning. He squinted at chirping sparrows and searched the leaves upset by his flat feet. At noon he wheeled Ellie Walker, a ninety-year-old spinster, to lunch on creamed potatoes and meatloaf. At two he sat with Hal Sloan, who screamed a lot and sometimes pinched the dark-eyed recreation therapist. When the Baptist children's choir came, he stroked the hair, he thought platinum threads, of a big-eyed little girl and smiled with gapped teeth. And, again at dusk, he inspected the crackling brown oak leaves around the entire perimeter of his home. At nine he slept and dreamed whatever morons dream.

Now read the story of Luther Miller as it was originally written:

LUTHER MILLER

Luther Miller was a moron
Who walked the nursing home hill
Every morning
He squinted at chirping sparrows
And searched the leaves upset
By his flat feet
At noon he wheeled Ellie Walker
Ninety-year-old spinster
To lunch on creamed potatoes
And meatloaf
At two he sat with Hal Sloan
Who screamed a lot and sometimes pinched
The dark-eyed recreation therapist
When the Baptist children's choir came
He stroked the hair he thought platinum threads
Of a big-eyed little girl and smiled
With gapped teeth
And, again at dusk, he inspected
The crackling brown oak leaves
Around the entire perimeter
Of his home
At nine he slept and dreamed
Whatever morons dream.

Faye Angelo,
Hinds Junior College, Raymond, Mississippi.
Reprinted from *Teaching English in a Two-Year College*,
10 (May 1984): 263.

Did you feel the impact of the word "moron" in the first line ("Luther Miller was a moron") more forcefully than you did when you read "Luther Miller was a moron who walked the nursing home hill every morning"? Think about your reaction to each line. Did you see meaningful parts of sentences in the poem that you overlooked in the paragraph? Did the poem make you think about something or feel something that the paragraph didn't? What kind of a person is Luther Miller? Is he a "moron"? What is a moron?

All of the sentences in "Luther Miller" are well written, whether they are in the poem or in the paragraph, but the poem enables the reader to see the importance of even the smallest details.

As "Luther Miller" illustrates, a typical day in someone's life can reveal a great deal about that person. Think of someone you know (yourself, for instance), or even someone you have never met but have often observed with interest. See what you can learn about that person by making a chronicle of a typical day in that person's life. Think about what you want to say about that person, and then say it in a poem or in a paragraph.

Drawing Generalizations

Both in school and on the job, you will often be required to summarize detailed information—to examine specific data and arrive at logical conclusions about what the data say. Read the following information regarding absenteeism in an urban elementary school and think about what the numbers mean.

After examining the data, ask yourself, "What have I learned about the causes of absenteeism in the Watson Elementary School?" "What do I know about the absentee child that I didn't know before?" Write a brief profile of the typical absentee child in Watson Elementary; in other words, write a paragraph describing the characteristics of chronic absentees at Watson.

WATSON ELEMENTARY SCHOOL ABSENTEE REPORT

Total school population	560
Number of chronic absentees	53
(Chronic absentee = student who misses 20 or more days per year)	
Living with both parents	5
Living with single parent	41
Living with someone other than parents	7
Living with parent who abuses drugs	28
Living with parent who abuses alcohol	36
Living with siblings who abuse drugs or alcohol	23
Living with siblings who are chronic absentees	29
Living in a high crime area	41
Living in a home with no telephone	25
Living in a home with no washer or dryer	10
Living in a home with no alarm clock	19

19 *Spelling and Apostrophes*

SPELLING PROBLEMS

All types of writers have one thing in common: they make spelling mistakes. Some of the most successful writers in the world misspell words from time to time. Familiarity with the language, however, usually prevents these writers from making a great many spelling errors. Inexperienced writers often make more spelling errors because they haven't done enough reading and writing to connect the sound of words with the look of words—especially those words that are not spelled the way they are pronounced.

If you have serious difficulties with spelling, you should take a closer look at your writing. Even though the number of errors you make may seem overwhelming, you will probably find that many of those errors are the same type of mistake. Thus, even though you may have ten or fifteen spelling mistakes in one paragraph, your problems may be limited to two or three types of errors. Once you find your individual patterns of error, you can start reducing your spelling mistakes. You may discover, for example, that you misspell words that you don't pronounce distinctly.

Incorrect		*Correct*
jist	instead of	j*u*st
contac	instead of	contac*t*
sanwich	instead of	san*d*wich
then	instead of	th*a*n

ir rev ve lant	instead of	ir *rel e* vant
Feb u ar y	instead of	Feb *ru* a ry

Perhaps you tend to misspell words that are not spelled the way they are pronounced. Silent consonants, for example, often cause spelling problems.

The silent *b* in words like debt and doubt

The silent *g* in words like sign, reign, and foreign

The silent *h* in words like while, what, ghetto, and exhaust

The silent *k* in words like knife, knock, knuckle, and knew

The silent *gh* in words like night, fight, sigh, and righteous

Silent vowels can also cause problems, especially the silent *e* in words like love, breathe, and ninety and the silent *e*'s that make *le* endings sound like *l*. Thus, people sometimes write *cattl* instead of *cattle* or *motorcycl* instead of *motorcycle*.

Other spelling problems are caused by two-letter combinations that produce the sound of another letter.

A *ph* that sounds like an *f*

phone	sophomore
pharmacy	morphine
trophy	sophisticated

A *gh* that sounds like an *f*

laugh	rough
graph	tough

A *ch* that sounds like a *k*

chemistry	school
chrome	echo
parochial	anchor

EXERCISE 19A: FINDING MISSPELLED WORDS

Correct any misspelled words you see in the following sentences.

1.   I read an article yesterday about kemical additives in chicens.

2.   By the time I was finished, I had nots in my stomack.

3. Now I loath the tast of chicken.

4. In fact, I'm not even abl to look at one.

5. I start thinking about my poor littel cromosones.

6. Chemical additives are sometimes nercessary, but they can also mak peopl sic.

7. That's why consumer protection organizations are offen at odds with chemical kompanies.

8. They are fighting for the rights of the averag American consumer who doesn't always no wat he or she is eating.

9. Sometimes the battls uncover rather startling information.

10. Undoubtedly, chemical teknology can save lives, but it can also destroy them.

Words that are supposed to have double consonants are also frequently misspelled. Here are some of the most commonly misspelled words:

accommodate	embarrass	parallel
beginning	immediately	possession
necessary	approximately	written
committee	occasion	success
correspondence	occurrence	recommend

243

EXERCISE 19B: WORDS WITH DOUBLE CONSONANTS

Sound out each of the following words and divide them into syllables according to the way you pronounced them. Then look up the words in your dictionary and see if you pronounced them correctly. Copy the word down exactly as it appears in the dictionary and pronounce it, syllable by syllable.

1.   accomplishment _____   _____

2.   curriculum   _____   _____

3.   dissolved   _____   _____

4.   interruption   _____   _____

5.   aggravation   _____   _____

6.   naturally   _____   _____

7.   syllable   _____   _____

8.   questionnaire   _____   _____

9.   college   _____   _____

10.   professor   _____   _____

   Homophones cause problems for both good and poor spellers. Homophones are words that sound alike but differ in spelling and meaning. Some examples are:

to	two	too	principal	principle	
there	their	they're	through	threw	
your	you're		weather	whether	
hear	here		whole	hole	
whose	who's		affect	effect	
no	know		led	lead	
new	knew		medal	metal	
forth	fourth		desert	dessert	
won	one		accept	except	

EXERCISE 19C: USING HOMOPHONES

Break into small groups and choose ten of the sound-alike word sets above. Then write ten sentences using one set of homophones in each sentence. If you're not sure what some of the words mean, look them up in your dictionary.

EXAMPLE: I *knew* what he meant, even though the word was *new* to me.

1. _____
2. _____
3. _____
4. _____
5. _____
6. _____
7. _____
8. _____
9. _____
10. _____

Plural endings are another common source of misspelled words, especially if the words end in *y* or *ey*. If this is one of your problems, the following guidelines should help:

When a noun ends in *ey,* just add an *s* to form the plural:

valley   valleys
attorney   attorneys

Similar sounding word endings, especially *ible/able* and *ence/ance,* always cause spelling problems. You cannot solve these types of errors by simply studying rules. You have to get to know the words through increased reading and writing. Following are some common examples:

respons*ible*   prob*able*
flex*ible*   adjust*able*
incred*ible*   veget*able*
convert*ible*   debat*able*

experi*ence*   appear*ance*
exist*ence*   mainten*ance*
independ*ence*   attend*ance*
obed*ience*   perform*ance*

245

EXERCISE 19D: WORD ENDINGS

Change each of the following verbs into nouns by adding an appropriate word ending: *ance, ence,* or *tion.* If the word ends in a silent *e,* drop the *e* before adding the word ending. If the word ends in *y,* change the *y* to *i* before adding anything. Otherwise, just connect the word ending to the root word.

EXAMPLES:

Verb	+	*Word Ending*	=	*Noun*
inherit	+	ance	=	inherit•ance
reassure	+	ance	=	reassur•ance
comply	+	ance	=	compli•ance

	VERB		WORD ENDING		NOUN
1.	insure	+	_____	=	_____
2.	transfer	+	_____	=	_____
3.	disappear	+	_____	=	_____
4.	produce	+	_____	=	_____
5.	guide	+	_____	=	_____
6.	forbear	+	_____	=	_____
7.	calculate	+	_____	=	_____
8.	cohere	+	_____	=	_____
9.	transform	+	_____	=	_____
10.	interfere	+	_____	=	_____

Other common misspellings are caused by a number of factors. Careful proofreading can often help eliminate errors like the following:

Incorrect		*Correct*
grammer	instead of	grammar
seperate	instead of	separate
untill	instead of	until
recieve	instead of	receive
gose	instead of	goes
alot	instead of	a lot
with out	instead of	without

Once you have identified your individual patterns of misspelling words, you can start improving your spelling, but you can't do it without a dictionary. A dictionary not only shows you how to spell a word; it also teaches you how to pronounce the word and tells you what the word means. Seeing the syllabification and pronunciation of a word is very helpful. You can then sound out the word and see how the spoken word corresponds to the written word. For example, once you see the word *in•ter•est•ing* in a dictionary and notice that it has four distinct syllables, you may never again misspell the word like this: *in•tres•ting*.

Careful proofreading is, of course, indispensable in eliminating spelling errors. Learning to proofread *word by word* is the key to successful proofreading. Sometimes, you have to pretend that you are looking at someone else's writing. Writers often find others' mistakes more quickly than they find their own. You might try proofreading lines from right to left or beginning at the end of your paper instead of at the beginning. It's harder to overlook spelling errors when you proofread in these ways.

EXERCISE 19E: PROOFREADING

The following verse will sound familiar to you, but many of the words have been misspelled. Proofread the passage carefully, using your dictionary to check correct spellings. After you have corrected the misspelled words, read each line word by word from right to left and see if you missed any misspelled words.

Twas the nite befor Cristmas and all thru the howse,

Not a creeture was stiring, not even a mouse.

The stokings were hung by the chimny with caer,

In hopes thet St. Nickolas soon wood be there.

The childrn were nesseled all snug in there beds,

Wile visuns of sugar plums danced in their heds.

An Ma in her kirchief and I in my cap,

Had jist setled down for a long wintr's nap,

When out on the roof there a rose such a clater,

I sprang to the flore to see wat was the matter

Away to the windo I flu in a flash,

Tor open the shutters and through up the sash.

The moon on the brest of the nu fallen sno,

Gave the lustre of midday to objecs below,

Then wat to my wandring eyes did apear,

But a miniture slay and ate tiny rein deer

With a littl old driver so livelie and quik

I new at a moment it must be St. Nik.

More rapid then eagels his courses they flew

With a sleigh ful of toys and St. Nickolas to,

And he wistled and shouted and called them by kname,

Now Dashr, now Dancer, now Prancr and Vixen,

On Comit, on Cupid, on Donner and Blitzen,

To the top of the portch to the top of the wal

Now dash away, dash away, dash away all!

THE APOSTROPHE

Many of the words you use in your everyday speech are contractions—two words shortened into one. For example:

Contractions
I *do not* = I *don't*
You *will not* = You *won't*
They *cannot* = They *can't*

Contractions
I am = I'm
It is = It's
You are = You're

Contractions
He *is not* = He *isn't*
They *are not* = They *aren't*
She *was not* = She *wasn't*
They *were not* = They *weren't*

As you can see from these lists, many contractions are formed from the combination of *not* and a verb. In contractions, *not* is shortened to *n't*. An apostrophe stands for the missing letter *o*.

Sometimes an apostrophe is used in place of more than one missing letter:

Contractions
I will = I'll
He will = He'll
She will = She'll
You will = You'll
They will = They'll

Contractions
I have = I've
He has = He's
She has = She's
You have = You've
They have = They've

Contractions
I would = I'd
You would = You'd
She could have = She could've
You should have = You should've
I would have = I would've

Three contractions in particular are often misused because they sound like other words. They are:

it's	sounds like	its
who's	sounds like	whose
you're	sounds like	your

Use *it's* only when you mean *it is*. Use *who's* when you mean *who is*. And use *you're* when you mean *you are*.

EXERCISE 19F: USING CONTRACTIONS

Substitute contractions to make the following song titles read the way they were originally written.

1.   "It is impossible"

2. "I cannot give you anything but love"

_____

3. "I am sittin' on top of the world"

_____

4. "I do not want to set the world on fire"

_____

5. "They will be comin' round the mountain when they come"

_____

6. "I will be seeing you"

_____

7. "I am sorry"

_____

8. "We will be together again"

_____

9. "She is always a woman to me"

_____

10. "It is a sin to tell a lie"

_____

The apostrophe is also used to show possession. For example, "Mrs. O'Leary's cow" means "the cow that belongs to Mrs. O'Leary." Sometimes writers worry about where to put apostrophes. Most possessive nouns are governed by two simple guidelines:

To show possession for a singular noun, add an 's.
To show possession for a plural noun, add an s'.

For example, "I have to find the _boy's_ parent" means that there is only one boy. "I have to find the boys' parents" means that there is more than one boy.

Singular Possessive	Plural Possessive
college's	colleges'
animal's	animals'
welder's	welders'

The need for an apostrophe is frequently overlooked in expressions such as these:

one day's pay
three week's vacation
two month's salary
four year's work

Here are a few more things you should know about apostrophes:

1. Even if a noun ends in *s*, you still add an *'s* to show possession.
   Dickens's novel = the novels written by Dickens
   Joneses' neighbors = the people who have to keep up with the Joneses

2. To show possession in a compound subject or completer, just add an *'s* to the second noun.
   Dick and *Jane's* lives were spent communicating in three-word sentences about their pets.
   Spot and Puff's lives were far more exciting than *Dick* and *Jane's.*

3. If a noun is a hyphenated word, add *'s* only to the last part of the word.
   My *mother-in-law's* car . . .
   The *Vice-President's* favorite dessert . . .

251

4. Don't confuse possessives with plurals.

   Incorrect: The Jefferson's are coming for dinner.

                      It's hard to keep up with the Jones's.

   Correct: The Jeffersons are coming to dinner.

                      It's hard to keep up with the Joneses.

EXERCISE 19G: USING APOSTROPHES

In the following sentences, add apostrophes where you think they are needed.

1. Ernie called his paper "The American Doctoral Degree: Its Use and Abuse."

2. In his paper, he took a critical look at higher educations most cherished degree.

3. He noted that, in the United States, earned professional doctorates first appeared in the late eighteenth century.

4. The first doctorate was a medical degree granted in 1770 by Kings College (now Columbia University).

5. Approximately 100 institutions granted the Ph.D. before 1900.

6. Ernies paper also dealt with the practice of awarding honorary doctorates.

7. The practice began in 1692 when Harvard awarded an honorary degree to its first president, Increase Mather.

8. Today, nearly 9,000 honorary doctorates are awarded each year.

9. Apparently, however, these doctorates are no longer used solely for the purpose of awarding scholarly achievement.

10. Today, an honorary doctorate is often a universitys way of thanking a benefactor.

11. Actually, the honorary degrees tarnished image began after the Civil War when granting honorary degrees became an academic fad.

12. Between 1870 and 1900, hundreds of doctorates were handed out to persons with nonacademic backgrounds.

13. One of these doctorates was not even awarded by a college; it was awarded by Philadelphias Central High School!

14. A few colleges and universities refuse to grant honorary degrees.

15. For example, Stanfords first president resolved that no honorary degrees would ever be given at Stanford, and no one at Stanford has ever disregarded his wishes.

WRITING FROM READING

Taking Ownership of Your Writing

To a great extent, our writing is a reflection of our experiences. That's one of the factors that makes writing so interesting. No two people write in exactly the same way. Just as no two writers discussing the same topic necessarily make the same point, neither will they necessarily use the same means to arrive at their points.

Consider the two approaches to the same topic presented below. One was written by a physics professor, Ernest Zebrowski, Jr.; the other was written by one of his colleagues, a writing instructor. The main idea in both is essentially the same (a sentence is something that is used to express a thought), but each illustrates the point in a different way.

PHYSICS PROFESSOR

Whether a sentence is expressed in words or in symbols, it always provides a way to express a thought. An equation, for example, is really just a sentence that uses symbols instead of words to express a thought. $3 + 3 = 6$ is a perfectly legitimate sentence with a subject, a verb, and an object:

Subject	Verb	Object
Three plus three	equals	six.

Mathematical sentences are read from left to right too, just like English sentences. ($5 > 2$ reads "Five is greater than two.") An equation, then, is simply a shorthand way of expressing a thought with numbers instead of words.

WRITING INSTRUCTOR

A sentence is a group of words that expresses a *thought*. In fact, the word *sentence* itself is derived from a Latin term, *sententia*, which means "a way of thinking." The sentence has been around for thousands of years, but, with the invention of the printing press in the fifteenth century, the sentence gained new prominence. Now hailed as "the basic unit of composition," the sentence can be found almost anywhere. One can even find sentences chiseled on tombstones, scribbled on subway walls, or programmed onto electronic screens. Some are simple, some are compound; some are wordy, others are concise; some are exciting, others are boring; but no matter how they are described, they all have one thing in common: they all express a thought.

Break into small groups and choose one of the topics listed below. Then think of different ways of developing that idea. Think of different audiences, different methods of development, different attitudes toward your topic (for example, a humorous approach versus a serious approach) and think of different ways of organizing your thoughts. Instead of presenting your main idea at the beginning of a paragraph, you might lead up to your controlling idea and place your topic sentence at the end of the paragraph. Compare your decisions with those of other groups in your class. See if they came up with any good ideas that your group didn't think of.

Americans often waste their spare time.

Whoever complained about living a dog's life didn't know my dog.

You can fool some of the people all of the time and all of the people some of the time, but you can't fool Mom.

Anyone can present information, but not everyone can teach.

Children grow up too fast today.

20 *Word Choice*

In studying writing, you need to focus on three different things: organization of the paragraph (and later, organization among paragraphs), structure of sentences, and finally, word choice.

Every time you write, you sharpen your writing skills. You can learn overall organization within a short time, perhaps only a semester. You can learn sentence structure in a relatively short time also, although it may take a little longer than a semester. Word choice is the area in which you can always learn more and can always improve.

Your ability to choose the right words to fit your purpose depends greatly on your understanding of the qualities of words. You need to keep in mind that words are not actual things that can be passed back and forth; words are only *symbols* for the things, ideas, and feelings that you try to communicate. The process of communicating through words is complex indeed, but a useful method for classifying words according to their qualities is *general* versus *specific* and *abstract* versus *concrete*.

GENERAL VERSUS SPECIFIC WORDS

General words name (put a label on) a whole class or group; specific words apply to a member of a class. Thus, *game fish* is the name or label applied to a very large class of fish, so *game fish* is a general term. *Muskellunge*, a member of that group, is specific. Consider the following examples:

General	Specific
tree	loblolly pine
bird	emperor penguin
myth	Golden Fleece
structure	Grand Coulee Dam
car	Fiat Spider
boat	inflatable dinghy

The distinction between general and specific is relative: *mountains* is more general than *Appalachian Mountains,* but *Stone Mountain* is more specific than *Appalachian Mountains.* The choice of a general word or a more specific one is not a matter of right or wrong; the choice should depend on purpose. Very often, however, you can immediately improve your writing by replacing general words with more specific ones. For example, the general word *say* could be replaced by a more specific word such as *mutter, mumble, whisper, drawl, shout,* or *screech.*

ABSTRACT VERSUS CONCRETE WORDS

Abstract words or terms name ideas, qualities, or concepts—things you cannot see, touch, taste, weigh, or measure. For example, *beauty* names an abstract quality, a set of ideas and values apart from any object or individual.

Concrete words or terms name things that you can see, touch, taste, weigh, or measure. For example, such words as *fishhook, orange,* and *locomotive* name things that you can see or touch or test with your senses.

General and specific words, abstract and concrete words—all have their place and purpose in the language. But when you want to appeal directly to your readers' senses, you need to use concrete words. Concrete words have image-making power because they are understood through the senses of sight, sound, smell, taste, and touch.

The dress she wore was *pink with white polka dots.*
All the food tasted of *lard and tin.*
Parked in the shade after the hard drive, the old Buick *ticked quietly.*
The pine needles *prickled* between his toes.
The *odor of the hog pen* clung to his overalls.

DARN PINE NEEDLES!

EXERCISE 20A: BEING SPECIFIC AND CONCRETE

Change the following sentences to make them more specific or concrete or a combination of both. Notice how the sentences become more interesting as you make them more specific and concrete.

EXAMPLE: *General:* The basketball player played a good game last night.
Specific: Moses Malone scored thirty-eight points and grabbed twenty-four rebounds last night.
Concrete: Leaping and whirling, shooting from every corner of the court, Moses Malone dazzled the screaming fans and the Detroit Pistons last night.

General: She was rich.
Specific: Rhonda inherited $30 million.
Concrete: Rhonda wore elegant soft furs and as much gold as Mr. T, she owned a lavender Rolls Royce and several flashy sports cars, and she had beach-front estates in all the major resorts of the world.

1. The magazine was popular.

2. The injury was painful.

3. The animal was big.

4. The room was noisy.

5. The game is dangerous.

6. His bedroom was messy.

7. The man was a crook.

8. The job was good.

9. The police officer was harsh.

10. The child abused drugs.

WORDINESS

Try to eliminate those wordy phrases that creep into your writing. Try not to use two or three words where one would do. Note how each of the following phrases can be replaced by a single word:

in the event that	if
at the present time	now (or today)
during the time that	while
round in shape	round
bring to a conclusion	conclude
because of the fact that	because

Also, avoid the *overuse* of such words as *very, truly, certainly*, and *actually*. These words seldom add anything to your message, so they can be eliminated without changing your meaning.

EXERCISE 20B: ELIMINATING WORDINESS

Rewrite the following sentences to eliminate as many words as possible without changing the meaning.

1. During the time that he was in class, the band was rehearsing outside the classroom window.

2. In this modern day and age, we should not have millions of unemployed youths.

3. Because of the fact that Juanita had never seen Sergio's older sister, I am of the opinion that she must have expected someone very different from Marguerite.

4. They planned to bring the investigation to a conclusion before the election.

5. In the event that I see Jake, I'll give him your message.

6. Florida is a state that offers the finest water sports in America.

7. The turtle's shell is oval in shape, with a distinctive crimping around the edges.

8. We were given the choice of choosing whether or not we would stay at the base camp.

9. The important essentials for the climb had been supplied by the British.

10. Because of the fact that he is a great story teller, they agreed to take him along on the trip to Oregon.

CHOOSING SUBJECTS AND VERBS

Choosing the correct words is the main job of the writer. It is the correct word, the colorful word, that entices people to read what you have written. Since the most important words in a sentence are the subjects and verbs, let's concentrate on those first.

Subjects

If at all possible, choose subjects capable of action, for this gives your sentence movement and vitality. If you choose a subject such as "the sidewalks," you have chosen a subject that cannot act. Sidewalks cannot act; they cannot jump or debate or throw a kiss. As a result, you will be compelled to use a linking verb or a verb of being rather than an action verb.

Often you can rearrange sentences so that actors can replace passive subjects and action verbs can replace *to be* verbs. Instead of "The sidewalks were slippery" or "The ice was dangerous," you could change the sentence to read: "People inched along the dangerous ice."

You should also try to be specific when you write. Instead of making a general statement such as "The results were spectacular," you could say specifically

The new training program resulted in athletes' running faster, jumping higher, and throwing farther.

or

The committee discovered that Joe had exaggerated, Stella had denied her previous statement, and Larry had skipped town.

or

Mary raised her English grade from a D to a B, Debbie improved her reading level from 6.4 to 8.9, and Bill changed from chump to champ.

You can see from these sentences that the original sentence—"The results were spectacular"—doesn't tell the readers very much. If you, as a writer, are specific, readers will understand you better. Again, remember that some words are general: *medicine, food, furniture.* Other words are specific: *Bayer aspirin, French fries, love seat.* And still other words are in between: *painkiller, potatoes, living room furniture.*

Sometimes it is fun to "layer" words—that is, to see just how many words you can get between a general word at the top and a specific word at the bottom. Each word on the ladder should be a little more specific than the word above it. For example, let's start with a very general word:

institution

next, we put

educational institution

next,

college

next,

community college

next,

community college of Beaver County.

A name of something is fairly specific, but you could continue the process by adding a part of the institution:

classes at CCBC
English classes
English 155, Lecture C.

See if you can make a list of seven or more words, each more specific than the one above it, starting with each of these general words:

Recreation

Entertainment

Living things

When you write sentences, try to make your subjects and verbs as specific as possible. Instead of just taking the first word that comes to your mind (which is usually a general word), try to get a more specific word that tells the reader a great deal more. Instead of just using a verb like *laughed,* for instance, use a word that tells the reader what the laugh was like—was it a titter, giggle, snicker, teehee, roar, or chuckle?

DENOTATION AND CONNOTATION

Words have two main types of meaning: *denotation* and *connotation.* The denotation of a word is its core meaning, the meaning that points to the thing or idea for which the word stands. In defining words, the dictionary deals primarily with their denotations. The word *clan,* for example, refers to a group or social unit claiming a common ancestor and following the same chieftain.

The *connotation* of a word is the suggestions and associations the word is capable of arousing. The word *clan,* for example, may have quite different associations for different people. For those from a large, close-knit family, *clan* may evoke positive images of family weddings, reunions, and other celebrations. For others, *clan* may suggest kilts, tartan tweeds, and Scottish Highland chieftains. For still others, *clan* may evoke negative images of family feuds (the Hatfields and McCoys) or racial injustice (the Ku Klux Klan).

Several words may have the same *denotation*—that is, they may point to the same person or thing; yet they may have quite different *connotations.* Consider the words *burly, stout, corpulent, fat,* and *obese.* All might be applied to the same physical condition, but the word *burly* has a generally favorable connotation, whereas *fat* and *obese* have strong negative connotations. In addition, the connotation may change with the context in which the word appears. A *slim* paycheck, for example, is not as desirable as a *slim* body.

The main point is this: if you are to communicate your meaning to your readers accurately, the words you choose must have not only the right denotations but the right connotations as well. There are many fine distinctions in connotation, so the range of choices may be enormous. Mark Twain once said that the difference between the almost right word and the right word was the difference between the lightning bug and lightning.

The right word.

The almost right word.

EXERCISE 20C: DENOTATION AND CONNOTATION, SENTENCE LEVEL

In each of the following sentences, both words in each set of parentheses have the same denotation, but very different connotations. For each sentence, choose the word with the correct connotation. Notice how the whole meaning of the sentence would change if you chose the other word. (Use a dictionary if you are unsure of the meaning of any word.)

1. Jennie is a great (politician, senator).

2. She (shuffles, strides) into the Senate (proudly, arrogantly), and her speeches are (bold, impudent).

3. She uses her (skill, craft) in getting (monumental, important) legislation passed.

4. She (memorizes, studies) every bill with an (objective, indifferent) attitude, then supports or opposes it (stubbornly, determinedly).

5. Jennie is (plump, fat) and a bit (dirty, unkempt) but always (merry, silly).

6. On the other hand, I hate Senator Exbob who is a (sober, humorless) (lawyer, shyster).

7. He's a (skinny, slim) man who wears (cheap, inexpensive) clothes.

8.   He is constantly (plotting, planning) in his (cautious, cowardly) way to impress some (important people, bigshots).

9.   He has a lot of (nerve, courage) and is a (devoted, fanatical) campaigner.

10. He is a (thrifty, miserly) man with a (curious, snooping) nature and is a/an (proud, arrogant) creep.

EXERCISE 20D: CONNOTATION AND DENOTATION, PARAGRAPH LEVEL

In the following two paragraphs, underline the words you think are connotative. Then, on the basis of these connotative terms, determine the attitude expressed by each paragraph.

The instructor I remember most warmly was both amusing and effective. He bounced, smiling, into the classroom. He shouted a genial "hello" to the class, tossed his suit jacket at the nearest empty chair, and, striding to the lectern, grasped its sides. He bent toward us with an eager expression and sparkling eyes. When he began to speak to us, however, his voice grew intense, rising and falling to highlight and emphasize his facts and theories. He ranged widely over his subject until he wanted to underscore an important point, and then he revealed the depth of his knowledge by detailed discussion. His enthusiasm and his knowledge made him my favorite instructor.

The instructor who sticks in my mind was boring and incompetent. He stumped, scowling, into the classroom. He yelled an indistinct "good morning" to us, even if it was afternoon. He buttoned up his jacket as if to protect himself from us, strutted over to the lectern, and grabbed its sides. He leaned away from us, his boredom exposed in his dull eyes. When he began to speak, however, his voice seemed to stick at about two notes, making no distinction between important points and superficialities. He bumbled on through his lecture, exposing his narrow, shallow acquaintanceship with his subject. His boredom and his ignorance made him an incompetent pretender of an instructor.

263

METAPHOR

A *metaphor* is an imaginative comparison. It does not literally compare two things of the same class, such as the administrations of Presidents Lincoln and Grant. Rather, it compares two things that could not be compared in any literal sense. Metaphor, in other words, uses nonliteral comparisons to describe and identify one thing in terms of another. For example, when a poet wrote, "My heart is like a singing bird," she did not mean that her heart had feathers, that it was capable of trilling bird calls, or that it slept with its head tucked under its wing. She meant that she was very happy. By comparing her feelings to the image of a singing bird, she made herself sound happier than she would have sounded if she had just said "I'm very happy."

One purpose of metaphor is clarity. For instance, another writer entitled his book about his childhood *The Golden Age.* He was, of course, not referring to metal or color but to the precious quality of gold to emphasize how precious his memories of childhood were. *Memory* is an abstraction—that is, a word that cannot be understood through the five senses but only through the intellect. (*Color* is an abstract word; you can't see it. But *green* is a concrete word; when you hear the word *green*, you can see that color.) Since these precious memories are an abstraction, it is rather difficult to communicate their precise sense. All abstractions differ somewhat from one individual to another, just as memories differ. However, the idea of a wonderful time is clearly communicated by the phrase "the golden age."

In a famous metaphor, General Sherman said, "War is hell." Literally, of course, this makes no sense; war is armed conflict between nations; hell is a theological idea concerning damnation. There is, however, no question about what Sherman meant. Two abstractions have been made emotionally and intellectually clear.

Another purpose of metaphor is emphasis. Had Sherman said, "War is dangerous and uncomfortable and painful," readers would all agree, but they would not pay much attention to him. The metaphor he chose, however, is so vivid that it makes a strong and memorable impression. Another vivid metaphor, this one from the Bible, says "All flesh is grass." Needless to say, flesh is *not* grass, but the point the metaphor makes is that life is short. Grass dies at the end of each growing season, and human life, too, is relatively brief. Therefore, to say that flesh is grass stresses the brevity of life.

Sometimes a writer will go from a literal statement into a metaphorical statement to *intensify* or add a new quality to an idea. For instance, Robert Frost began one poem with the botanical fact that the apple, pear, plum, and rose all belong to the same botanical family, the *Rosaceae.* In the last two lines, he moved into a metaphor that compared his beloved to a rose.

THE ROSE FAMILY

The rose is a rose,
And was always a rose.
But the theory now goes
That the apple's a rose,
And the pear is, and so's
The plum, I suppose.
The dear only knows
What will next prove a rose.
You, of course, are a rose—
But were always a rose.

Robert Frost,
West Running Brook
(New York: Holt, Rinehart,
1928), p. 7.

Frequently, a metaphor goes beyond a single comparison and becomes an *extended metaphor*—that is, a cluster of related comparisons. In the following poem the poet states in the underlying metaphor that a life is no longer than a winter's day. She then extends her metaphor by comparing a short life to a very short day in which only breakfast is eaten. Other, longer lives have a midday meal as well, and still others are long enough to have supper also. The metaphor makes the point that all lives, long or short, must end, and that all living must be "paid for" in trouble and pain.

Our life is nothing but a winters day,
Some only break their fast and so away,
Others stay dinner, and depart full fed,
The deeper age but sups and goes to bed.
Hee's most in debt, that lingers out the day,
Who dys betimes, has lesse and lesse to pay.

Margaret Burnell (1687),
quoted in Walter de la Mare, *Come Hither*
(New York: Macmillan, 1932), p. 234.

EXERCISE 20E: USING METAPHORS

Try writing out your interpretations of the following metaphors.

1.   Life is just a bowl of cherries.

_____

2.   My love is like a red, red rose.

_____

265

3. A mighty fortress is our God.

_____

4. Life is a carousel.

_____

5. Does the road lead uphill all the way?
   Yes, to the very end.

_____

6. My mind to me a kingdom is.

_____

7. My love is like to ice, and I to fire.

_____

8. Your support has let me hit the ground running.

_____

9. Stop changing your mind; you're always reversing your field.

_____

10. With rue my heart is laden
        For golden friends I had,
    For many a rose-lipped maiden
        And many a light foot lad.

    By brooks too broad for leaping
        The lightfoot boys are laid;
    The rose-lipped girls are sleeping
        In fields where roses fade.

> A. E. Houseman, *Shropshire Lad*
> (London: Faber & Faber, 1896), p. 211.

_____

_____

_____

WRITING FROM READING

Word Choice

No writer pays as much attention to word choice as a poet does. Because a poem is short, each word must carry as much meaning as possible. The poet weighs and balances each word of the poem so that he or she conveys, in relatively few words, the precise idea and the exact emotion intended.

Verse as well as poetry demands careful selection of words because no two words mean *exactly* the same thing. *Verse* and *poetry* are themselves two words that illustrate this point. Although they both denote a particular form of literature, they connote differing ideas of the quality of that literature. Poetry deals with lofty thought and soaring emotion (notice how the words *lofty* and *soaring* connote a heavenward sort of direction). Verse deals with commonplace observation expressed in clever language.

Look at the following verse written by a nine-year-old child in the fourth grade:

> Babies howl,
> Children whine,
> Bears growl,
> Owls moan,
> Losers weep,
> But Big Boys
> Don't cry.

The first five lines are two-word, parallel sentences that emphasize that all living things complain. The *howling* of babies suggests the infants' rather animal objection to hunger pangs and wet diapers. The *whining* of children implies a somewhat toned-down despair of getting their own way. The *growling* of bears and the *moaning* of owls indicates the sounds those animals make as they express their discontent with their worlds.

When the author reaches the fifth line, he is beginning to focus on his precise meaning: life is hard. The sound he wants us to hear is the weeping of life's losers. He comes to his point with the last two lines, swinging into the contrast on the word *but*. Big Boys—an ultimate goal—rise above complaint, even if complaining is justified.

Notice how the author of this verse identifies himself as a child. You'd know he was very young from his writing. Babies and children, bears and owls are characters that people a child's world. Grownups don't set as their goals the behavior of Big Boys. Neither do little girls, so you know the author is a little boy. You also know that he has the psychological and moral insight to realize that manhood demands that he rise above feeling sorry for himself. To express this insight, he uses the truism that adults have foisted on little boys for generations: Big boys don't cry. His words and phrases are childlike, but his insight is sadly mature.

Now consider the following verse, in which a grown man recalls one of childhood's more frustrating experiences:

BOBBY'S FIRST POEM

It rely is ridikkelus
how Uncle Charley tikkles us
at eester and at mikklemus
upon the nursery floor.

and rubbs our chins and bites our ears
like firty fousand poler bears
and roars like lyons down the stares
and won't play enny more.

Ogden Nash, ed.,
The Moon Is Shining Bright as Day
(Philadelphia: J. B. Lippincott, 1953), p. 38.

The choice of words in the verse communicates much of the meaning. For example, the words *mikklemus* (Michaelmas) and *nursery* indicate that the poem is British rather than American, for Michaelmas is not an American holiday, and American kids play in playrooms, not nurseries.

Write a short paragraph in which you say what specific word choices communicate to you. For example, what's conveyed by the title in the name *Bobby* and his *First* poem? Why are so many words misspelled and evidently mispronounced? Did you ever have an uncle like Uncle Charley? What kind of person is Uncle Charley? How is the last line a contrast to the first seven? What psychological question does Bobby bring up? Remember to limit your analysis to the words in the poem.

21 *The Topic Sentence*

If a teacher asked you to write a paragraph about your pet, how would you start out? If you start out without much thought, you might come up with sentences like these:

My pet is a goldfish.
My horse is named Sheila.
I have a pet parakeet.
I love my dog Harry.
Let me tell you about my cat.

If you start out with a sentence like one of these, you will probably not be able to write a good paragraph. None of these sentences offers you any direction or focus. Your paragraph might turn out something like this:

Let me tell you about my cat. She was a pretty good mother, but we gave all her kittens away. She is very playful, and she will play with anything: a mouse, catnip, a spool of thread, a ping pong ball, an old sock. My cat's name is Ginger. My sister loves cats. Sometimes Ginger just wants to be left alone, and she'll hiss at you if you bother her. Her kittens were adorable. She's a picky eater. She'll eat cat food, but only the most expensive canned kind. My father is not crazy about cats. He tolerates Ginger, but I love her. She doesn't know any tricks at all except those *she* made up. I don't think she's very smart. She likes to get into a paper bag and fight it. She can get in and out of any place she wants to, though. We can't keep her out of the

bedrooms or even the house. Maybe she is smart! She would probably be classified as an alley cat, but she has some Persian in her. She's a great cat.

THE PURPOSE OF A TOPIC SENTENCE

The group of sentences you have just read looks like a good paragraph, but it doesn't read like a good paragraph. A paragraph is a series of sentences on a *single narrowed subject.* Did you feel, as you read about Ginger, that you were reading a series of unrelated thoughts, that you were being jerked from one idea to another? You were indeed—and that's because there is no unity or "oneness" to the paragraph. What's more, a "paragraph" on any of the other sentences at the beginning of this chapter probably wouldn't be much better because none of those sentences is a *topic sentence.*

A topic sentence has all the attributes of any other sentence—that is, it is complete, clear, and well worded—but it also has an *attitude.* An attitude is a word or phrase that tells the reader *what you are going to say about the subject.*

The reason that the paragraph about Ginger the cat is so disjointed is that the writer started with a sentence that was not a topic sentence. It had no attitude. "Let me tell you about my cat" gives the writer no focus and no guidance on what to say about the subject.

Before you start to write, you should decide what you want to say about your subject. Suppose you choose to write about your cat. Do you want to discuss the cat's appearance? The cat's personality? The cat's intelligence? The feelings of the family members toward the cat?

Once you have decided what you want to say about your cat, you must announce this decision in the topic sentence, which is usually the first sentence of the paragraph. Depending on what you want to tell about your cat, you might use any of the following sentences. (The attitude has been italicized. The subject, in all cases, is the cat.)

My cat Ginger is *beautiful.*

My cat is *playful, but only when she wants to be.*

My cat is either *very dumb or very smart.*

My cat evokes *different responses* from every member of the family.

Not all paragraphs have topic sentences. And not every piece of writing needs to *open* with a topic sentence in order to have a clear focus. But most of the writing you do and much of the writing you read in school is expository writing, which means writing that *explains.* A standard expository paragraph usually begins with a topic sentence.

Starting a paragraph with a topic sentence that states the main idea helps both the writer and the readers. It helps the writer stick to the subject, and it helps the readers focus on what the writer is telling them. When a writer is explaining a point, he or she can help the readers keep important details in focus by stating the main idea first. Many writers make their main points at the beginning of a paragraph and then go on to explain them; much expository writing (many of your textbooks, for example) thus opens with paragraphs that state the main ideas. Note, however, that frequently—in narrative or descriptive prose, for example—a writer can make his or her idea clear to the readers without stating it explicitly in an opening topic sentence. A topic sentence, in other words, may be placed at any point in the paragraph, even though it usually appears somewhere near the beginning or end.

Read the following paragraph, and notice how much easier it is to understand than the previous example. This paragraph is unified by its topic sentence.

Everyone thinks that my cat, Ginger, is very dumb because she never listens, but the truth is Ginger can be pretty smart when she wants to be. She can get into and out of any place. Once she caught a mouse and tried to bring it in the front door. My mother screamed and slammed the door. Ginger immediately climbed the trellis to the second floor porch roof, entered my parents' room through a window, and deposited her prize on the bed. Once she got into a supposedly locked closet and opened all the wrapped presents in it. She also invents games for herself. She taught herself ping pong, for example. After watching part of a game, she leaped on the table and started batting the ball back to me with her paw. She played quite a bit for three or four

271

weeks and got really good. She also made up a game with a paper bag; she would walk into it, knock it over, and walk out the other side. If we tried to catch her, she would vary the side she came out of—and beat us every time. I think Ginger is smart; she just doesn't like our games and our orders. She does everything her way.

EXPRESSING AN ATTITUDE

Usually, the subject of the paragraph is the subject of your topic sentence. The subject tells the readers what the paragraph will be about. The attitude tells the readers what the rest of the paragraph will explain *about* the subject.

If the topic sentence does not have an attitude, there is nothing more to say; if it were a conversation, it would be a dead end.

John: The President made his State of the Union address last night.
Mary: Right.

John: It snowed again yesterday.
Mary: Right.

John: Johnny Carson has been on TV for many years.
Mary: Right.

Notice the difference if your sentence has an attitude.

John: The President's State of the Union Address was the *best* I've ever heard.

Mary: Really? Why do you say that?

John: This is the *worst* winter we've ever had.

Mary: Why do you think so?

John: Johnny Carson is a great entertainer.

Mary: Convince me.

In each of these examples, the conversation will go on because John must *explain* his statement; he must support his statement by facts, reasons, arguments, comparisons, contrasts, definitions, examples, or analysis. Therefore, he has a reason to write a paragraph—a series of sentences that develop his idea. A topic sentence must have an attitude that is *capable of development.* If the sentence has no attitude, there is nothing further to say, and no development is necessary.

EXERCISE 21A: RECOGNIZING GOOD TOPIC SENTENCES

Put an *X* on the blank in front of each sentence that would be an acceptable topic sentence.

____ 1.   "20/20" is a television news magazine show.

____ 2.   "20/20" is a very educational TV program.

____ 3.   The BMW is a remarkable automobile.

____ 4.   BMWs are manufactured in Germany.

____ 5.   Mary is a secretary.

____ 6.   Mary is the perfect secretary.

____ 7.   Thirty-two million people in the United States are disabled.

____ 8.   The disabled are often ignored by architects when they design "public" buildings.

____ 9.   Many Americans go camping every year.

____ 10.   Camping is fun.

EXERCISE 21B: IDENTIFYING SUBJECT AND ATTITUDE

Underline the subject and circle the attitude in each of the following sentences. If a sentence has no attitude, circle the number.

1. The teacher's job is a tough one.

2. Being a good parent is the toughest job there is.

3. Television is a waste of time.

4. Many television programs are educational.

5. High-rise apartment buildings are dangerous if there is a fire.

6. My boyfriend wears an earring.

7. Mardi Gras means Fat Tuesday.

8. Driving a taxi is a fun job.

9. "St. Elsewhere" is the best show on television.

10. Extremists of any kind are frightening.

EXERCISE 21C: IDENTIFYING SUBJECT AND ATTITUDE

Now try some sentences that are a little more complex. Underline the subject and circle the attitude in each of the following sentences. Remember that the subject is what the paragraph is about. The attitude tells what the paragraph will say about the subject.

EXAMPLE: *Topic sentence:* Of all the (romantic) places in the world I think the Royal Hawaiian Hotel on Waikiki Beach is tops.

What will the paragraph be about? Royal Hawaiian Hotel.

What will the paragraph tell about the Royal Hawaiian? Most (romantic.)

Topic sentence: Although I enjoy my job, my (greatest pleasure) is a demanding, frustrating, exhilarating round of golf.

What will the paragraph be about? Golf.

What will the paragraph tell about golf? (Greatest pleasure.)

1. Becoming a private in the army must be frustrating for someone who is used to being the boss.

2. After graduation, we had a party no one will ever forget.

3. Of all the boring jobs around the house, dusting is the worst.

4. Having believed in God all my life, I was frightened at the atheist's speech.

5. The worst remedy for truancy is in-school suspension.

6. My only true love is baseball.

7. My first date with Kim was a disaster.

8. Of all my classes, my favorite is English.

9. The toughest thing about college is not the classes, nor the work, nor the homesickness; it's the food.

10. Lori's dream of becoming a star died Thursday night.

WRITING FROM READING

Topic Sentences

> *It is hard for me to decide what to do when every important person in my life expects something different from me.* My mother expects me to spend all my time on college work. She expects me to get an A in everything. When I showed her my first-semester grades, a string of B's of which I was rather proud, she snorted. "It seems to me that anyone who sat in class for as long as you did should get an A in *something!*" On the other hand, my dad doesn't want me "to worry my head" about difficult courses and impossible professors. "It'll be O.K.," he says, "we'll work it out." My older sister demands a great social life. "Don't spend all your time on books," she warns. "College is the place to have fun." My roommate, who is president of the sorority, looks hurt when she feels I don't do my share of work there. My grandfather warns me against becoming so involved in books and being so career-minded that I'll turn off all prospective husbands and deny him any great-grandchildren. My Aunt Gracie just screams, "No drugs, no drugs, stay away from drugs!" It's no wonder I fit the description of a "crazy, mixed-up kid."

The topic sentence (set in italics) in this paragraph gives the writing unity. Without the topic sentence, you would have merely a series of sentences telling of advice or direction given the writer by a group of people important to her. Only with the addition of the topic sentence does the paragraph have a clear focus from the beginning.

In order to get a closer look at how writing styles vary, try this little research project. Form a small group with four of your classmates. Each of you choose a different textbook and then select a chapter from that textbook as your research base. First, count the number of paragraphs in the chapter and record that number. How many of these paragraphs have topic sentences? From the total number of paragraphs in the chapter, what percentage contains topic sentences? Compare your findings with those of other members in your group. Now find the total number of paragraphs from all of the five different chapters and calculate the total percentage of paragraphs that contain topic sentences.

From your findings, what conclusions can you draw about the use of topic sentences in your textbook sample? Did the frequent use of topic sentences depend in part on the subject matter of the text or on the particular chapter you chose to analyze? Did one author use more transitional paragraphs than another? (Transitional paragraphs are usually very brief; they act as bridges from one paragraph to another. They rarely contain topic sentences.) Were the chapters with more topic sentences easier to understand than those with few topic sentences, or was the difference too insignificant to measure?

Now take a closer look at the *placement* of topic sentences. How many paragraphs opened with a topic sentence? How many topic sentences appeared somewhere in the beginning (in the first one or two sentences)? How many appeared at the end of a paragraph? How many appeared somewhere between the beginning and the end of a paragraph? Did the textbooks differ very much in the placement of topic sentences? Compare your response to this question with those of other members of your group.

What have you learned about the use of topic sentences in your textbook? What have you learned about the placement of topic sentences in your textbook? Record your conclusions and compare them with those of the other research groups in your class. See if you can find any areas of strong disagreement.

Conduct the same research project using five articles from different magazines. See if you find any significant differences in the number of topic sentences used in your textbooks and the number of topic sentences used in the magazine articles. (Don't choose five news magazines or five sports magazines. Try to get different types of magazines.)

22 *Paragraph Unity*

As you learned in Chapter 21, most of the writing you do in college is *expository* writing, which explains something. In expository writing, you choose a topic and develop it so that your readers understand your point and, ideally, agree with you.

To gain understanding and agreement, a good paragraph needs unity, logical order, and coherence. This chapter considers paragraph unity.

The root of the word *unity* means *one*. To achieve unity in your writing, all you really have to worry about is oneness. You make a statement about *one* thing or idea, and you choose all of your details to support that one idea.

HOW TO ACHIEVE UNITY

Selection of Details

Like a photographer, you must focus your readers' attention on one main idea. You provide this in your topic sentence. Every succeeding sentence you write must relate back to that topic sentence. Any sentence that is not relevant to the topic sentence blurs the focus, so you must delete it from the paragraph. Each sentence should add something to the idea you are developing. When you think you have enough supporting details to make your idea clear, you then write a concluding sentence which sums up what you have just said.

When your paragraph is unified, all of your sentences have a clear relationship to each other and all explain your main point. When your paragraph is not unified, you are apt to confuse your readers about what your idea really is because you have digressed from that idea or even contradicted it.

Here is a first draft one student wrote of a paragraph:

> I have a terrible dog. He's a nuisance morning and night because he barks every time someone comes close to our house. Once he barked like mad at two o'clock in the morning. When we finally went downstairs to shut him up we saw that someone had tried to jimmy our back door. Another annoying habit that dog has is digging in the garden. Last summer he dug up three young tomato plants. One day when he was digging he found the wallet my husband had lost the year before. He isn't very friendly with other dogs who come into our yard and jump on the children playing. He chases them right out. Perhaps the worst thing he does is get underfoot all the time. Wherever I go, he wants to trot right along beside me. When I go to bed, he sleeps on the rug at the foot of the bed. When I sit down to read or knit, he sits in front of me with his head in my lap and his brown eyes glowing with love. You know, when you think of it, he isn't such a bad dog after all.

As you can see, this paragraph lacks unity, for the ending is in direct contradiction to the topic sentence. The best way to unify this paragraph would be to rewrite the topic sentence to something like this:

My dog's bad habits always turn into something good.

The first step toward unity is to decide precisely what you want to say and to put it in words as expressively as you can. Once you know exactly what you want to say, you will have little difficulty avoiding irrelevant supporting details. The topic sentence, obviously, is of vital importance in achieving unity.

Organization of Ideas

The next step toward unity is to organize your material. The standard expository paragraph has three parts:

1. A topic sentence
2. Supporting detail that develops the topic sentence
3. A concluding sentence that sums up and ends the discussion of that particular topic sentence.

An old joke, sometimes called "the preacher's three," can be used to compare an expository paragraph to a sermon. First, the preacher announces his text to his congregation—*he tells'em what he's going to tell'em*—just as your topic sentence does. Then, *he tells'em*, as your selected supporting details do. And third, *he tells'em what he's told'em*, just as your concluding sentence does.

To develop a unified paragraph, you need to have a plan in mind. The plan may be as simple as having one clear controlling idea (topic sentence) and several points to support that idea. As you write down ideas and details to develop your paragraph, quite often you will see a pattern of organization emerge. You may see that you need to put the details in the right time sequence, or in the order of increasing importance, or in some other pattern of organization that will seem natural and sensible to your readers.

As you already know from the preceding chapter on the topic sentence, a good topic sentence has a subject plus an attitude toward that subject. A unified paragraph demands unity in both subject and attitude.

If your topic sentence says, "History and literature are my favorite subjects," you should not discuss your lack of enthusiasm for math. Since math isn't mentioned in your topic sentence, bringing it up in the development interferes with unity of subject. Your dislikes are not mentioned in the topic sentence either, so if you talk about your dislikes in the development, you spoil your unity of attitude.

UNITY OF SUBJECT

History and literature are my favorite subjects. These subjects appeal to me because they deal with people. History talks about what people did and what happened to them. Literature talks about individual persons and how they feel about things. When I study history and literature, I feel that my understanding of life is growing little by little. I like psych and sociology for the same reason. These subjects, too, are concerned with people from a theoretical rather than an actual point of view. For example, a story might *show* one character kissing or kicking another. But the psychological approach would tell *why* he kissed or kicked. Nevertheless, whether it's showing or telling, I like subjects that are concerned with people.

Since your topic sentence says that you are going to discuss history and literature, you are limited to discussing only those subjects. Your statements are therefore irrelevant from the sentence "I like psych and sociology . . ." on to the close of the paragraph.

You can achieve unity in this paragraph in one of two ways. First, you can change your topic sentence to something like:

> History and literature are my favorite subjects, but I like psych and sociology for almost the same reasons.

With this as a topic sentence, you can talk about all four. Second, you can achieve unity without changing the topic sentence simply by dropping all references to psych and sociology and expanding on your enjoyment of history and literature, as in the ending for this paragraph:

> . . . little by little. I like history and literature because I can live in the worlds those subjects create. I am not restricted to my own time and place; I can cross the Delaware with Washington or I can experience a first battle with Johnny Tremaine.

UNITY OF ATTITUDE

> History and literature are my favorite subjects. These subjects appeal to me because they deal with people. History talks about what people did and what happened to them. Literature talks about individual persons and how they feel about things. When I study history and literature, I feel that my understanding of life is growing little by little. The only thing I don't like about history is that some teachers go on and on about all kinds of little details, such as what General Overstreet ate for breakfast the day before the Battle of Gettysburg. In literature, sometimes the only writers you hear about are the big names like Hemingway and Faulkner, until you finally get tired of hearing about them. I'm sure that a lot of kids lose their appreciation for history and literature long before they get out of high school.

Since your topic sentence says that history and literature are your *favorite* subjects, that *favorable attitude* should be reflected throughout the paragraph. As soon as you start discussing what you *don't like,* you shift the attitude and you destroy the unity of the paragraph.

You can achieve unity of attitude in two ways. First, you can rewrite your topic sentence:

I like history and literature, but I don't like the way they are often taught.

With this as a topic sentence, you are free to talk about both your likes and your dislikes. Second, you can drop the sentences that do not refer to your topic sentence. In this case you would drop everything that follows ". . . little by little."

Your concluding sentence should reinforce the controlling idea of your topic sentence. The topic sentence and the conclusion must be unified in both subject and attitude. One way to check that your paragraph is unified is to determine whether your topic sentence and conclusion express the same controlling idea. Above all, make sure that your concluding sentence actually does conclude and does not introduce a new idea.

EXERCISE 22A: DETERMINING THE SUBJECT AND ATTITUDE

For each of the following possible topic sentences, indicate what both the subject and the attitude would be.

EXAMPLE: He found school a terrible bore.
Subject: school
Attitude: boring

A writer writing about a personal experience should make a point.
Subject: writing about a personal experience (Notice that a subject
can be more than a single word.)
Attitude: make a point

Stories can be as real as life to children.
Subject: stories
Attitude: as real as life (Notice that the attitude can be more than a
single word.)

1.   Quitters are not heroes.

Subject: _____

Attitude: _____

Arrogant people are often insecure.

2. King David was no saint.

   Subject: _____

   Attitude: _____

3. Arrogant people are often insecure.

   Subject: _____

   Attitude: _____

4. Soft-hearted people often spoil their pets.

   Subject: _____

   Attitude: _____

5. Affirmative action protects racial and ethnic minorities and women against discrimination in schooling and in jobs.

   Subject: _____

   Attitude: _____

EXERCISE 22B: ENSURING UNITY

The following paragraph contains several sentences that do not support the topic sentence. Strike out the irrelevant sentences that interfere with unity.

Of all human relationships, the longest lasting one can be among siblings. Friends, no matter how dear to you, parents, children, and spouses are all vital to you for a shorter period of time than your brothers and sisters. You can even have a warm feeling for your dog. Many of the events of life separate you from your friends—new jobs, marriage, transfers to other parts of the country, just growing older. Parents usually die before you do. Children grow up and leave the nest. Some children, of course, have no desire to go to work so they stay home long after most children have gone out on their own. Spouses usually have not shared the first fifteen years of life with you. I have a friend, however, who has known his wife since he was six. She lived next door to him and they played together as kids. Your brothers and sisters, however, have shared your life from the very earliest days and, with any luck, will be close to you until the end.

WRITING FROM READING

Finding Controlling Ideas

Some of the following paragraphs have been taken from a sociology textbook,* and some have been taken from a travel guide.† See if you can find the controlling idea in each of them. Underline the topic sentence, and then, following each paragraph, identify the subject and attitude expressed in that topic sentence.

> <u>Some cultural experience is common to all mankind.</u> Everywhere infants are nursed or fed by older persons, live in groups, learn to communicate through language, experience punishments and rewards of some kind, and have some other experiences common to the entire human species.

Subject: cultural experience
Attitude: common to all mankind

After you have identified the subject and the attitude in each topic sentence, read the paragraph again and see if they all demonstrate both unity of subject and unity of attitude.

---

* Paul B. Horton and Chester L. Hunt, *Sociology*, 3rd ed. (New York: McGraw-Hill, 1972), pp. 87 and 129–131.
† Gordon and Jane Rietveld, *Greece Aegean Island Guide* (Englewood Cliffs, N.J.: Prentice-Hall, 1982), pp. 131–132, 87.

To a far greater degree than most people recognize, one's behavior in a particular situation is a result of the needs, pressures, and temptations of that situation. There is ample evidence that many people who would not cheat a blind newspaper man will cheat the national supermarket chain if they get a chance to do so; war veterans who did not rob their neighbors back home "liberated" many articles from the enemy population; people do things as part of a mob which they would never do as individuals. War atrocities are committed by all armies, including American armies (Taylor, 1970). Whether a surrendering enemy is shot or taken prisoner depends more upon the circumstances at the moment of surrender than upon the character of the capturing troops.

Subject: _____

Attitude: _____

At the very least, hostile glares and unkind remarks await the group who deviate from the cultural norms (or the member of a deviant group who deviates from *their* group norms), but this is hardly "persecution." A denial of civil rights or an unequal enforcement of laws, however, might justifiably be termed "persecution." For example, Hamersma (1970) test-mailed stamped letters addressed to the Young Lords in Chicago, a group of Latin revolutionaries, and found that the letters were frequently delayed, opened, or never delivered. Huessenstamn (1971) found that when a selected group of students added Black Panther decals to their cars and attempted to continue driving in their usual manner, their traffic tickets multiplied astronomically! These are two recent experiments which document the perfectly obvious fact that deviants suffer some forms and degrees of punishment in all societies.

Subject: _____

Attitude: _____

Many primitive societies succeeded in controlling the behavior of individuals through their mores, reinforced by the informal controls of the primary group, so that no formal laws or punishments were necessary. But with large populations and more complex cultures, formal governments, laws, and punishments are developed. Wherever it becomes possible for the individual to become lost in the crowd, informal controls are inadequate and formal controls are necessary. For example, in a clan of one or two dozen adult kinsfolk, informal food sharing is whatever he can catch, while informal group pressures can be trusted to prevent laziness and control greed. But in a village of hundreds of persons, it would be impossible to keep tabs on each person informally; individual laziness and greed would make a system of informal food sharing unworkable. Some *system* of assigning work and distributing rewards becomes necessary. Thus, with larger populations and cultural complexity comes a shift to impersonal secondary group controls—laws, regulations, councils, and formalized procedures.

Subject: _____

Attitude: _____

Although Karpathos is a modern town, there is an undeniable Italianate look along the waterfront. This decorativeness goes well with the sight of a young Greek boy in lime-green shorts and a tangerine jersey, or a pretty girl sashaying by, purple shoes strapped above her ankles, wearing a golden yellow dress. You might see a stout man in a pink shirt and baggy blue trousers, or a black-and-white dog bounding down the street and flopping down next to a harborside table where uninhibited men are eating flaky, buttery *Baklava*, walnuts and pastry layered almost an inch thick and nestled in a spicy syrup. Time: 10:00 A.M.

Subject: _____

Attitude: _____

Patmos is considered to be one of the most sacred of the Aegean Islands. Here, in A.D. 95, St. John the Divine, by tradition identified with the Apostle John, was banished by the Romans. During his exile, he dictated *The Book of Revelation* to his disciple Prochoros. Immortality was given to the island by his words, "I, John, who also am your brother and companion in tribulation, and in the Kingdom and patience of Jesus Christ, was in this isle called Patmos . . ."

Subject: _____

Attitude: _____

Now see if you can write your own paragraph demonstrating both unity of subject and unity of attitude. From the following list of details, see if you can discern a subject and an attitude toward that subject. Once you have decided on a controlling idea, develop a paragraph using some of the details provided. When you have finished, compare your paragraph with those of your classmates. Did you arrive at the same controlling idea? Talk to each other about your choice of topic sentences and your ease or difficulty in developing those topic sentences. Was one person's topic sentence easier to develop than another's? Why?

Sappho of Lesbos was born in the town of Eressos.

Lesbos is an island in the Aegean Sea.

Sappho was a Greek poet.

Many women write poetry.

My mother writes poetry.

My dad is always teasing her about it.

Sappho was born around 600 B.C.

Plato called her "the tenth muse" because she wrote such beautiful verse.

Other late Greek writers agreed with Plato.

Plato said that Sappho wrote with impeccable purity.

He said that she had complete command of the language.

Supposedly, the Greek poet Alcaeus was her lover.

Sappho presided over a school for young maidens.

She encouraged them to write love songs.

She was devoted to these maidens.

When they left to get married, she would compose beautiful bridal odes for them.

Her poetry projected much passion and tenderness.

She often wrote about love and the beauty of nature.

The word *lesbian* evolved from the supposed relationship between Sappho and her young disciples.

Some writers of antiquity accused Sappho of immorality.

These accusations are not supported by most modern authorities.

Sappho had a daughter named Cleis.

Today, there are only a few surviving fragments of her writing.

She introduced the metaphor into language with phrases never heard before, such as "white as milk" and "more precious than gold."

The notion that Alcaeus was her lover is not supported by any written evidence.

Tall tales and legends are often associated with the lives of famous people.

George Washington supposedly cut down his father's cherry tree and then refused to lie about it, but this is a legend.

Everyone thinks that George Washington had false teeth, too, but that's not true either.

23
Paragraph Coherence

Coherence means holding together. The sentences in a unified and coherent paragraph are not just isolated bits of thought or information. They must be closely tied together so that your readers never read blindly but are able to see a basic pattern of development—a logical progression with no missing links of thought. Thus, if you want to communicate clearly, you must present your ideas in logical order, and you must provide connecting links from sentence to sentence within the paragraph.

Coherence does not come automatically. You need to give careful attention to how you arrange the ideas and details that you plan to include in your paragraph. Remember that your readers expect some logical pattern of development. You might, for example, arrange factual details in the order of increasing importance, or use comparison or contrast to illustrate a point, or present the details of a story according to an exact time sequence. Whatever method of development you use, the readers must be able to see that the sentences of the paragraph are linked together in a logical pattern to form a connected whole.

The most important steps in achieving coherence are:

1. Line up your ideas and sufficient details to illustrate or support them.
2. Arrange your ideas into a logical pattern.
3. Provide the connecting links needed to relate one sentence to another.

HOW TO ACHIEVE COHERENCE

Some of the main devices you may use to link the sentences within a paragraph include: (1) using transitional words and phrases; (2) using pronouns for reference; (3) repeating key words or phrases; (4) using parallel wording; and (5) enumerating.

Using Transitional Words and Phrases

To logically link the thoughts in your paragraph you must carefully choose transitional words and phrases to suit your *purpose.* Following are some common connectors:

to show addition:	also, furthermore, too, and again, in addition
to show comparison:	similarly, likewise, in the same way
to show contrast:	but, yet, nevertheless, on the contrary, on the other hand, nonetheless
to show concession:	although, even though, no doubt, granted that
to show a result or a conclusion:	thus, therefore, consequently, finally, as a result, in conclusion
to show emphasis:	in fact, indeed, certainly, surely
to show time:	before, after, afterward, first, second, last, later, in the meantime, for the moment
to introduce an example:	for example, for instance, in fact, that is, as an illustration

The transition need *not* be the first word or words in the sentence. Often a much smoother paragraph results from putting the connecting links *within* the sentence.

> The Department of Transportation, *for instance,* . . .
> The Soviet government, *consequently,* . . .

Using Pronouns for Reference

Using pronouns such as *he, she, it, these, we, those,* or *they* to refer to a subject named in a previous sentence aids paragraph coherence. Note how the pronouns in the following example help to knit this brief paragraph together:

Few people think of Florida as being home on the range, but *it* has some of the finest herds of beef cattle in the nation. *These* are the hump-shouldered descendants of Brahmin cattle imported from India to improve the native breeds. Today, *they* roam the flat grasslands north of Lake Okeechobee and land reclaimed from the Everglades. *They* are rugged animals that stand up to the heat, the insects, and the diseases of the tropics that would destroy other breeds. Almost unnoticed, Florida has grown to be one of the leading cattle-raising states.

Repeating Key Words or Phrases

Repeating key words or phrases often aids paragraph unity and coherence. Note how the repetition of key words ties the following sentences together:

The most dynamic element in a *capitalist* economy is the consumer's *freedom* of choice and the *competition* generated by that *freedom*. Granted sufficient *freedom* to operate, the *capitalist* system rewards those producers who offer consumers the most in goods and services at the lowest possible prices. *Competition* generated by the *capitalist* system demands that even the most efficient producers constantly work to bring out improved products or adopt more efficient methods to meet the needs of consumers. It is the *freedom* to compete in the marketplace that makes *capitalism* a dynamic system.

Using Parallel Wording

Repeating a sentence pattern and wording can add clarity and emphasis to your writing. For example, if you wanted to show enthusiastic support for a farm-state governor, you might line up your main supporting points in a series of parallel sentences.

He helped the farmers to . . .
He helped the farmers to . . .
He helped them to . . .
He helped them to . . .

Enumeration

In reporting an accident, describing a process, or giving instructions, the simplest and most direct transitions may serve you best: First, . . . Second, . . . Third, . . . Fourth, ... This basic method for guiding a reader through any step-by-step process is called *enumeration*, and it can serve you well as long as you do *not overuse* it.

For example, if you were telling someone how to fill cracks in a plastered wall, you could add clarity and coherence to your instructions by using enumeration.

First, you add water gradually to the spackling compound and mix it until you have a smooth, firm paste. Second, you spread the paste along the crack with a putty knife and squeeze it in firmly. Third, you add thin layers of paste until the crack is completely filled and the surface smooth. Fourth, . . .

EXERCISE 23A: SUPPLYING TRANSITIONS, SENTENCE LEVEL

Select the transitional words or phrases which seem most suitable to link the following pairs of sentences.

1.   He had been arrested more than eighty times on charges ranging from petty theft to drug dealing. _____, he had spent a total of less than a year in jail.

2.   All of the boys in the family had gotten into some sort of trouble at one time or another. _____, Ricky had been caught trying to rob a gum-ball machine.

3.   Lorenzo worked at a fast-food restaurant four nights a week and played in a

Stick 'em up!

band on weekends. _____, he was able to keep up his grades and finally get an engineering degree.

4. Some people feel that the federal government has a duty to protect and support the American family farm. Some, _____, believe that farmers are in trouble precisely because they have come to depend too much on government programs.

5. Many people seem to regard federal aid grants as a waste of taxpayer's money. Urban renewal grants, _____, may generate many times the amount of the grant in private investment.

6. It might be comforting to think that our welfare system takes care of all the truly needy. _____, the thousands of homeless who roam the streets of our cities can no longer be ignored.

7. The department of justice operates a witness protection program. _____, some of the witnesses given new identities under the program have launched new careers in crime.

8. Abraham Lincoln was born in a log cabin in Hardin County, Kentucky. _____, Springfield, Illinois, generally referred to as Lincoln's hometown, attracts about a half a million visitors to various historical sites associated with Lincoln.

9. Today, some people think of the Civil War as a distant struggle wrapped in a romantic haze. For the young soldiers on both sides, _____, the Battle of Gettysburg was a desperate and bloody struggle.

10. The mayor had refused the protestors' request for permission to march to the courthouse. _____, there was a nasty traffic jam when the angry marchers came down the main street.

EXERCISE 23B: ORDER AND TRANSITION WITHIN THE PARAGRAPH

Rearrange the sentences in the following paragraph in a logical sequence. Then rewrite the paragraph, adding any connecting words that are necessary.

The car that my younger brother Jeff bought last summer turned out to be no bargain. (1) By the end of the summer the car was hauled away, squashed flat, and fed into the crusher. (2) One of Jeff's friends put his foot through the floor. (3) The metal floor pan on the passenger side had completely rusted out. (4) The frame of the car had been bent so that the front wheels were permanently out of alignment, and the rear wheels refused to follow the front. (5) It finally quit running when a radiator hose popped and the engine got so hot that the valves began to melt. (6) After a delivery van smashed a rear door and half of the trunk, Jeff said that the car had to tiptoe past the junkyard.

EXERCISE 23C: SENTENCE COMBINING AND TRANSITIONS

By combining sentences and adding transitional words and phrases, put the following information together to form a coherent paragraph.

The waterspout is a strange phenomenon.

It is most likely to be seen in the South Pacific.

Clouds and the surface of the ocean become joined.

They are connected by a twisting column or spout.

The column may look like a massive pillar of water.

It is a cloud.

It is like the funnel cloud of a tornado.

It is formed by condensation of water vapor.

The inside of the column or spout is a partial vacuum.

The churning spout swirls across the ocean's surface.

Some surface water is drawn up the spout.

Tales have been told of whole ships being sucked up by waterspouts.

The stories are fanciful nonsense.

A waterspout is an awe-inspiring sight.

The waterspout may appear quite rapidly.

It may run its brief course and disappear within minutes.

WRITING FROM READING

The Joy of Discovery

One of the joys of reading and writing is discovering thoughts that never occurred to you before. How often, for example, have you thought of physical pain as "an intimate friend"? The following paragraph might give you some food for thought.

> A "war" on pain is not quite the same as a "war" on cancer or heart disease. The latter are undesirable under all circumstances, insults to our bodily integrity, and therefore "enemies." Pain, on the other hand, is often an intimate friend who warns and protects us. By young adulthood most of us would possess gnarled stumps instead of hands and fingers were it not for pain's warning signals, which are transmitted along the naked nerve endings originating in our fingertips. In addition, pain can protect us from the perils of our inner world. The vague tinge of chest discomfort first experienced while working outdoors on a cold winter morning may forewarn the potential heart attack victim to stop working and seek medical attention. Because of its usefulness, therefore, we wouldn't want to eliminate pain altogether, only control it.

Richard N. Restak, *The Brain: The Last Frontier*,
pp. 335–336. Reprinted by permission of Doubleday
& Company, Inc.

Emotional pain, like physical pain, often has positive as well as negative effects. Think about some experiences in your life when something good came out of something bad. Jot down anything that comes into your head. Just keep writing for five or ten minutes, and don't worry about grammar or spelling or punctuation. This is called "free writing." The purpose of free writing is to get your thoughts down on paper—no matter how disorganized or strange or incomplete they may sound to you at first. Sometimes you can discover feelings you didn't even know you had. When you are finished with your free writing, read it aloud and see if you have reached any conclusions about your experiences.

Index of Possible Topics

Following is a list of possible topics for your writing. As you look over the list, think about the topics in terms of a memorable experience that you've had, an experience that taught you something or made you feel good (or bad). Or think about describing someone you know or some place you've been. Or think about expressing an opinion that tells the reader what *you* think about something.

Write about an experience that taught you:

1.   To think before you act
2.   To respect age
3.   To spend more time with your family
4.   To change your priorities
5.   To be less critical of others
6.   To appreciate your parents
7.   To appreciate your roots
8.   To have more confidence in yourself
9.   To be compassionate toward someone you don't like
10. To appreciate your education

Describe:

11. A blind date
12. A childhood prank
13. Your first birthday
14. Your first attempt at public speaking
15. Your first job interview

16. Your boss
17. Your football coach
18. Your doctor
19. Your auto mechanic
20. Your workshop
21. Your school cafeteria
22. Your grandmother's attic
23. An embarrassing experience

Express an opinion about:

24. Misleading commercials
25. Comic strips with a message
26. Unusual pets
27. Rip-offs
28. Preschool con artists
29. Violence in fairy tales
30. Human characteristics in animals
31. Funny incidents in Sunday School
32. Famous cowards
33. Two types of diets
34. Two types of students

Tell about:

35. Your most interesting vacation
36. Meeting your future in-laws
37. Making a crucial decision
38. Winning a championship game
39. Losing your job
40. Taking your first plane ride
41. Reading a good book
42. Training a pet
43. Becoming a vegetarian
44. Living on a farm
45. Two types of salespeople
46. Different types of friends
47. Different approaches to comedy

48. How movie heroes and heroines have changed
49. How attitudes toward work have changed
50. How education has changed
51. How musical tastes have changed
52. How the role of women has changed
53. Clever alibis
54. Annoying salespeople
55. Unusual occupations
56. Ridiculous fads
57. Interesting friends
58. Exceptional athletes
59. Single parents
60. Computer crime
61. Video games
62. Inspiring teachers
63. Fast-food restaurants
64. Workaholics
65. Perfectionists
66. Chauvinists
67. Grandmothers
68. Married life

Relate:

69. Drinking and driving
70. Economic needs and career choice
71. Quality and price
72. Laughter and mental health
73. Drugs and sports
74. Personality and choice of car
75. Personality and style of dress
76. Television and reading habits
77. Working and going to school

Discuss:

78. Peer pressure and cheating
79. Censorship on television

80. Smoking in public places
81. Public employee strikes
82. Women in the clergy
83. Generic food products
84. Mandatory class attendance
85. Dress codes
86. Motorcycles
87. Phobias
88. Overcoming physical handicaps
89. Your favorite hobby
90. The biggest challenge of your life
91. The effects of television
92. The effects of advertising
93. The effects of a smile
94. Your favorite holiday
95. Violence in sports
96. How to budget your time
97. How to save money
98. How to survive holiday shopping
99. How to survive a dentist appointment
100. How to survive English class

Index